John Rogers, the People's Sculptor

JOHN ROGERS (1829–1904)

John Rogers

The People's Sculptor

BY

DAVID H. WALLACE

WESLEYAN UNIVERSITY PRESS

Middletown, Connecticut

Library of Congress Catalog Card Number: 67–24107
Manufactured in the United States of America
First edition

Contents

Illustrations

WITHIN THE TEXT

WITHIN THE CATALOGUE

All of the above-mentioned illustrations courtesy of The New-York Historical Society, New York City, except Nos. 3 and 19 courtesy of the Society for the Preservation of New England Antiquities; No. 20 courtesy of the Gladys A. Hawkins Memorial Museum, Hannibal, Missouri; Nos. 102B, 188, and 200 from *Rogers Groups: Thought and Wrought by John Rogers,* by Mr. and Mrs. Chetwood Smith; No. 112C courtesy of the Toledo Museum of Art; No. 187 courtesy of the Essex Institute, Salem, Massachusetts; and Nos. 99B and 102A, photos by the author.

Introduction

In America, before the Civil War, sculpture was an art patronized almost exclusively by the rich. Marble and bronze were expensive materials which only the well-to-do could aspire to bring into their parlors. At the same time, sculpture was so highly regarded, as the noblest of the arts, that even the middle-class householder was eager to own a piece of statuary. For some this need was met by the importer of English parians and small French bronzes in the larger cities or by the itinerant Italian image-vendor who peddled his plaster busts and classical figurines in the cities, towns, and villages of the eastern seaboard. The general hunger for statuary was still largely unsatisfied, however, when the "Rogers Group" appeared on the scene just before the Civil War.

Between 1860 and 1893 the American public bought about eighty thousand of John Rogers' putty-colored plaster statuettes at an average price of about fourteen dollars. The Rogers Group was indeed almost as much of a necessity to a well-appointed Victorian parlor as the antimacassar and the chromo of George Washington. "A popular ancedote of a later day," wrote Allan Nevins in *The Emergence of Modern America,* "told of a tramp who assured his benefactress, "You can realize how poor we were, ma'am, when I tell you that my parents could never afford to buy Rogers' Weighing the Baby.' "

No American sculptor has remotely approached Rogers in popularity, and the reasons for this are not difficult to see. No other American sculptor has ever been so completely at one with his contemporaries in taste, in spirit, and in human sympathy, and none has made his works so readily available to the general public. In the following verses, published in *The American Queen,* January 18, 1882, W. R. Croffut pleasantly summed up what John Rogers meant to his generation:

John Rogers! Laureate of home!
The Muses fly to meet you;
Behold, the humble millions come
With grateful words to greet you.
Where other art is seldom met,
In silent, rustic places,
Your statuette is quaintly set
A witness for the graces.
You touch our prosy life, and lo!
Where all was dead and barren,
The green leaves grow and blossoms blow
As on the rod of Aaron!

. . .

Of love and war, of joy and woe,
Of pleasure, pain and healing,
You've learned to know the secret, so
You sweep the chords of feeling.

. . .

And so the grateful millions come
With pleasant words to meet you,
John Rogers! Laureate of home,
The muses fly to greet you.

In this study of his career, I have sought to show how it happened that John Rogers, scion of Puritan ministers and Yankee merchants, became an artist instead of a dealer in dry goods — and the chief Realist among American sculptors at that, rather than another genteel sacrifice laid by Boston on the altar of Italianate Neoclassicism. I have sought to show also by what means Rogers won and held his position as America's most popular sculptor and to assess the effect on himself and on his contemporaries of his lifetime devotion to realistic popular art. Of Rogers' personal life, except as it affected his artistic development, I have said relatively little. As Russell Lynes has said in *The Tastemakers,* it was almost "abnormally normal," and the recital of its incidents would add little to an understanding of John Rogers' role in American nineteenth-century culture.

This study is based almost entirely on material in the Rogers Collection of The New-York Historical Society, acquired by gift and purchase from the Rogers family in 1936 and 1955. Of particular interest in this collection are the hundreds of letters written by John Rogers and a few to him (1837–1904); two personal account books (1848–50 and 1866–86); four scrapbooks of press clippings spanning his entire professional career; one working sketch book (c. 1870–78); some early landscape sketches; a very brief dictated autobiography, to which Mrs. Rogers added many pages of information on her husband, their children, and various Rogers and Francis relatives; Alexander Parker Rogers' typed "Recollections of my Father"; and many photographs of the artist's family and his works. Also at The New-York Historical Society is the most complete collection of the artist's work, including almost all his published works in plaster, thirty-seven of the original bronze models, and several unpublished works.

A few other Rogers manuscripts are in the possession of the New Canaan Historical Society, New Canaan, Connecticut; the Massachusetts Historical Society; the New York Public Library; and the Archives of American Art, Detroit, Michigan. The records of Rogers' business, if still extant, have not been located.

In the very early stages of my research I had the privilege of visiting and corresponding with the late Miss Katherine R. Rogers, the last surviving child of John Rogers. She very graciously showed me about the Rogers house and studio on Oenoke Ridge in New Canaan, searched among family papers for material I might otherwise never have seen, and cheerfully answered many questions about her father and his work.

In preparing the catalogue of Rogers' works I have drawn upon the resources of many institutions and private collectors of Rogers Groups. I am particularly indebted to the following: Albany Institute of History and Art, Albany, New York; American Antiquarian Society; Brooks Free Library, Harwich, Massachusetts; Essex Institute, Salem, Massachusetts; Fleming Museum, University of Vermont, Burlington; Lightner Museum of Hobbies, St. Augustine, Florida; Manchester Historic Association, Manchester, New Hampshire; New Canaan Historical Society, New Canaan, Connecticut; Society for the Preservation of New England Antiquities, Boston; Harold Warp Pioneer Village, Minden, Nebraska; Mr. and Mrs. William M. Hawkins; Mr. J. Edwin Huey; Dr. Harry Mackler; Mr. and Mrs. William E. Stone; and Mr. Albert L. Partridge.

Finally, I wish to record my indebtedness to *Rogers Groups: Thought and Wrought by John Rogers,* the pioneer study of Rogers' life and works, written by the late Mr. and Mrs. Chetwood Smith and published for them by Goodspeeds, Boston, 1934. The present study, though more comprehensive, is designed to supplement that earlier work, not to supplant it. Its charm assures it a permanent place in any collection of Rogers' works and memorabilia.

John Rogers, the People's Sculptor

CHAPTER I

Poor Relations

ONE DAY early in the year 1849, while suffering from an acute eye infection, young John Rogers met a dentist friend in Boston who invited him into his office to see a little clay figure he had modelled.

> I took a great fancy to it [Rogers recalled years after]; immediately went to Charlestown to an address, which he gave me, of a pottery; and there I got some clay & carried it home; whittled some modelling sticks, & set up my first figure. I was quite successful. I could work on it without straining my eyes and found it a great resource and enjoyment.

Rogers' pocket account book fixes the date of this happy encounter as April 2, 1849. Under that date, between two payments for medicines, he recorded the expenditure of thirty cents for "clay for models" and ten cents for "Charlestown omnibus." Thus simply, in his twentieth year, began the career of the artist who was to become the most popular of American sculptors.

There was certainly little in John Rogers' family background to suggest the course his life would take. For six American generations his ancestors had been clergymen or merchants (with the notable exception of a great-great-great-grandfather, John Coney, one of Boston's early silversmiths). Both his grandfathers, Daniel Denison Rogers of Boston and John Derby of Salem, were men of wealth and high social standing in early nineteenth-century Massachusetts. By the time the future sculptor was born, however, his immediate family's social position was unsupported by wealth. This fact dominated the boy's early years.

Through his mother, John Rogers was kin to the Derby family of Salem, whose rise to mercantile power in the middle of the previous century culminated in the awe-inspiring career of Elias Hasket Derby (1739–99). One of the few early Salem merchants who did not begin as a sea captain, "King" Derby revolutionized the trading habits of Salem in the years immediately following the Revolution. In 1784 he sent the bark *Light Horse* to the Baltic to open direct trade between America and Russia. In 1784 also he sent the *Grand Turk* on the first New England voyage into the Indian Ocean and on to China. Encouraged by the immense profits from these experimental voyages, Derby decided to concentrate on trade with the Far East. His success and that of his fellow merchants ushered in Salem's golden age, which lasted through the War of 1812. "In all this period," writes James Duncan Phillips, the historian of Salem, "one cannot escape the conclusion that in daring initiative, willingness to take risks and the skillful execution which resulted in great success, Elias H. Derby stood head and shoulders above all the rest."

With the passing of "King" Derby in 1799 the family's pre-eminence in commerce quickly waned. The division of his million-dollar estate among his seven children was fatal to the Derby shipping empire. Deprived of the great merchant's unifying control and capital, the tightly knit organization he had built up could not withstand the strains of family jealousies and the pressures of competition. Other Salem merchants, many of them former Derby employees, profited by the weakening of the Derby interests, so that by 1810, the peak year of Salem's prosperity, the heirs of Elias Hasket Derby were already far down the list of Salem shipowners.

John Derby, the oldest son, though head of the family after 1799, did not have the energy and drive of either his father or his own younger brother, Richard Crowninshield Derby, who moved to Boston. He did manage, however, to keep the Derby name from disappearing entirely from the Salem shipping register and he served as a director of the Salem Bank and of the Salem Marine Insurance Society. He lived well, but not ostentatiously, in a pre-Revolutionary house on Washington Street that had been done over in the Adam style in 1786 by Salem's carver-architect, Samuel McIntire. Here, in comfort and security, the five children of John and Eleanor Coffin Derby grew up.

Sarah Ellen Derby, born in 1805, was the oldest of the children, followed by Mary Jane, Elizabeth Laura, Martha Coffin, and George. Sarah Ellen and Mary Jane spent their schooldays at a boarding school in nearby Beverly, where they received instruction in French, botany, embroidery, and drawing. Later, to complete their education as gentlewomen, the two girls were sent to Boston to be "finished" by their elegant Aunt Martha, Mrs. Richard Crowninshield Derby.

Despite the similarity of their training, the two girls were strikingly different. Sarah Ellen was an acknowledged beauty — tall and slender, with thick wavy hair of a dark reddish tint, light brown eyes, and regular, almost classic features, carrying herself with quiet dignity and "alluring reserve." The younger girl, on the other hand, was known for vivacity and brilliance of mind, rather than for beauty. Sarah Ellen, it was said, compelled the passerby to stop and look; Mary Jane compelled him to stop and talk. The future of both, however, seemed foreordained. They would find rich husbands and, like Jane Austen heroines, enjoy in their own establishments the same pleasures and comforts to which they had been accustomed in their father's house.

Sarah Ellen was the first to be married. If her youngest sister Martha is to be believed, the marriage was one of convenience, not love. Sarah Ellen's heart, Martha said later, was set on marrying "a Dr. Reynolds of Boston." Her mother, however, said "No, she must marry that rich Mr. Rogers," and marry him the obedient Sarah Ellen did, on June 5, 1827.

John Rogers of Boston, who won the hand if not the heart of Sarah Ellen Derby, was himself something of a catch. Though only "moderately good looking," at twenty-seven he was apparently well established as a merchant in Boston, having two years before inherited from his father approximately a quarter share of an estate valued at a little over $400,000. A moderately intellectual graduate of Harvard College, unathletic, quite talkative "on certain subjects" (not specified), Mr. Rogers was obviously a solid, sober young man to whom prudent parents could safely entrust a loved daughter.

Not the least of young Rogers' assets, moreover, was a lineage of unusual distinction, even for Massachusetts. He could boast of direct descent from Nathaniel Rogers (1598–1655) of Ipswich, acclaimed by Cotton Mather as "one of the greatest men that ever set foot on the American Strand"; from John Rogers (1630–84), fifth president of Harvard College; and from two other, less prominent, divines, John Rogers (1666–1745) of Ipswich and Daniel Rogers (1707–85), who gave up a Harvard tutorship to follow George Whitefield in 1740 and established the "New Light" church at Exeter, New Hampshire. Marriages with descendants of Governor Thomas Dudley, General Daniel Denison, and Richard Clarke had given the family added social importance. When the nineteenth century opened, wealth had been added to the family's good name by the energy of Daniel Denison Rogers (1751–1825). A dry goods merchant who moved from New Hampshire to Boston during the Revolution, he accumulated a considerable fortune before his death. Daniel Denison Rogers, it was said, was distinguished by "the warmest and most affectionate feeling, and a judgment remarkable for its correctness, coolness and foresight." These same qualities, like his "united to great industry," were to reappear in his grandson, the sculptor John Rogers. They were lacking, however, in his own elder son, the sculptor's father.

If young Mr. Rogers' riches were, as his sister-in-law asserted, his chief recommendation in the eyes of the elder Derbys, they had made a sad choice for Sarah Ellen. The simple truth was that John Rogers was not a good businessman. Despite his six years in trade and the handsome capital derived from his father's estate, within a year of his marriage Rogers found himself in serious financial difficulties. Part of the trouble may have been in the partnership of Holmes and Rogers itself, for the probate records of Daniel Denison Rogers' estate show that the firm was over $36,000 in debt to the elder Rogers at the time of his death, while John himself owed his father over $15,000. These debts alone must have reduced his acquired capital seriously. But the real blow came from an unexpected quarter. According to family tradition, John Rogers secured notes amounting to about $40,000 for his sister Elizabeth's husband, Jacob Tilton Slade. Elizabeth died in 1826, leaving three small children, and in April 1827 Slade left Boston. When it became apparent that Slade had no intention of returning, his brother-in-law John Rogers found himself liable for Slade's unpaid debts. The financial blow was one from which Rogers never fully recovered, despite several efforts to retrieve his losses. Sarah Ellen Rogers, though never really poor, had to forgo forever the comfortable standard of living to which she had been accustomed. The knowledge of his failure in this respect was a constant source of discomfort to her husband. Perhaps conscious of her lukewarm feelings toward him at the time of their marriage, he felt doubly conscience-stricken at having involved her in his subsequent troubles. Mrs. Rogers, for her part, bore her trials with dignity and courage. If she was bitter, she carefully kept her feelings to herself. Her husband, perhaps unwisely, tried to sound them, but as he later told their son John, "he could never get her to say that she loved him, all she would say was 'don't doubt of my affection.' "

For the first three years of their marriage Rogers and his wife remained in Boston, where their first child, Ellen Derby, was born on March 23, 1828. For the birth of her second child, however, Mrs. Rogers returned to Salem. There, in the home of his Derby grandparents on Washington Street, John Rogers, Jr., was born on October 30, 1829. He was baptized soon after by the great Unitarian preacher William Ellery Channing, long a good friend as well as pastor of the baby's Rogers grandparents.

By this time the young father had given up hope of making his way in Boston. Like so many men of his time, he turned his gaze westward, hoping

JOHN ROGERS' BIRTHPLACE

The Pickman-Derby House, Salem, Massachusetts, from a lithograph by Pendleton after a drawing by Mary Jane Derby, Rogers' aunt. The house was torn down in 1915.

to find there the land of promise. During the summer of 1830, when little John was about ten months old, the family of four made the long, slow trip to Cincinnati. There, in the rapidly growing "Queen City" on the Ohio River, Mr. Rogers made a new start as a sawmill owner in partnership with a Mr. Goodwin, who apparently provided most of the capital.

The new business prospered at first. Mr. Rogers was able to take a house on fashionable Fourth Street, one block west of Vine, and the family was soon at home in Cincinnati society, or at least the Yankee portion of it, for a sharp division existed between the rather standoffish New Englanders and the "Buckeye" natives. Mrs. Rogers fitted easily into the circle of married ladies whom the minister-litterateur James H. Perkins described as "scarcely to be equalled in any city for intelligence, and what is better, excellence beyond compare." Mrs. Rogers also attended the meetings of the Semi-Colons, a literary society whose informal membership included the as-yet-unmarried Harriet Beecher. The Rogers' exile in the West was further lightened by the presence of Sarah Ellen's younger sister Mary Jane who first visited them during the winter of 1831–32 and returned in 1833 as the bride of the Rev. Ephraim Peabody, whose Unitarian Church stood in Fourth Street just two doors east of the Rogers house.

Mr. Rogers did not make his fortune in the lumber business in Cincinnati, as he had hoped. Bad luck seemed to dog him. During the terrible cholera epidemic of 1832 his partner died, leaving Rogers with hardly enough capital to carry on. By July 1833 Mr. Rogers was, according to his friend Perkins, "satisfied that he cannot find in town wherewithal to live." The Cincinnati directory for 1834, published early that year, lists Rogers and Goodwin's Hamilton Steam Saw Mill on Front Street west of Western Row as "not now in operation."

If Mrs. Rogers was discontented, she took pains to hide the fact. Her son remembered her as always cheerful, though quiet in her ways. Among her many friends there were some who sensed the strain she was under. James Perkins speaks of talking with her of "the uncertainty of human hopes and the high rate of wages, of which she, poor woman, has had far more experience than I." Young Mr. Perkins, with the romanticism of one exempt from woman's cares, continued:

> and yet I know not why I should call her poor; she has a husband that loves her and is ready to do all and sacrifice all for her; she has children that might gladden any woman's heart; she is respected and beloved by all that know her; and while actual want stands aloof I cannot but think her happier than nine tenths of those who have not a wish that wealth can gratify that is not gratified.

For Mrs. Rogers, however, these must have been unhappy years. Besides having to do household work to which she was unaccustomed and share her husband's financial worries, she suffered personal losses during these years which weighed heavily on her. In the space of three years she lost three members of her family — her brother Nathaniel in 1830, her father in 1831, and one of her own children, Laura Derby, who died in September 1832 at the age of three months. To be separated from the rest of her family at these times of sorrow made doubly hard the bearing of them. The prospect of a return to Massachusetts which Mr. Rogers decided on in 1835 must have been more than welcome to his wife.

Neither John, Jr., nor his sisters Ellen and Laura (born in 1834 and named for the baby who had died two years earlier) was old enough to remember much of their life in Cincinnati. Although they must have seen Mrs. Trollope's famous Bazaar and may have seen the Western Museum whose frightening wax work Inferno was the handiwork of young Hiram Powers, just starting on his phenomenal rise to fame as a sculptor, these sights left no permanent impression. What John remembered instead were two events which would excite any child. One involved a free-running pig which got into his Aunt Peabody's garden and stole a fish. John, aged four, chased the thieving pig down the street, retrieved the fish, and brought it triumphantly to his father, who rewarded the little boy's efforts by throwing the fish out the window, whereupon another pig came along and ate it up. Twenty-four years later John memorialized the incident in an illustrated poem for his parents' thirty-first wedding anniversary.

The other memorable event of John Rogers' early childhood in Cincinnati was the painting of his portrait at the age of five. More than forty years later he spoke of it to his sister Ellen: "I can recollect perfectly going to sit for it, and once you were with me and Beard was painting my knee, when you discovered a little mouse & chased it round while I had to keep my seat much against my will." The portrait was painted specially for John's grandmother Derby. James H. Beard, the artist, a young man who had come to Cincinnati just a year or so before, had built up a thriving trade in portraits of children, usually with animals. The demand was stimulated, according to Mrs. Rogers, by the death of a child, which caused other parents to hasten to have portraits before their own were lost to them.

Beard's portrait of John Rogers shows him as a blue-eyed, blond, curly-headed cherub with a firm mouth, his arms thrown about the neck of a rather wild-eyed collie. According to Mrs. Rogers, "Beard had not a dog in his room, but saw a child in something that attitude playing in the street

JOHN ROGERS AT THE AGE OF FIVE
Oil portrait by James H. Beard, 1834.

with a cross dog." John's mother was especially pleased with the expression on his face: "He caught Johnny's laughing eye from his jumping up to catch a mouse that happened to come out of his hole just as he was getting very tired sitting."

One other incident of this early part of his life John Rogers remembered, the long journey by stagecoach and canal boat from Cincinnati back to Massachusetts, during the summer of 1835. The family was back in Boston, where Mrs. Derby was now living, before August 1 when Mr. and Mrs. Rogers paid a visit to their Cincinnati friend, James H. Perkins, and announced their new plans. John Rogers' mother had died in 1833 and, from the subsequent sale of the Rogers mansion on Beacon Hill, he had realized more than $14,000. With this new capital, Rogers was going to try his hand at a new business, raising silkworms.

The creation of a native silk industry had been an American dream since early colonial times, but the dream gave no promise of becoming reality until 1826 when a new variety of mulberry tree, the *morus multicaulis,* was introduced. Its rapid growth, easy propagation, and immense leaves were expected to revolutionize the domestic silk industry. Under the patronage of Congress and the active promotion of the nation's nurserymen, interest in the raising of *multicaulis* trees and silkworms grew with amazing rapidity until, by the mid-'thirties, as one writer put it, "everyone seemed to be infected with a strange frenzy." From New England to Georgia and west to Ohio, professional and amateur horticulturalists alike rushed to plant trees and pluck from them easy profits.

In Massachusetts the fever raged with special intensity. The Governor's Message in 1836 contained this sanguine prediction:

> If anticipations are warranted, silk will become the staple product of the country, both for consumption and exportation, second to no other branch of industry and source of wealth.

The center of mulberry and silkworm culture in the state was the Connecticut Valley town of Northampton where Samuel Whitmarsh, an enthusiastic convert from tailoring to the silk industry, had settled in 1829, sinking all his capital into a large mulberry plantation and cocoonery, to which he added in 1836 a silk manufactory at Florence, a nearby village. One of the most active promoters of silk culture throughout the 1830s, Whitmarsh had unbounded faith in the possibilities of the domestic silk industry. "The raising of silk is as interesting as it is profitable," he wrote. "It is not laborious or difficult nor does it require large capital. It is happily within the means of the most humble, and offers all who will undertake it a rich return." One nurseryman, it was reported, realized a profit of $30,000 on 30,000 trees grown on a single acre.

Although he had no experience in agriculture, Mr. Rogers embarked on his new venture with great enthusiasm. Leaving his wife and children in Cambridge for the time being, he went alone to Northampton in April 1836, rented a house, and set about planting his trees and seeds. The work, he found, was less easy than advertised. After planting two thousand trees with the assistance of a hired man and boy, he was almost too tired to write home, but his spirits were high and he felt renewed confidence in himself. "It is . . . a source of pleasure to me," he wrote to his wife, "to think that I am now beginning to do something which I trust will one day afford me the means of adding to your enjoyments, and that at no distant period I shall so retrieve my pecuniary affairs as to be able to command whatever may in any way contribute to your gratifications." By June Mrs. Rogers, who had been ill, was well enough to make the journey to Northampton and they were soon comfortably settled in the house Mr. Rogers had taken.

Charmingly situated on bluffs skirting the widespreading meadows of the Connecticut, which have given the town its popular name of "the Meadow City," its main street lined with ancient elms, Northampton in 1836 was a small rural village distinguished from neighboring hamlets by a few shops and some fine homes clustered about the Hampshire County Court House. Farming was still the chief occupation of the inhabitants, although Samuel Whitmarsh's silk mill at nearby Florence would soon provide employment for sixty operatives.

The house which Rogers had rented, and which he later bought from the Rev. Edward Hall for $1,800, was located on Elm Street on the present site of Smith College. "It was," Mr. Rogers wrote, "a very pleasant house, surrounded with beautiful elm trees, and in the neighborhood of many fine houses and gardens." Besides pleasant neighbors, particularly the family of Judge Samuel Hinckley, Northampton offered the city-bred Rogers family a taste of rural life which they enjoyed. Mr. Rogers delighted in the life of a gentleman-farmer. Besides taking his family on "many delightful walks and rides" about the neighborhood, he played host to visitors from outside, including the Prussian Minister Baron Renier whom he escorted on a tour of local sites of interest like Sunderland Cave, Laurel Hill, and Amherst College. He also served on the Elm Street School Board and as an assessor in the Second Church.

As always, Mrs. Rogers quickly made friends. Only three weeks after her arrival, a local lady was writing to a mutual friend in Cincinnati that "her calm loveliness has an attraction for every one. . . . In *her,* beauty seems to be the real type by which moral qualities are expressed in the outer man. . . . When I see Mrs. Rogers, I can't help thinking how one particle of affectation or artificiality in any of its forms would ruin this pure emblem of virtue. And her children seem to be after the same pattern. With such treasures, Mr. Rogers cannot know the *bitterness* of poverty."

John, Jr., who was almost seven when they moved to Northampton, always looked on his years there as the happiest of his childhood. He was, "like most other boys of his age," as his father said, "more fond of kites and balls and stilts than books." Soon after their arrival he began to go to the Elm Street School, a little unpainted schoolhouse at the foot of Round Hill. More memorable to John, however, was the cider mill at the corner of Elm and Paradise Road (now the site of the Smith College quadrangle), around which he and the other boys used to gather. The proprietor used to keep a cup especially for the boys' use. "When he ground sweet apples," Rogers recalled in his old age, "it soon got known amongst the school boys who drank quarts of it." Another favorite diversion Rogers remembered was picking chestnuts on nearby Round Hill where not long before had flourished George Bancroft's and J. G. Cogswell's famous Round Hill School. Best of all, however, were the excursions to the top of Mount Holyoke, the view from which Rogers considered one of the finest he had ever seen.

John's life was not all idle pleasure, however. As befitted the oldest son (his brother Henry was born in Northampton in 1837) of a farmer, as Mr. Rogers considered himself, young John had his share of chores to do. There was a cow to milk and he later recalled how proud he was when he could show his pail full to the strainer. He was also charged with carrying in "all the wood which was burned throughout the house in cold weather." More fun, and certainly more rewarding, was his work on his father's mulberry plantation. When he was about eight, he was able to join the people employed to pick mulberry leaves at ½ cent a pound. One day he picked 75 pounds. With the 37½ cents thus earned, the independent boy felt rich enough to buy his own shoes, which he says he did from that time on. He also had his own garden in which he raised all sorts of melons to sell to his father. When he begged to be allowed to go with his sister Ellen to visit at Nahant, however, Mr. Rogers felt he could hardly trust him there, "unless he was chained to a post, so that he could not fall from the rocks." His caution may have been the result of a disastrous fall John had had just a few weeks earlier at Northampton's open-air Fourth of July tea party. "Johnny was there," father Rogers wrote to his nephew Daniel Denison Slade, "and had a grand frolic with the other boys, and a plenty of cake to eat. He was unlucky enough however towards evening to slip down and soil his nice white pantaloons, so badly that he was obliged to leave the party and make the best of his way home, the most retired way he could find."

His six years in rural Northampton left a deep impression on young John Rogers and gave him a permanent love of country life which was to exercise a strong influence on his artistic career. Northampton, as he remembered it, was a place of unending delight.

> What real comfort we used to take in our large garden in Northampton [he wrote to his mother in May 1857]. Such delicious melons we used to raise. I can recollect with what pride I wheeled an enormous great water melon in my yellow wheelbarrow down to Judge Lyman's. I think I never felt prouder in my life than when I trundled that along & people would stop & look at it & I thought it all came out of *our* garden. And then the currants & tomatoes & the great apple tree in the corner of the garden & I can recall them all before my eye as plainly almost as if I were there. It was the happiest part of my life. Everything stands before me in the brightest colors — the rides we used to take with Grandma on summer evenings in an open barouche down by the river & the chestnuts we used to go after on Round Hill . . . , the cows I used to milk, the hop vines over the barn.

However much John enjoyed rural life, to his father it eventually brought only a renewal of his earlier disappointments. In the fall of 1839, after a decade of frenzied speculation, the *multicaulis* boom suddenly came to an end. Various reasons have been given for the collapse, including failure of the mulberry crop because of hard winters and disease and overproduction of the trees, but the effect was universally disastrous. Trees which had sold in the summer of 1839 for as much as $500 a hundred could scarcely be disposed of for ten cents a hundred the following year. Thousands of cultivators lost their whole investment, among them Rogers' friend and adviser in Northampton, Samuel Whitmarsh.

Since the silk industry as a whole was not affected by the collapse of the speculation in *multicaulis* trees, the market for mulberries continued and the cultivation of other varieties produced a temporary revival of interest after 1839. Five years later, however, a combination of cold weather and widespread blight put an end to the raising of mulberries for silk in the United States.

Rogers himself apparently survived the *multicaulis* panic of 1839, for in October 1840 he won a number of premiums at the fair of the Hampshire, Hampden, and Franklin Agricultural Society in Northampton. At that time he had 73,720 mulberry trees, and ranked fifth among local cultivators. A third prize for silk cocoons indicates that he was also running a cocoonery. He was still in business the following March, when a premium for raw silk was awarded him at the Society's annual meeting, but less than a month later Mr. Rogers had decided to sell out. An advertisement in the *Hampshire Gazette,* April 7, 1841, announced to the public that John Rogers would offer at public auction on April 15, his "4 acres of prime land" on West Street by Mill River. The property was sold to Enos Cook of Northampton for $475, at a loss of 25 per cent on the original investment. The house on Elm Street remained in their hands till 1844 when it was sold to William Adam (of the Florence Community), at an even greater loss. Mr. Rogers' second attempt to make his fortune had ended in total defeat.

The harassed family took temporary refuge in Walpole, New Hampshire, on the sheep farm of William Powell Mason, Rogers' wealthy brother-in-law. Arriving in the dead of winter, young John was delighted with their new home, particularly by the "fine prospect all round us" and a steep hill nearby, "where we have made a fine coast." His mother, however, was near collapse after the "hurry and confusion of moving." "I feel rather too blue to impose myself on anyone," she wrote in a brief note to her mother soon after their arrival in Walpole. "I cannot feel much at home yet & fear I never shall — at least that I shall never be happy here." Their temporary home was situated on the top of a bluff and was fearfully cold in winter. Designed only for summer use, it had only open fireplaces and straw carpets. John later remembered that he frequently had to break the ice in his water pitcher when he got up in the morning. Since there was no school within three miles, the children recited their lessons to their father.

Their stay in Walpole lasted only a few months. Later in 1841 Mr. Rogers found a situation in the Boston Custom House and moved his household to Roxbury, then a suburb of Boston. After renting three different houses, Mr. Rogers eventually bought No. 85 Cedar Street, where he and Mrs. Rogers spent the rest of their lives. Mr. Rogers was to remain in the Custom House until 1843 when he became Treasurer of the newly-formed Vermont and Massachusetts Rail Road at a salary of $1,500. He made no further attempts to resume his disastrous business career.

THE ROGERS FAMILY, 1849

Left to right: Mrs. John Rogers Sr., Clara, Ellen, Henry, Martha, John Jr. (the future sculptor), Laura, John Rogers Sr., and the twins Bessie and Fanny.

CHAPTER II

A Practical Education

JOHN ROGERS, JR., left Northampton when he was twelve and completed grammar school in Roxbury three years later, in 1844. The next step in his education, if he was to follow the customary course for Boston boys of his class, should have been his entrance into the Boston Latin School where he would study the classics for three years in preparation for Harvard College. His father's circumstances made this impractical, however; since it would be too expensive to send John to college, there was no point in sending him to the Latin School.

It was for boys in just these circumstances that the English High School had been founded in 1821 "to furnish young men who were not intended for a collegiate course of study and who had enjoyed the usual advantages of the public schools, with the means of completing a good English education and fitting themselves for all the departments of commercial life." The curriculum, ignoring the classics, included only practical subjects: reading, composition, logic, geography, arithmetic, algebra, navigation, surveying, natural and moral philosophy, modern languages, and drawing. A forerunner of the modern high school, in the middle of the nineteenth century the Boston English High School was looked upon as a model. One American educator ranked it second only to West Point in thoroughness, while an English observer wished that there were a hundred such schools in England.

When John Rogers entered the school in 1844, it had just moved from Pinckney Street to a new building on Bedford Street which it was to share for the next thirty-odd years with the conservative Boston Latin School. The headmaster was Thomas Sherwin, a former mathematics tutor at Harvard, engineer and surveyor, and author of several algebra texts. During his thirty-two years as head of the English High School, from 1837 to 1869, Sherwin exerted a profound influence on the school and on the thousands of boys who came under his charge. His aims, it was said, were to give his pupils a thorough understanding of the subjects they studied, to teach them to think for themselves, and to encourage manliness of character. In his passion for science he was ahead of his time, at least in the educational field. "I have often thought that a good knowledge of chemistry, geology, zoology, and botany is a better qualification for a teacher in the school under my charge," he once said, "than perfect familiarity with all the Latin and Greek that was ever written." With this John himself would have agreed, for by his own admission he did not like Latin.

In his methods Sherwin was equally forward-looking. Making little use of textbooks in his classes, he is said to have preferred to unfold his subject with homely illustrations from life and nature, as well as frequent blackboard demonstrations to clarify problems in mathematics, navigation, astronomy, and mechanics. Sherwin also did away with corporal punishment in his school, on the theory that the boys would keep out of mischief as long as the teacher aroused their interest and kept them busy. When censure was required, it was administered privately; honest effort met with public praise. The headmaster familiarized himself with the home background of each pupil and when they left school helped them to find jobs. As an associate wrote after Sherwin's death, "There was a reality about him, a freedom from arrogance and pretension, show and routine," which earned him the affection of his pupils and the respect of all.

Although the English High School course lasted three years, at this time only a quarter of the entrants completed it. John Rogers left at the end of his second year, possibly for financial reasons, or possibly because he did not particularly enjoy school. By his own estimate he was an average student, best in mathematics and algebra, but when the opportunity offered he was glad enough to escape from his studies. In August 1846, a few months after he had left school to go to work in Boston as a store clerk, John wrote to his sister Ellen of a friend who was about to undergo the "torture" of a two-day examination. "If I had kept on with my studies," he wrote, "I suppose I should have entered with him, but I feel better satisfied where I am, than if I was preparing myself for some profession. I know what an examination is, from my experience at the English H. School, too well to envy him. . . ."

John Rogers owed more to his two years at the English High School than he realized or would admit. The training he received there in mathematics, mechanics, and surveying undoubtedly led to his choice of engineering as his profession a few years later. The same training helped him greatly during the ten years he spent as a mechanic and draftsman before turning professional artist in 1859. Even after he had taken up sculpture, he found his knowledge of mechanics useful.

Although from a cultural point of view it can hardly be counted an advantage, Rogers' lack of classical training in high school may also have played an important part in his development as an artist. When he visited Italy later, Rogers reacted strongly against classical tradition in art. This reaction, so different from that of earlier American sculptors, marked Rogers off from his predecessors and helped turn American sculpture in new directions. How much the character of his schooling influenced his feeling toward classicism it is impossible to say, but it is likely that his comparative unfamiliarity with Roman and Greek literature explains, in part, his later rejection of artistic conventions based almost entirely on classical sources.

In Rogers' artistic development the most immediately significant part of his training at the English High School was the instruction in drawing he received there. Of his teacher we know little more than his name, Edward Seager, and that he introduced the study of drawing at the school in 1844 and remained until about 1850. Several drawings in pencil made by Rogers on his 1849 trip to Spain testify to the thoroughness of Seager's instruction; they are literal and detailed views of buildings, showing a good knowledge of perspective and shading — in short, the work of a competent draftsman rather than an artist. Indeed, the very fact that Seager was an instructor at the English High School suggests that he was primarily a skilled draftsman who could be expected to fit his pupils for the drawing requirements of surveying, engineering, or related professions.

This introduction to the graphic arts made more than a casual impression on John Rogers. According to his own account he immediately set his heart on becoming an artist. The idea met with little encouragement from his family, however. Despite their remote connection with the eminently successful painter John Singleton Copley, who had been their mother's uncle-by-marriage, neither John Rogers, Sr., nor his lawyer brother Henry Bromfield Rogers felt that the life of an artist offered sufficient financial returns to be seriously considered, at least in the absence of transcendent talent. If John did seriously wish to become an artist at this early date, he was overruled by his elders and obliged to turn his talents to more mundane uses. His interest continued though, for he was still taking lessons from Seager a year and a half after his withdrawal from the High School.

If John did receive any encouragement from within the family it probably came from his Aunt Mary Jane, whose husband, the Rev. Dr. Ephraim Peabody, was now minister of King's Chapel at Boston. As a young woman, Mary Jane Derby had shown some talent as an artist, going so far beyond the usual schoolgirl repertory of fruit pieces and landscapes as to design a painstakingly detailed lithograph of her father's house in Salem. Serious trouble with her eyes, supposed to have been brought on by the close work involved in such artistic productions, had forced her to abandon her pencil soon after her marriage, but Aunt Peabody was always ready to encourage artistic talent in others and no doubt did so in the case of her nephew.

His half-formed plans of becoming an artist checked by the more practical dictates of his elders, John left high school in June 1846 to take his first job. Possibly through the influence of Headmaster Thomas Sherwin, who knew the family of one of the proprietors, John was hired as a clerk by the Boston dry goods dealers, Jewett, Tebbetts & Green. After a brief vacation with an uncle and aunt at Walpole, and an overnight visit with his sister Ellen, who was taking Dr. Wesselhoeft's fashionable water cure at Brattleboro, Vermont, John went to work in the store at 44 Milk Street probably sometime in September. He was just short of his seventeenth birthday.

At first business was very heavy at the store and frequently it was ten or eleven at night before John got out, with several miles still to walk to his home in Roxbury. Next morning he had to be up at five and walk back to Boston. After three weeks of this, his mother reported to Ellen, John was worn down and thin. With winter approaching, it was decided that he should stay in Boston with his grandmother Derby and come home on weekends. John was not enthusiastic about the idea at first, apparently, but by the end of the winter he admitted to Ellen that it was "very agreeable to pass the winter in the city, but in the summer," he added, "I like to live at my country seat, in the bosom of my family, surrounded with lilacks, grape vines & clouds of dust." Despite his joking tone, John really meant what he said. Neither this first winter of semi-independence nor the following years spent away from home lessened his very close attachment to his parents and his brother and sisters. It was evidently a happy home, in spite of the financial cares which Mr. Rogers was never able wholly to banish, and there is no evidence that young John ever felt the need of rebelling against it.

Of all the family, now brought to its full complement by the recent arrival of the twins, Bessie and Fanny, John was closest to his older sister Ellen. Playmates in childhood, in adolescence they became correspondents, for Ellen's chronic poor health kept her away from Roxbury for long periods. To Ellen John wrote often and freely about his own activities and feelings, what was going on about him, and what the rest of the family was doing. The correspondence began haltingly enough in June 1846 with a letter from John to Ellen at Northampton, the first letter he had ever written without first making a copy, as he proudly informed her; the letter ended with the firm request that hereafter she should write to him directly and not to their father with a little postscript to John, Jr. During the next four years few letters were exchanged, since Ellen and John were both home most of the time; those that John did write were generally brief and full of apologies for his inability to write as much as his sister. A typical opening sentence reads: "With me it is always the hardest part of a letter to begin it, particularly out of so small an assortment, as my stock of news consists of." Gradually, however, his stock of news increased and his aversion to writing abated; the flow of letters swelled until John was writing once or even twice a week; the letters became, in fact, a sort of diary in which is recorded most of the story of John Rogers' early career. The preservation of this series of letters, John's side of it at any rate, was probably due to Ellen's fondness for her brother, but it was certainly not against his wishes. "Be careful *not* to burn, or otherwise destroy," he wrote at seventeen, "such valuable documents as this and the other letters I have written to you."

Outside his family, the young dry goods clerk's chief interests were reading, mechanical experiments, and drawing. In October 1847 he joined the Mercantile Library Association, which offered a series of lectures, beginning with one by Daniel Webster, as well as the use of a reading room where he thought he would spend his evenings when there was nothing else to do. But for him the most exciting event of the season was not the appearance of Dickens' latest novel, *Dombey and Son,* which Ellen urged him to read at once.

> I went into the Mechanics Fair yesterday afternoon [he reported to his sister on September 26], and staid there four hours. I believe I saw everything, for I took each hall separately, and beginning at the outside, gradually came to the center. . . . The entrance is in Faneuil Hall; here are displayed all kinds of dry goods, needle work, furniture &c. &c. There were some cakes of soap near the door, two or three feet square and eight or ten inches thick. They were beautifully shaded and ornamented with stars made of different coloured soap. Another very pretty thing was a case with a number of dageurotypes [sic] of Tom Thumb, taken in his principal characters. They were very well done and looked as natural as life. Passing into Quincy Hall there were all sorts of machines and new inventions, some of them very curious. The most amusing part of the exhibition here, was an Electric Magnetic Battery. Any body that wanted to take a shock could do so. Once in a while a stout man would come up, and they would give him such a shock as to lay him flat on the floor, then he would get up and sneak off, looking about as sheepish as any body need to. Dr. Morton had some beautiful specimens of artificial teeth and one set in operation, moved by a spring. But there were so many things there it would be almost useless to try to give any description of them. There has nothing interested me so much for a long time.

Certainly the life of a clerk behind a dry goods counter was not nearly so interesting, nor did it offer much promise for the future. By the time his eighteenth birthday came around on October 30, 1847, John was beginning to think of going back to school. And the following April he was very happy, as he said, to leave Messrs. Jewett, Tebbetts & Green's shop to accept a position as "rodman" or surveyor's assistant with the Boston Water Works.

The subject of popular agitation as early as 1825, the Water Works were authorized by the State Legislature in 1846. The first Board of Water Commissioners was then appointed and work began on the aqueduct. The line of the conduit pipe from Lake Cochituate (formerly Long Pond), the source of the water supply, to Brookline was divided into three divisions. The first or Western Division, from the lake to the Newton Lower Falls–East Needham road, a distance of 5½ miles, was surveyed in July and ground was broken at Cochituate on August 20, 1846. E. Sylvester Chesborough was Chief Engineer of the Division; T. E. Sickles, the Resident Engineer, with M. Conant, William E. Furgurson, and G. H. Hyde as assistants.

Because of quicksands and a high water table near the lake, the laying of the conduit in the Western Division was expected to be especially difficult, slow, and expensive and on April 1, 1848, the Water Commissioners reported that this section would probably be the last to be finished. The challenge was taken up with spirit by Chesborough, Sickles, and their assistants and every effort was made to meet it. It was just at this time that John Rogers joined the Division as a very junior assistant, probably on the recommendation of his uncle, Henry Bromfield Rogers, a prominent lawyer, alderman of Boston, and one of the Water Commissioners.

Boston's new water system was to be carried from Lake Cochituate through a brick conduit covered with earth. The only exposed parts were the crossing of the Charles River and a valley in Needham, where the pipe was to be carried by stone arches in a severely simple style "indicative of a prudent economy, but at the same time such as would not degrade the character of a great public work, or give offense even to a fastidious taste." In the Western Division, however, all the work was to be underground. Built of brick masonry eight inches thick and laid in "hydraulic cement," the conduit pipe was in section an egg-shaped oval, large end down, the greatest width five feet and depth six feet four inches inside. The pipe rested upon four feet of earth and was to be covered by a great earthen embankment four feet high and eight feet wide at the top.

Rogers' part in this great undertaking was a small one, but for a boy who hoped to become a civil engineer the experience was stimulating. Besides working as a rodman on the works themselves, John also acted as errand boy for Sickles and the other engineers, making frequent trips to Boston, chiefly to buy or order pieces of equipment and to pay bills. His salary was $39.00 a month. After more than a year behind a dry goods counter at $50 a year, an out-of-doors job with an adequate salary and a future was just what he wanted. That he gave satisfaction is evident from a letter to his Uncle Henry in October:

> My Dear Uncle,
>
> I most heartily thank you for your valuable present of a gold watch and chain, which I received from you this morning, and assure you that I feel more than satisfied in your selection, but am somewhat embarrassed in returning my thanks for so costly a present.
>
> It is very gratifying to know that you have heard such good accounts of me from those in whose employ I am, and you need not fear but my ambition to succeed in the profession that I have commenced, is fully equal to the wishes you entertain for me.
>
> Your interest in my success, I will ever consider a sufficient inducement to overcome all obstacles that may lie between my present position and my future hopes, and with a knowledge of your esteemed friendship, I will ever remain
>
> Your Affectionate Nephew,
> John Rogers, Jr.

The work at Cochituate had its elements of excitement, too. The Western Division engineers, Chesborough and Sickles, were determined to be the first, rather than the last, to complete their work and their enthusiasm was transmitted to the workmen. Working at top speed during the summer of 1848, they completed the laying of the pipe through the Western Division shortly before August 20, second anniversary of the ground-breaking. The two other sections were completed only a couple of months later.

To celebrate the completion of the work, Sickles determined to let the water in and go through in a boat. He was to be accompanied by Chesborough and John B. Jervis of New York, consulting engineer to the whole Boston Water Works. Mr. Jervis declined, as did Chesborough, which was just as well, for the triumphal progress was something less than stately. At the last minute, Sickles invited John Rogers to fill one of the vacant seats. John, who was about to leave for home on the train, of course accepted the invitation. Explaining his failure to appear in Roxbury as expected, he thus described the opening of navigation through the Cochituate Aqueduct:

> We provided ourselves with overcoats, and after some delay, occasioned by dams in the arch, we started about seven o'clock in the evening with cheers from those assembled to see us off. There were three of us — Mr. Sickles, Mr. Ferguson and myself, I sitting in the bow of the boat and, in fact, being the first one that ever went

> through the division in a boat. We met with some difficulty once in a while from dams and timbers &c which had not been taken out and from the crazy sort of boat that we had, which would dip water with the least movement to the right or left. We found it much more laborious to propel it than we had anticipated, but after four hours of this sort of fun, we arrived at East Needham, the end of the division, a distance of nearly six miles. There we got out and drove home, taking our tea a little after twelve. So much for glory! I would not have missed the chance of going down on that occasion for a good deal.

One part of the fun John omitted to tell his father, though he mentioned it to his sister Ellen to shock her a bit, no doubt. Their occasional stops to bail out the boat were occasions also for mixing up brandy punches, "just to keep the damp out, *that's all.*"

For the first time in his life, John was living away from home and comparatively free of parental control. There is no doubt he enjoyed it. Though he made frequent weekend trips to Roxbury, he spent most of his free time in or around Cochituate from April to December and took his fun where he found it. It was all innocent enough, for John was not the sort of boy to sow very wild oats, but his sense of fun expressed itself more freely at Cochituate than it is likely to have done at home.

> I find [he wrote to Ellen in August] that I have got to be quite a hand amongst the girls and I suppose that you will be surprised to hear that I have just had a kiss from one of the prettiest that you can find anywhere round. O——h! but didn't it taste good. But that is only one from an innumerable number which have been accumulating from the prettiest girls round. I have been out sailing or walking on moonlight evenings most every night with them and go home about twelve or one o'clock. Cochituate isn't so bad a place after all.

This sort of thing was hardly calculated to give comfort to a fond sister, much less a fond mother!

Nor did it go unnoticed in the little village of Cochituate. Rumors reflecting on the moral character of several of the young engineers eventually came to their ears. To check this whispering campaign, John and two of his co-workers, one of them the Resident Engineer, devised an elaborate prank which apparently had the desired effect. After printing up a set of rules and regulations for "The Cochituate Gossiping Club," they distributed them secretly to the worst of the town's taletellers. Then John dressed himself up as a girl and went walking one evening with Mr. Sickles. Making certain that they were seen, they boldly went into the works office and locked the door. The subsequent revelation of the plot and the obvious discomfiture it caused certain parties in the village gave Rogers and his fellow-conspirators the greatest delight.

Not all of John's leisure was spent in such larks. In March, shortly before going to Cochituate, he had spent $1.50 on an encyclopedia. His five other book purchases during the ensuing year were mainly technical — *Davies Surveying, Davies Legendre, Index Rerum,* and *Mechanics Companion* — but one title, *Rosa Lee,* suggests rather lighter reading, and from earlier and later remarks we know he did read Dickens. In the way of improving entertainments Cochituate had little to offer besides an occasional concert or lecture, such as Mr. Wade's on phrenology in August (at which John had his bumps read for fifty cents). He was close enough to Boston, however, to go to the Museum (actually a theater) a few times, as well as to Horticultural Hall to see Hiram Powers' famous marble statue, "The Greek Slave," then the subject of much comment, both favorable and unfavorable, among Boston art-lovers. John, however, made no comment other than to record the cost of seeing it, $.25.

This visit to the "Greek Slave" would suggest that John had not altogether abandoned his interest in art and his account book bears this out. Although his drawing lessons from Mr. Seager had ended by January 1848, the pupil continued on his own. From time to time he bought various artist's supplies — crayons, pencils, a drawing board, charcoal, drawing paper — and on September 3 he even recorded the expenditure of ten cents paid to a "bog trotter" who stood for his portrait. This last is lost, but a number of landscape drawings in pencil have survived, including some of scenes at Cochituate. Though adequate as representations of things seen, these drawings show no particular evidence of a pictorial gift. They were no better, no worse than most of the work of a host of amateurs stimulated by the introduction of art education in nineteenth-century schools. Rogers himself may have been aware of his limitations, which would help to explain why he was so easily diverted from his wish to become an artist. Still, the artistic impulse existed in him, awaiting only the opportunity to express itself in another form.

This opportunity came quite unexpectedly. Early in December 1848, still working outdoors at Cochituate, John Rogers caught a severe cold. This caused an inflammation of the eyes which stubbornly persisted and finally, about the 13th, he was forced to give up his job and return home to Roxbury for treatment. This was a great disappointment, for he had enjoyed his nine months on the job and left several good friends there. Worst of all, the condition of his eyes made it questionable whether he would ever again be able to do the close work involved in civil engineering. The future, lately so bright, suddenly looked bleak indeed. Barred from his usual resources, reading and drawing, John whiled away the time at home as best he could, paying occasional visits to his friends at Cochituate, going to occasional lectures and concerts, and running in to Boston now and then for variety.

It was on one of these Boston jaunts that he met the friend whose amateur work in clay inspired him to take up modelling himself. The subject of Rogers' first clay figure, like the identity of the "young dentist" who inspired him to model it, is today unknown. Among his papers, there is a pencilled list in his hand of over forty titles of figures or groups he modelled or projected during his early, amateur years. Although the titles are not listed throughout in the order in which they were made, it may well be that the first one on the list — "Dutchman" — was also the first to come from his hand.

Although Rogers found in modelling "a great resource and enjoyment" during the difficult days when his sight seemed permanently impaired, the idea of becoming a sculptor did not at first occur to him. At the time, his first object was to cure the inflammation in his eyes. It was with this in mind that in July 1849 he was sent to Spain on a trip financed by his Grandmother Derby and Uncle Henry Rogers. Like today's tourist with his camera, John had brought along his sketchbook and charcoal to record the sights, thereby largely negating whatever benefit the sea voyage had done his weak eyes. Four of his drawings from the trip have been preserved, one of Gibraltar from the water, three of Moorish remains in Granada. The most interesting, an unfinished view of the Court of Lions in the Alhambra, shows to perfection the painstaking literalness which would probably have prevented Rogers from ever attaining the rank of a Darley in the field of illustration. Every detail of ornamentation with which the Moorish gate framing the view was covered is recorded with religious accuracy on an almost microscopic scale. Though Rogers completed only half the picture, intending to copy the corresponding half at a later time, the work took him the better part of four days.

A similarly literal approach to the art of Spain is apparent in young Rogers' few comments on the subject. In the Cathedral at Malaga a series of sculptured scenes from the Bible elicited this comment: "They are as large as life, or nearly so and are well executed, though not very agreeable to look at." The Lion fountain in the Alhambra struck him as not showing "any great skill in sculpture." At the Carthusian Convent in Granada he saw paintings and carvings but was more impressed by the quality of the marble than by the handling of it. The Generalife at Granada also had paintings which he looked at dutifully, but it was "the fine views and delicious air" of the place which really attracted him.

Rogers returned to his family in October with lots of stories to tell, sketches to show, but little if any improvement in his eyes, for whose benefit the voyage had been undertaken. If he had had any hope of resuming his interrupted engineering career, this was dispelled by the state of his eyes. For the winter he would have to stay at home and try further treatment, and in the spring look about for a job which would not overtask his sight.

With time on his hands, a state of affairs he never enjoyed, Rogers turned again to his clay and modelling sticks. At least one of the figures he did during the next nine months is known by name: "The Apple Woman."* In his account book there is a separate little account, dated January–March 1850, recording the expenditure of $34.10 for having several plaster casts made of this figure. On the credit side was listed only $2.00 from a Mrs. Quincy. This brief, unbalanced record gives considerable point to Rogers' later statement; "I would have been glad to take this up as a business, but my relatives thought it offered a poor support, and favored another offer which I had for a position in a machine shop." John was too practical not to see the wisdom of their advice, and too cautious by nature to take a chance and give all for art. Bowing for the second time to the practical dictates of older and wiser heads he accepted the machine shop offer. In July 1850, at the age of twenty, he left home for Manchester, New Hampshire, there to learn the machinist's trade.

* "Checker Players" [Catalogue, No. 3] may also have been done at this time, since Rogers later referred to it as one of his first pieces.

CHAPTER III

Learning a Trade

IN 1850 Manchester was a young and thriving mill town. Although small mills had existed around the Amoskeag Falls early in the century, it was only ten years since the "new mills" had been built on the east bank of the Merrimac River and the town of Manchester laid out. Just back from the river bank, lined with massive cotton factories, foundries, and machine shops, stood the "blocks" of company houses, neat brick rows marching up the hill toward the upper town. Beyond them, on the high ground, a model town had been built, its regular plan pleasantly broken by a number of small parks. In the lower town lived the mill hands; above, the company officials and independent tradespeople. In 1850 the two elements of the population were still fairly homogeneous, but the tide of Irish immigration was gradually displacing the Yankee girls who had at first made up the vast majority of the mill hands. Before John Rogers left in 1856, Manchester had seen its first anti-Catholic, anti-Irish riot.

The Amoskeag Corporation, Manchester's industrial heart, was a complex enterprise. Besides several large mills which turned out cotton goods and muslin de laine, the Corporation maintained a foundry and several machine shops for making and repairing machinery, not only for the Manchester mills but for factories in other New England cities as well. A year before Rogers came to Manchester, the machine shops had begun manufacturing railroad locomotives. In 1851 the various departments of the Amoskeag machine shop alone employed a total of about 500 men.

John Rogers probably owed his job in the Amoskeag machine shop directly to William Amory, president of the Amoskeag Manufacturing Company, a Bostonian known personally to John Rogers, Sr., and Henry Bromfield Rogers, both of whom were also Amoskeag stockholders. Lacking any experience as a mechanic, John entered at the apprentice level, although there is no indication that he was bound, as machine shop apprentices normally were, for a term of three years. An apprentice's pay was nominal —

50 cents a day the first year, 66 2/3 cents the next, and 83 1/3 the third—but at the end of his term he was practically assured of a steady job and good pay thereafter, in Manchester or elsewhere, for fully trained mechanics were much in demand.

Rogers arrived in Manchester on July 15, 1850. The same afternoon at one o'clock he was put to work in the shop where cotton machinery was made. By the end of the second day, when he wrote home for the first time, he complained that his neck was "suffering martyrdom" from "leaning over a bench all day." His day was a long one. "In the first place the bells are rung at about 4½ in the morning; that is to get up. At seven minutes before five they ring a second time and then we have to go into the shop and commence work. At seven we wash and go to breakfast and come back a quarter before eight. At half past twelve to dinner and back quarter past one and to tea at seven when I have felt so tired I have been to bed soon after."

In answer to a nervous inquiry from his mother he reported that he had "hardly perspired at all. . . . It may be because I dress very coolly as I take off coat & waistcoat and neck cloth and roll up my sleeves and put on a light straw hat." The dirt was harder to contend with. "My hands get almost black before I have been in the shop five minutes but they keep growing blacker and blacker till at last they get a regular shining black polish like a new air tight stove and you may imagine what a job it is to wash them three times a day before eating. . . . I have almost used my nail brush up for I am bound to have them clean once a day."

Thanks to his natural aptitude and perhaps a little to Mr. Amory's interest in his welfare, Rogers made rapid progress. After less than a week he was set to "much finer work" and in another week he was promoted from hand work to a machine lathe. Machinery fascinated him. "It appears singular," he told his mother, "but nearly all the work in iron is done or assisted by machinery. If a bar is to be turned perfectly straight, all that is to be done is to put it in the lathe and wait till it is done." Frequent variations in his duties helped to relieve the monotony of a fourteen-hour day; now he was turning pieces in the engines, now filing and polishing them in a lathe, now fitting joints and filing iron pieces by hand.

There was danger in the work, too, to add excitement. "I burnt my tongue rather singularly the other day," he wrote home in November. "The chips of iron that are cut by the turning engines are as hot as a cinder, and as I was leaning over my work whistling one of these chips flew into my mouth and it was some time before I could sputter it out. We have to look out for our eyes," he added. "Some of the boys have scars on their eyes caused by hot chips. I never got any bad ones in yet." His report of another, more serious, accident on Christmas Eve was little calculated to add to the holiday spirit in Roxbury.

> We have had several accidents at the shop today. First, the main shaft in our room broke & as all speed was on it made a great disturbance. It was close to where I was at work. This afternoon the chain to the large derrick in the foundry broke by the weight of a tub of melted iron containing five tons of the metal & went completely over one man from head to foot & strange to say, though he is pretty badly burnt, yet he is not dangerously. It went over another man's face & burnt his whiskers off & that was all. They say that when iron is so hot it runs off before it burns & the reason this man was burnt so was because of his clothes.

On the whole, John was satisfied with his new job. Despite a feeling of superiority toward the "low sort of fellows" who made up most of the shop force, he liked working with his hands, and felt that he was on his way to a useful, respectable, and profitable career. He had the pleasure, too, of knowing that he was giving complete satisfaction to his employers. Amos Buxton, his foreman, even went so far as to tell John he would part with every hand he had before he would part with him. No praise could have pleased him more, unless it was that of his friends and relatives. Even his Uncle Peabody, the rather dour minister of King's Chapel in Boston, began to think well of his nephew, something of a change of heart, John felt.

Although he felt "rather desolate" the first few days in Manchester, Rogers would not admit to homesickness, "though I must say," as he wrote to his father, "I have thought it no small change from the comfort of home with kind friends all about me." New friends were soon forthcoming, but no boarding house could supply the comforts of home. Mrs. Fifield, his first landlady, though "a very clever old woman," kept a table not entirely to John's taste. "The eating is fair to middling" he reported to his mother. "Breakfast and tea seem to be thought more of than dinner for then we always have pies and doughnuts and good bread and butter and sometimes berries and milk. For dinner we have had no meat except boiled ham and one day beefsteak. They generally give us a dish of boiled pork and peas or something of the kind and bread & butter." In Manchester, he also noted, they had the "curious fashion" of having Sunday dinner about one and tea a little after four. In summer breakfast was from 7:00 to 7:45, after two hours of work, dinner from 12:30 to 1:15, and tea at 7:00. In winter the schedule changed, breakfast coming before the 7:00 o'clock opening time, and tea at 7:30 in the evening. Rogers preferred the winter breakfast schedule as he disliked going to work with an empty stomach and appreciated having one meal for which he did not have to scrub his hands. When Mrs. Fifield moved in November, Rogers took a room in No. 6, Machine Shop Block, the home of C. P. Crane, Superintendent of the Machine Shop. Though Crane was not popular in the Shop, where he was privately known as "the old bird," Rogers found him agreeable enough in his own home. He moved again, however, the following March to No. 94, Machine Shop Block, a company house rented by Mrs. Nancy Richardson, whose son Charles (later Paymaster of the Amoskeag Corporation) became one of John's closest friends. With the motherly Mrs. Richardson, Rogers at last found an acceptable substitute for home.

Social life in Manchester, like its eating habits, struck a suburban Bostonian as rather amusingly provincial. In his letters home, particularly to his sisters, he described it with a superior air which was only partly put on. "There is such an *entirely* different set of people here that, of course, the parties are in correspondence," he told Ellen. Most of the town's gay life centered upon public "levees, picnics, and select parties" which were advertised every few nights, "ninepence a ticket, some of them." The following description of one of these affairs undoubtedly amused his sisters.

> The long-wished for time arrived last week for blowing out the lights, as the 20th of March is the last day we light up and now we get out at dark. One of the corporations had a "blow-out Picnic" to celebrate the happy event. All the operatives were entitled to a ticket and as they were mostly girls they had the privilege of giving a ticket to their "fellers" but no one else was admitted, except by favor. I happened to be a favored one and I was thankful for the opportunity for I knew it would be a novelty to me. When I first went there the girls were all sitting round the sides of the hall rather stiffly, three or four hundred of them and in the centre were the refreshment tables. To prevent confusion it was all distributed on the plates. Each one had an apple, an orange, a few raisins, some cake and candy. Pretty soon they started the "string game" which I have forgotten whether I ever described to you but I guess the Dr. can. The hearty relish with which the girls would kiss the beaux and be kissed by them was a luxury to see. (Now Laura you needn't think I did anything of *that* sort). The refreshments were eaten and the tables were cleared off and the fiddles played and we danced, we did. It was amusing to see the tastes in dress. One was particularly striking. She had on a black dress, white scolloped [?] apron trimmed with black bows, sky blue kid gloves & blue scarf. She thought she was making a dash and she was as tickled and happy as a child. I was sorry afterwards that I didn't dance with her for the sport of it. Another had a large lace cap with a border of gold lace round it about two inches broad &c &c. I was walking round the hall with a friend looking after the pretty girls and had settled on a pair of twins as the prettiest girls in the room. We were walking near them and admiring them when we heard one of them say "I swow! I'm almost

squeezed to death." Romance was at a discount with us. However, I danced with her afterwards and she used no more emphatic expressions so I put it down as a slip of the tongue.

Even the amusements enjoyed by the young people of "the better kind" seemed a bit hearty to this city-bred young man. "I have often thought," he wrote, this time to his father, "if you would only be looking in and see our games, what you would say. You might not think that everything went on quite so much in Boston fashion as they did at the dance you came to here. However 'when you are in Rome you must do as the Romans do.' The forfeits which are given here would make considerable commotion if they were enforced amongst a set of the young folks of Roxbury in playing a game of button."

More sophisticated entertainment was provided by such visiting attractions as Señor Blitz, the ventriloquist, whose routine Rogers found practically unchanged since he had seen him in Northampton more than ten years before, and Richard Henry Dana, whose Lyceum lecture on *Macbeth* Rogers dismissed as "stupid." Much more enjoyable to the practical young mechanic was a series of lectures by Louis Agassiz before the teachers institute. "What a grand man he is," Rogers wrote after hearing the great naturalist. "I think it is splendid to hear a man talk who is so wrapt up in his subject & understands it so thoroughly."

Much to his delight Rogers discovered soon after his arrival that the Hookset Brick Yard a short distance up river from Manchester offered a supply of modelling clay which he later described as the best he had ever found. Since he was still having trouble with his eyes and could do little reading, he resumed his modelling. Perched on a high chair in Mrs. Richardson's kitchen, he spent many an evening and Sunday working at his little clay figures. One night, he later recalled, he worked all night and was still at it when the family came down to breakfast.

Only a few of the subjects he modelled during his first two years in Manchester are mentioned in Rogers' letters. "Robinson Crusoe," made as a present for Uncle Henry at Christmas 1850, was generally well received at home, the only criticism coming from another uncle, Dr. George Derby, who thought Crusoe's cap should have been on his head. "He must recollect," the artist explained, "that Robinson is *at home* — in his house — and has manners enough to take his cap off." Uncle Henry, though he had not favored John's making a career in art, was proud of his talent nonetheless and acknowledged the gift in "a beautiful note."

"Haymaker," a boy with a rake and jug, was made for Benjamin Kent,

Roxbury schoolteacher and librarian of the Roxbury Athenaeum. Mr. Kent came up to see it in Manchester in March 1851 and, although he "*attempted* to criticize" some of the details of the figure, was so pleased with it that the very same night he sat down and wrote over a hundred lines about the scenes of his boyhood.

Rogers had scarcely completed his "Haymaker" before he set to work on another figure which he christened "The Old Bachelor." This was intended for sale by lottery at Roxbury's May Fair, the annual charity bazaar organized by the ladies of the community for the benefit of the local missionary to the poor. John recommended that it be given a glass case to protect it and hoped that it would be drawn by one of the family, for, as he said "I have taken more interest in it than I did in the last." His fellow workmen were quite impressed with it, too. "Well, I swow," said one, "if that ain't considerable of a git up." "Unprotected Female" was probably made this same spring and taken home to Roxbury. Of this nothing is known other than the intriguing fact that Rogers hoped it would be put out of sight when his Grandma Derby visited Roxbury.

Being far enough from home so that he could get to Roxbury only occasionally, Rogers made of writing to his family a regular Sunday habit, one he kept up until his marriage. No longer did he complain, as he had some years before, that he had nothing to write about. Among other things, it gave him a chance to impart some elder-brotherly wisdom to his younger sisters. A letter to sixteen-year-old Laura in December 1850 conveniently summarized for her and for us some of his practical conclusions on the conduct of life, based on twenty years of experience and Yankee education:

> Mother says you will leave school next year. I suppose you are glad of it. You will keep up your studying when you leave I hope. *Go it while you are young. . . .* Now I am in rather a moralizing mood I will give you a few of my standard maxims. The first one which you can most frequently use and which will save you a great deal of vexation and waste of time is — *never ask another to do what you can as well do yourself* — for it is a sign of laziness and *lazy folks take the most trouble.* You try it a few times & see if you don't feel more cheerful than when you ask someone else to do it for you & they make mistakes and after all you have to do it yourself. And again — *make friends & keep them.* You can never have too many.
>
> "Small service is true service while it lasts;
> Of Friends, however humble, scorn not one:
> The daisy, by the shadow that it casts,
> Protects the lingering dew-drop from the sun."
>
> *A stitch in time saves nine.* This relates to your sewing & when you come to do your own sewing as I do you will see the force of it. *Waste not want not.* You have heard

of this before. Don't forget it. *Haste makes waste.* Do whatever you are about promptly & quickly, but *never in a hurry and flurry.* These are my standard ones and I have seen the advantage of them all. You may have them for a new year's present.

Even more revealing of John's highminded but uncomplicated view of life is a letter he addressed to his older sister Ellen in January 1852. Despite a trace of not very convincing fatalism, it is filled with the confidence in human perfectibility and the determination to get ahead which he carried with him throughout his life.

It has crossed my mind repeatedly, in thinking of the New Year, "Where may I be another N. Year." I may be dead, and I may live to realize all my plans for the future. We *may* die and we *may* live. It is our duty to be prepared for the one, and for the other, with some aim in view, to move steadily on. Our ambition cannot be too high. The farther off the mark the more diligently we must toil to acquire it. I believe a person may accomplish almost anything, if they go to work with a full determination to do so. . . . I am thankful for possessing a cheerful heart and a persevering nature and with these I can overlook most of the lighter troubles in life, and, if I am permitted to live, I hope I may be a useful man to society. "Act well your part, there all the honor lies."

During the first half of 1852, the part he was to act was still in doubt. After eighteen months at machine work in the shop, in February John was at last promoted to the drafting room. The change was welcome, as it meant his learning something new, and it made him feel that he was getting ahead. Mr. Amory even held out the prospect of his becoming a travelling agent for the company. But by April Rogers' thoughts were running in a different channel. For two months he had been making drawings of locomotive engines. The next step, he felt, was to gain experience in running a locomotive, after which he would turn to the study of marine engines. "As long as I want to be a thorough mechanic I should get some knowledge of all parts of the business," he reasoned in a letter to his father, "and as soon as I have acquired a pretty good knowledge of one part push on to the next."

This ambitious plan apparently met with approval both at home and with Mr. Amory. Later that summer Rogers did in fact go on the road between Manchester and Concord, not as an actual engineer, but as an observer. His father, according to Mrs. Rogers, approved highly and Mrs. Rogers herself expressed her pleasure at his "spirit and determination," though she was worried about possible accidents, especially getting dirt in his eyes, which still troubled him. John met this problem by applying his inventive mind to making a pair of goggles.

By late September John was ready for his next step, the study of marine engines. On the recommendation of Mr. Amory and Mr. Bayley of the Amoskeag Machine Shop, he decided to go to New York and apply for a job at the Novelty Iron Works at East Twelfth Street and Avenue C overlooking the East River. Arriving in New York on October 1st, he was received rather coolly by Horatio Allen, one of the owners to whom he had been recommended, but he did get a job in the machine shop. His wages, 75 cents a day, or $4.50 a week, were little, if any, more than he had been earning in Manchester, but the working day was shorter, ten hours Monday through Friday and nine on Saturday. After working twelve to fourteen hours a day in Manchester, John relished the prospect of long evenings. He quickly felt at home in the shop, enjoyed the work, and discovered to his surprise, for he had a Bostonian suspicion of New York, that his fellow workmen were a much better class of men than he had expected. In addition Mr. Allen held out the hope that he might get an engineer's berth on a ship through his connection with the Novelty Works. For the moment, at least, he had every reason to congratulate himself for leaving Manchester.

Finding it difficult to get a suitable boarding house near his work, since the neighborhood swarmed with what he referred to as "nasty dirty irish" and Germans, with nearly every shop and cellar a "rum hole," John decided to try keeping house for himself. He finally found two unfurnished rooms, which he painted and whitewashed to hide the smudges commemorating past battles between men and mosquitoes. He furnished the apartment with bed, two armchairs, table, washstand, bureau, stove, and carpet at a cost of almost forty-five dollars. To his fellow boarders at Mrs. Smith's at No. 93 Avenue C, where he still took his meals, this move was taken as a preliminary to marriage. Rogers had a hard time convincing them otherwise, for they could hardly believe that a single man would go to the trouble of furnishing a room and living in it by himself. To John, however, it was well worth the trouble to have things just right. "Oh, Mother," he wrote as soon as he was settled in it, "you don't know how comfortable I am here. I'm as cosy as any old bachelor without a pretty little partner to make his bed & sweep his room can be. . . . The bed has not a wrinkle, the hems of the sheets come right side out, a nice clean towel is laid over the pitcher & there is a place for everything and everything in its place. The broom stands in the corner (the brush end up) & in fact I think Mr. Spellman could hardly find fault with the order everything is in. I think any slovenly girls would be afraid to apply to me for a husband if they should see my rooms *today*."

Rogers had an additional reason for wanting extra room and freedom. In his eagerness to get ahead he planned to use some of his spare time evening and weekends for mechanical experiments which would round out his practical training. To this end he set up in his extra room a work bench with a small vise, an anvil, and a lathe. Modelling in clay for the time being was forgotten.

These energetic efforts to improve his opportunities met with whole-hearted approval at home. His wealthy uncle, Henry B. Rogers, to whom John had diplomatically reported his plans and progress soon after reaching New York, was particularly pleased. So much so, in fact, that he was moved to offer his assistance in an unexpected and most acceptable way. Some time before, a New York specialist visiting John's Aunt and Uncle Mason in Boston had indicated that the young man's chronic eye trouble could be cured. Uncle Henry now offered to pay for the cure proposed by Dr. Elliott. John jumped at the offer, for he had practically given up hope of ever using his eyes freely again. "I frequently think how much I would do if I had my eyes," he had written to Ellen earlier that same year. "I certainly never felt the wish to read so strongly as since I have been unable. It may be for my good in the end," he added, "for if I ever *am* able to use my eyes again as I could once, I would make up for much lost time, now that I know their worth."

Dr. Elliott's fee of two hundred dollars, to be paid in full one week after the first visit, checked both John's and his uncle's enthusiasm, however, and on advice from another doctor Rogers consulted Dr. Carnochan, Professor of Surgery at the New York Medical College. Carnochan not only scoffed at Elliott's diagnosis of "amaransis," but offered a cure at a much smaller fee. All the doctors, it turned out, considered Elliott "an unprincipled Quack," because he held "the most mistaken idea" that a specialist in one organ was "as likely to cure a disease seated there as one who has a general knowledge of the whole system." Dr. Carnochan's diagnosis was "congestion of the eyes" and the remedy he proposed was simple, drawing off the congestion through the insertion of a seton in the patient's neck. The treatment, though painful, produced the desired result. By February 1853, after two months of it John reported marked improvement in his sight and a month later he was able to read easily by daylight and even for an hour or more at night without ill effect. "It seems to send my heart or something else in my throat just to think of it," he wrote joyfully.

John immediately began to read voraciously. He felt, he said, as if he had just waked up from a five-year trance and had much time to make up. The evening hours he had been spending at his workbench now were passed in an armchair with a book in hand. Feeling deficient in "general information," he proposed a plan of self-improvement beginning with American history after which he intended to take up British history. He joined the Mercantile Library in April and rushed through Irving's *Columbus* and Prescott's *Ferdinand and Isabella,* and started Bancroft's *History of the United States.* He even talked of studying French. This flurry of intellectual activity quickly subsided, however, when his eyes, no doubt over-strained, suffered a relapse. Though never as weak as before, Rogers' eyes were never strong enough to allow him to do much reading. His lack of "general information," derived partially from his poor sight, helped to foster the shyness and lack of ease in society that characterized his mature years.

Rogers' first taste of New York society, to which he was introduced during the winter of 1852–53, was something of a shock. Coming from the provincial society of Manchester, where he had enjoyed prestige as a Bostonian, he found himself at a distinct disadvantage in the metropolis. The tone of society was altogether different even from that of Boston. At his cousins', the William Wainwrights', he noticed, for instance, that when visitors came to the house no one took the trouble to introduce him. He was told that it was not the fashion to do so in New York. To his mother, John testily observed: "I trust I may be preserved from being a *fashionable* young man, that I may treat others with common civility." Going into formal company had never been his favorite amusement and his first New York experiences in that line made it no more attractive. His ideas, "scarce enough at any time," as he said, were driven out of his head whenever small talk was required. He consequently avoided the Wainwrights and their friends as much as possible, preferring the less intimidating society of simpler cousins in Brooklyn, the Charles Catlins. An added inducement to visit the Catlins was his cousin Helen, "The Brooklyn Beauty," with whom he carried on a mock flirtation. Helen Catlin became the mother of William Ordway Partridge, who came into prominence as a sculptor just as John Rogers' career was ending in the early 1890s.

The great event of Rogers' year in New York was the International Exposition at the Crystal Palace on Forty-second Street at Fifth Avenue, where the New York Public Library now stands. John "did" the exposition, of course, soon after his arrival in New York and reported many of its features to the family in Roxbury. His remarks on the sculpture exhibits are particularly significant, for they show even at this early stage his strong preference for action and expression in sculpture. After dismissing as "stiff and clumsily done" Baron Marochetti's colossal equestrian of Washington and as "curious but not pleasant to look at" Monti's "Veiled Vestal" and

"Circassian Slave," Rogers waxed enthusiastic over Kiss's wildly romantic "Amazon." "A finer piece of statuary I think I never saw. It is of colossal size and is remarkably spirited. The face alone of the woman is enough for a study. It is a perfect picture of terror and determination. The tiger attacks the horse in front, and she shrinks back, grasping the mane with her left hand, and with the right she holds a javelin in the attitude to strike the beast." Rogers' fascination with the facial expression of Kiss's "Amazon" foreshadowed the attention to personality which was one of the most distinctive characteristics of his own work as a sculptor. He was equally alert to character-revealing situations in real life. In a letter of 1850, for instance, he had described the accidental death of a factory girl and its effect on the onlookers: "I could not help watching the different expressions, as it is in such exciting times as these when a person's nature shows itself. One girl in particular struck me. She stood close by the dying girl. She was tall and well proportioned and the delicacy of her features showed more refinement than any other in the group, and her pale cheek, quivering lip and clasped hands, showing that all her feelings were with the sufferer, would have made a study for any artist."

Rogers spent a good bit of time at the Crystal Palace during the summer of 1853, but not as a visitor. His Manchester patron, Mr. Amory, had on exhibit a new steam furnace ("Baker's Furnace") in which he had an investor's interest. To Rogers he entrusted the job of superintending it, which involved chiefly keeping a careful record of its fuel and water consumption and comparing them with figures for the furnace used to heat the Crystal Palace. Rogers' name was to appear on the published report of the experiment, or so he was led to believe, and Mr. Amory pointed out the further advantage to him of meeting important people during the exhibition. Mr. Amory's talent for talking people into things made a great impression on young Rogers. "If I had only the same machinery in my head that moves his tongue," he told his father, "I would have no fear of getting along well in any business."

By the end of August 1853 John had come to the conclusion that Mr. Amory's "wonderful bump of hope" had proved misleading as far as his own interests were concerned. His progress at the Novelty Iron Works had been discouragingly slow. After nine months at machine work, he had tried in June to get into the drafting room, but Mr. Allen had offered him nothing better than a slightly different job in the machine shop. This convinced him that what little Allen had done for him in the past had been done as a favor to Mr. Amory.

Rogers was also astute enough to realize that Amory's willingness to let him come to New York had been motivated by self-interest. "I don't mean to say," Rogers explained to his father, "that he would not have done all he has for me disinterestedly for my sake alone, but I *know* the *chief* spring was to represent his interest in the furnace with Mr. Allen for he has talked that into me every time I have met him." The idea that he, a half-trained machinist, should have any influence with Allen struck Rogers as "a perfect farce." By August he was tired of being Amory's pawn, especially since Allen's indifference had been made plain by his refusal to give Rogers a promotion at the Novelty Works. "If I should ever get into the draughting room, which is all I should have any desire for," he told his father on August 28, "it would be by begging for it, and as for living on the charitable disposition of Mr. Allen, I'll not do it." In the circumstances, John felt he had no choice but to leave and did so almost at once.

Within two weeks he was back in Manchester, apparently still with Mr. Amory's blessing, for he was taken on as a journeyman in the same drafting room he had left a year before as an apprentice. His new job was making drawings for the cotton machinery manufactured in the Amoskeag Machine Shop. Learning the twelve thousand patterns involved, far from daunting him, struck him as "a capital exercise." That he could do this close work without ill effect was encouraging, too, after his past trouble with his eyes. Best of all, however, was the satisfaction of having money enough to support himself fully for the first time. Within six months, he was assured, he would be earning three dollars a day.

During the two and a half years Rogers spent in Manchester after his year in New York, he took a far more active part in the life of the little city. His sudden emergence was a direct result of his friendship with the new Unitarian minister who came to Manchester just about the time Rogers returned from New York. The Reverend Francis LeBaron was young, handsome, and unmarried. His discourses, Rogers reported, were "truly poetical" and filled with "most beautiful quotations." "He seems almost too superior a man for Manchester," John added. "It seems almost like a missionary among the Africans."

LeBaron took much the same view of his situation. "He was, perhaps," as one who knew him a few years later put it very delicately, "not altogether without a consciousness of possessing culture and intellectual gifts superior to most of those with whom he associated." In Worcester, Massachusetts, he had lately enjoyed the friendship of Edward Everett Hale and had collaborated with him on a translation of Lamartine's *Atheism among the*

People. In Manchester he had little reason to hope for such another kindred soul. All the greater, then, was his delight on meeting Boston-bred John Rogers at a parish party soon after his arrival. "When he came into the room," LeBaron recalled many years later, "he seemed like a beautiful Parian marble vase amid earthen pottery."

Sharing a feeling of superiority to the provincial society of Manchester, the parson and the mechanic were soon fast friends, spending every available minute together in chess, reading, riding, and improving conversation. Rogers, the younger by six years, was for a month or so highly flattered to be the intimate companion of so cultivated a man but, when LeBaron began to take him to task for occasionally seeing other friends, his enthusiasm quickly waned. Repelled by his friend's "extreme sensitiveness," John was tempted to write him off at once but, after discussing the situation in a letter to his sister, decided not to act hastily. In the end they reached an apparently satisfactory understanding which preserved both their friendship and Rogers' self-respect.

A few months later the two young men set up housekeeping together in the new Unitarian parsonage, with much advice and practical assistance from the ladies of the church. Rogers was delighted with the new quarters which included a room for the chemical experiments which were his latest enthusiasm. Under LeBaron's influence, he also took up the study of French, joined a reading class of which he became president, designed the Christmas decorations for the church, and even undertook to teach an evening drawing class for boys. This last, he said, gave him the satisfaction of feeling that he was doing a charity, although he found it something of a bore when he would have preferred to be in his laboratory.

Rogers' friendship with Francis LeBaron had another happy effect. To please and surprise the minister in the early days of their acquaintance, John took up his modelling sticks again after two years and in four evenings made for him a figure of an Irishman with a pig on his back. He was delighted to have done it so quickly, as he found it discouraging to spend a long time on one piece. The figure was a fragile one, however, and broke not long after. When two attempts to repair it ended in failure, Rogers felt, he said, "like stamping him completely out of shape" but, "after looking at it a while to get reconciled to it," he went back to work and succeeded on the third try. "I tell them here," he wrote home, "that I experienced religion when I concluded to go to work after the last catastrophe."

In his next work, intended as a gift for his shop foreman, Oliver W. Bayley, John let his imagination go. It portrayed a man in the grip of a nightmare.

> The "adversary" is quietly sitting on his chest looking him in the face [the artist explained]. One imp is pulling his hair out, whilst two others are engaged in sawing his legs off. A few snakes complete the picture.

"I might have made it a little more *horrible*," Rogers added, "but concluded it would answer as it was for all *practical purposes*." The group was received with such delight in Manchester that the artist used the same idea again a few years later in Hannibal, Missouri.

Modelling occupied a great deal of Rogers' spare time during the last two years he spent in Manchester. From a list of subjects he drew up about 1858, it appears that he made at least forty-five clay models between 1849 and 1858. Of these about thirty were done after 1853. Besides the "Irishman" and "Nightmare" already mentioned, his letters from Manchester mention only three models by name and five others designated simply as "figures."

"The Old Oaken Bucket," inspired by Samuel Woodworth's popular poem, was modelled in July 1855 and shown the following month in Nichols' fancy goods store in Boston. Rogers gave the original model to Mrs. Cushing Stetson, a Roxbury neighbor, and a replica to another family friend.

"The Black Knight and Friar Tuck in the Hermitage," drawn from chapter XVI of Scott's *Ivanhoe*, was begun in August 1855 and hurriedly finished for exhibition at the New Hampshire Agricultural Society Fair, held in Manchester on September 12–14. Professing to be rather ashamed of the work, the artist consoled himself with the thought that the country folk in attendance would hardly know the difference. "Such a collection of Doodledom I never saw before," he wrote home. The judges were sufficiently impressed, however, to award Rogers as a prize a copy of the Society's annual *Transactions*. "The Black Knight and Friar Tuck" eventually found a place, along with many others of his clay models, in the family parlor in Roxbury, but has long since disappeared.

"Little Nell in the Curiosity Shop," one of the last groups Rogers attempted in Manchester, was the first for which he had a live model, a little girl named Kitty Dodge. He was "about as successful in getting a likeness," he complained, as he had been with his mother, referring to an unfinished bust of Mrs. Rogers begun a year or two earlier. "It does not seem as if it would be so difficult as to make a figure from my fancy," he had written of this troublesome bust, "for it was nothing but an imitation of nature, a low branch of the art." Although he eventually overcame the difficulty, Rogers was perhaps fortunate that taking likenesses did not come easily for him, for an early proficiency in portraiture was the undoing of many an American sculptor who won temporary fame at the expense of creative development.

Although urged "to try something in the beautiful order" by his sister Ellen and by the poetic parson, Rogers wisely declined to do so. "That would require an accurate knowledge of the human figure," he explained, "which I have never had the least opportunity of studying." With no apparent thought of seeking an opportunity to study, he simply went on amusing himself and astonishing his friends by shaping in clay his "every day scenes."

Rogers' awakening interest in the life around him was reflected not only in his modelling but also in a change of attitude toward the lowly mill hands of Manchester. After his return from New York, he was less inclined to laugh at the awkwardness and unpolished manners of the factory girls and more concerned about the hardship of their lot. Noting the "great rejoicing" among the hands in 1853 over the shortening of their day to eleven hours, Rogers commented that "it was really wrong to make people labor fourteen hours including an hour and a half for meals, for they had no time left to themselves out of sleeping hours." The shop where he worked was already on an eleven-hour day, but he could well remember the time only two years before when he himself had enjoyed daylight leisure only on Sundays.

When a strike broke out in Manchester in March 1855, provoked by the restoration of the twelve-and-a-half-hour day in the cotton mills, Rogers' sympathies were all with the strikers. The new rule, he wrote, was "perfectly barbarous & especially coming so after working only 11 hours as they have done two years past." Although the strike had widespread public support, it collapsed after two weeks of parades, meetings, and threats of violence. To Rogers it had been the "most exciting time" he had ever seen and he was keenly disappointed at the outcome, even though it had no effect on conditions in the machine shop.

Rogers' sympathy for the underdog extended even to the Catholic Irish, for whom he had no particular love. When an anti-Catholic riot broke out in Manchester on the Fourth of July, 1854, he condemned "the grand crusade against the Catholics" as "an outrageous thing" and noted with chivalrous concern that his landlady's Irish servant brought home several friends every night to sleep because they were afraid to stay in their own part of the town.

Matured by six years' hard work as an apprentice and wage earner, John Rogers was ready to strike out on his own by the winter of 1855–56. Since his arrival in Manchester he had worked diligently to master every part of the trade to which he intended to devote his life. Starting at the bottom as a simple bench worker, he had learned to handle the traditional tools and to operate the new types of machinery which were beginning to transform the world of industry. He had spent over three years in the drafting room, learning to make carefully scaled drawings of textile machinery, locomotives, and marine engines. He had mastered the difficult art of patternmaking. Finally, in his last year in Manchester, he had been introduced briefly to the mysteries of the countinghouse. An apt pupil, eager and quick to learn, his performance had given full satisfaction to his employers, to his backers, to his family, and, quite as important, to himself. It was with a feeling of pride in past accomplishments and buoyant confidence in the future that John Rogers, Master Mechanic, left the Amoskeag Machine Shop to make his own way in the world. At twenty-eight he seemed at last to have found himself.

COCHITUATE POND

Pencil drawing by John Rogers, 1848, showing (right) the cut for the Boston Water Works aqueduct.

HANNIBAL FROM LOVERS' LEAP

Pencil sketch by John Rogers, 1856, showing the Hannibal and St. Joseph Rail Road shops (right) and the town later made famous by Mark Twain.

CHAPTER IV

Master Mechanic

"ALL THE STATIONERY that you packed away for me was undoubtedly meant as a gentle hint to write as soon as possible. So I will 'embrace this opportunity' as they say. I know how hard you tried to save me from any 'family scenes' before leaving and I got off much easier than I expected. You don't know how I dreaded the parting. Every little keepsake you gave me fairly upset me. I did not even dare to read Ellen's kind sisterly note till today, but I can thank you all now from the bottom of my heart. They are very dear to me and if a faithful endeavor to do my duty and an honorable course meets with success, you will never repent that I deserted my kind home for a distant state. . . ."

John Rogers was writing to his mother from Niagara Falls, the first overnight stop on the thousand-mile rail journey from Boston to Hannibal. The Hannibal and St. Joseph Rail Road, whose Master Mechanic Rogers was to be, was one of hundreds of small lines springing up throughout the western portion of the country. Organized only a short time before, the railroad was to connect the Mississippi River port of Hannibal with the town of St. Joseph on the Missouri-Kansas border. It had been a local enterprise at the start, but control had recently passed to a group of Boston financiers, much to the annoyance of the Missourians. By April 1856, when Rogers arrived on the scene, less than ten miles of track ran inland from Hannibal.

Rogers arrived at Hannibal on April 2. The machine shop of which he was to take charge he found to be a converted pork shed, a large stone building standing on the bank of the Mississippi River in the shadow of "Lover's Leap," a lofty bluff overlooking South Hannibal. Operations were in an embryonic state. A small steam engine had just been installed, but the setting up of machinery and other arrangements were to be left entirely to the new master mechanic, much to his delight.

Within a fortnight John understood why his predecessor had resigned.

> So many inconveniences is enough to drive one crazy almost. . . . In the first place the pork shed, which is a large building 150 by 200 ft., is covered with cottonwood shingles and the least spark sets it on fire. Four or five times some one has looked up at the roof and found it all in a blaze. Then there is a general scramble to get up there and put it out, which operation generally scatters the sparks and sets it on fire in half a dozen other places. That makes considerable excitement for a while. Then the pump that supplies the engines gets out of order and puts me in a fever. Then every little thing we want we have to send to St. Louis to get and after waiting a week or so we may get it and we may not. There is no end to the vexations. . . .

To these was soon added the threat of flooding during the spring freshets.

The work itself, once he got his bearings, turned out to be both challenging and interesting. In answer to family queries, John briefly described his job:

> I have about twenty men under me and have full control of them and the shop, managing everything to my own liking. Building common freight cars is the principal part of the work going on just now. Besides that I have been making tools for the shop to complete the stock already on hand. I have just finished a hand car, which is a small, light car worked by hand and have added several improvements of my own, which have been very much liked.

More complicated tasks challenged Rogers' ingenuity during the summer. One was to transform 25 freight cars into open passenger cars to carry five hundred school children and "any quantity of grown people besides" to a grand Fourth of July barbecue about ten miles out on the line. More interesting to the Master Mechanic, however, was the challenge presented by a new excavator which had been condemned on other roads. Rogers staked his reputation on making it work, made some alterations, named it the "Pioneer," and then sent it out on trial. The result was galling to say the least:

> It seemed to be unfortunate from the time it left the shop. In the first place, in unloading it from the cars they neglected some of my written directions and tipped it over, breaking the main frame. I took a man out and patched *that* up. Then they commenced to work it and something gave out. I took the long ride on horseback . . . and set it right. The day after I returned they sent me word that the main driving gear had broken from some unaccountable cause. I sent a man out with another one and had *that* repaired. . . . What makes it more provoking, the old machine which looks as if it could scarcely hang together is doing a great business right by its side. . . . I am just making another which I intend to have much simpler and which will accomplish nearly the same results. Experience is a great teacher.

Stimulated by these challenges to his inventiveness, Rogers soon glowed with self-assurance. After six years as an apprentice and journeyman mechanic, he found it very pleasant to be his own master at last. "I feel full confidence in my ability now," he wrote to his father in August, "to meet anything that may come up. You know," he added, "it is a quality that I was always rather deficient in, but responsibilities always bring self reliance, at least it has been so in my case." To a large degree, he felt, his success was due to his varied experience in Manchester, and particularly to his intimate knowledge of drafting and pattern-making, both rare accomplishments among mechanics in the western country. There was only one drawback to his present job, the salary. He had started at $1,000 a year, but felt this was much too low, since other men in similar positions on nearby lines were getting $2,500 and $3,000. There was a good chance that this situation would soon be improved, however, especially since the machine shop had recently been taken over by the railroad company from the contractors who had originally had it, but the increase, when it finally came, was only to $1,500. Still, he thought, the experience was valuable and, knowing who his backers were, he felt his chances for getting ahead were very good. He was perfectly content to stay on in Hannibal, at least for two or three years, before looking for a better job.

Hannibal, as a town, had turned out to be less deadly than John had expected. At first, in fact, he had been delighted with the appearance of the waterside village nestling "in a hollow surrounded by high hills," from which "superb views" of the Missouri and Illinois prairies were to be seen. A closer look at the town had cooled his enthusiasm somewhat. Most of the houses were one-story affairs and "not very elegant," the hotel where he first boarded was filthy and overcrowded, there was little building going on in spite of the railroad. "Unless they import some Yankees," he decided, "I'm afraid they will never make much of a place of Hannibal."

The same was true of the Missouri countryside just back of Hannibal, where land said to be richer than any in Illinois was readily available. "An enterprising Yankee farmer could make himself rich here in a little while," John wrote. As yet, however, the land along the route of the railroad was only sparsely settled and it was used chiefly for picnics. "You might go all over New England," he said, "and not find such fine spots as you meet all round here. The woods are all oak and maple and clear of underbrush and it gives the country a very different appearance from our solemn, old pine woods at home." Twelve miles back from the river was the little town of Palmyra with some of the prettiest country residences he had ever seen, as well as several young ladies' seminaries, where girls from all over the South came, as John said, for their "edication." Monroe City, a new settlement on the line of the railroad nearer Hannibal, consisted of five or six houses set on the open prairie. The nearest towns of any size were St. Louis and Quincy, Illinois.

Though deficient in man-made beauty, Hannibal did boast one natural curiosity of considerable interest, a limestone cave some two miles downstream. As soon as he was well settled in his work, Rogers paid it several visits. After the first, he decided to survey it and accordingly, on June 7, as he wrote to his sister Clara:

> I took an early start this morning to explore the cave. I got a compass, ½ a doz. candles, some red chalk and chart paper and commenced my exploration. I was in six hours and explored about a mile of it as I found by reckoning on my chart. I took the course of each passage and paced it off and was successful in getting it tolerably accurate as far as I went but it is such a perfect labyrinth of passages that it is a difficult matter to make a correct chart. The bottom is slippery clay in places and having my hands full of papers and compass and candle and chalk I could not help myself much and consequently I took some amazing coasts down into mysterious looking, black holes 15 or 20 ft. deep. I was quite a sight when I came out of the cave. My clothes were covered with mud and with the droppings of the candle....

John spent another Sunday in the cave the following weekend. This time he was better prepared. "With an ingenuity worthy of a Master Mechanic, I rigged up an apron with pockets to carry a bottle of black paint to mark the passages, a compass, extra candles, a luncheon and my chart, so I was pretty well loaded, with my chart swung round my neck, a lighted candle in one hand, my compass in the other and all sorts of things in my pockets." Thus armed, he burrowed into all the little passages he could find, creeping on his hands and knees and clinging to jutting pieces of rock. He was not romantic enough, however, to enjoy this sort of thing for very long. His chart of the cave remained uncompleted.

Twenty years later Mark Twain's *Tom Sawyer* would make this same cave familiar to thousands of readers. It is hard to picture Hannibal in other terms than those which Sam Clemens' vivid memory of his childhood have impressed on succeeding generations. But in 1856 Clemens was only a lad of twenty-one who had left Hannibal three years before and was just about to begin his Mississippi piloting days. John Rogers, coming to Hannibal as a stranger, was bound to see the town in quite a different light. He was an observant stranger, however, with an eye for local color.

Slavery, as one might expect, was the first thing to attract his attention. Though not such a fanatic on the question as his sister Clara, whose passionate abolitionism was a family joke, Rogers came to Missouri prepared to be shocked. He was, but not enough to make him an abolitionist. As far as he could see, the Negroes were a particularly jolly set of humans who enjoyed themselves more than anyone else at picnics and other outdoor entertainments. Only one instance of brutality found its way into his letters, and that more because of his surprise at the behavior of a respectable white woman than from any very strong sympathy for the downtrodden race. "The curse of slavery," which he said was very apparent in Hannibal and even more so in the back country, seemed to Rogers a curse on the white as much as on the black inhabitants. To it he ascribed the lack of enterprise which prevented Hannibal from taking spectacular advantage of its position as a river port and rail terminus. But seeing it at close quarters did not convert him to fiery zeal for its instant destruction.

Even the Kansas troubles which were coming to a head while he was in Hannibal stirred his interest only mildly. In August 1856, in answer to queries from home whether there were any disturbances in Hannibal "on account of Kansas," John reported: "I think there is less here than with you. I am not much of a politician you know but there seems to be but little said about it. The most I hear is in the papers I get from Boston." Even when war broke out in Kansas between the antislavery settlers and the "Border Ruffians" of Missouri, Hannibal remained quiet and Rogers confined his reaction to the comment: "I am afraid they will have a serious time before it is stopped without vigorous measures are taken by Government. It will, no doubt," he added calmly, "call a great many restless spirits there on both sides." Although he heard of a meeting called in an inland town to tar and feather a New Englander who "because someone had some spite against him" had been denounced as an abolitionist, tempers in Hannibal were even enough for John to get away with calling his hand-car the "Border Ruffian." The folks at home were concerned at his rashness, but John reported that the local inhabitants took it as a joke and felt "rather complimented than otherwise."

Although he took little interest in political issues, Rogers was curious to see an example of Western stump-speaking. The opportunity presented itself during his second summer in Hannibal. His description of a political meeting might be drawn from one of George Caleb Bingham's paintings:

> Tomorrow is election day for Governor of Missouri [he wrote to Ellen on August 2, 1857]. I suppose you know how candidates for office electioneer for themselves out west. Well, the two candidates for Gov. this year were here last Friday evening. I had often heard of two opposing candidates speaking on the same stage in reply to each other, but had never seen any of it and was consequently on hand at the present opportunity. I was amused but at the same time disgusted at the poor show for Gov. and how low human nature could come down even when aspiring to

> the high and dignified office of Gov. One of the candidates, whose name is Rollins, is a coarse rough-looking farmer. He spoke first, announcing himself as the candidate for Gov. of the American party, boasted of his services to the people, blackguarded his opponent who was sitting on the same stage with him and expressed his confidence that he should be elected & would be very grateful for all who would vote for him. His opponent Col. Stewart, who is President of our road, but rather a young man, unmarried & dissipated, replied to him, holding up *his* services and blackguarding his opponent. As Stewart was a bachelor it made a good butt for Rollins to twit him about. As for discussing any great questions it was scarcely referred to, but was almost entirely of a personal nature. There were quite a number of ladies present & I heard several express a dislike for Stewart for not showing them proper respect because as it was a warm night, when he got on the stage, he first pulled off his coat, then his cravat, unbuttoned his shirt collar & rolled his sleeves up above his elbows. Not a very dignified proceeding in a Gov. elect to say the least.

Such sensitivity to the proprieties was not characteristic of all Hannibal ladies, however.

> Did I ever tell you of a wedding I went to sometime last summer in a little log house near where I boarded? There was nothing very remarkable about it except one thing that rather amused me. The bride's father, a little old man who did not seem much interested in the ceremony, as soon as it was over instead of congratulating his daughter, stole off to bed & when we went to get our hats & shawls, there he was cuddled up in bed, snoring for dear life. The effect was rather startling to me but the log cabin community of whom most of the ladies were composed seemed to think it nothing strange & took it as a matter of course. . . .

The log cabin community to which Rogers referred in this letter just quoted comprised the greater portion of South Hannibal, close to the Hannibal and St. Joseph shop. Mrs. Elliott, with whom he boarded there for the first few months, lived in almost the only two-story house in South Hannibal. The other houses were, he wrote, "almost universally little one story buildings and though many of them were of brick, they seemed to be taken from the pattern of a log house, with only one room which serves as a bedroom and sitting room and a small kitchen and the front door opens right into the sitting room." In such a cabin lived one of Rogers' best carpenters: "He and his wife sleep at one end of the room, her father and mother sleep at the other end and quite a family of children share a trundle bed in the centre." These simple arrangements were hard for a well-bred Yankee to accustom himself to, especially when making evening calls. On one such occasion, he related: "A gentle female voice called out, after some hesitation, 'come in' — but I found the voice proceeded from a nightcap dimly seen through the bed curtains, so wishing her pleasant dreams I departed." "I strongly believe in love in a cottage," Rogers concluded, "but I should prefer it on a little different plan."

Hannibal's female population, to Boston eyes, included "some queer specimens," some of whom judging from his letters, were intent on catching the interesting young man from the East. "Most affecting stories are circulated here," he wrote four months after his arrival, "about a remarkably homely young lady and the Master Mechanic which are made up with extraordinary ingenuity without the shadow of a foundation." The young lady in question may well have been the Hoosier girl he later described as "a tall barrel with a very large punkin on top of it." This same young lady turns up again:

> The *fat girl* that I believe I told you of once as the daughter of my landlady [he wrote the following February] was up to her elbows, writing and receiving [Valentines]. I came upon her unexpectedly yesterday noon while she was writing them. Byron's poems and a large scrapbook were before her from which she was making liberal selections while note paper and valentines were scattered round with a perfect looseness. She showed some sample ones she had received. One was the cover to a ream of letter paper, such as you see on every ream, without any writing. Another was written but there were scarcely two words in succession spelt right. Still she seemed to regard it with a great deal of pride.

And again, two weeks later; in connection with Hannibal's Washington's birthday ball:

> The fairy that I board with who has been preparing for the last three weeks was perfectly radiant. You remember she is about the shape of a bundle of straw and weighs more than I do though she is but about sixteen. Her flaxen hair was all in a frizzle and her well developed figure was enveloped in pink and white airy nothings which gave her a very etherial appearance. The last addition which she made to her muslin dress was thirty yards of ribbon. She told me a day or two before the event that she could not go. "Why not?" said I. "I've got no company," said she in a doleful tone. It was most too strong a hint to be mistaken but I turned it off the best way I could. I finally compromised matters by promising her that I would dance with her once and *not* take her, but I didn't do that, for the dance that I had engaged with her she was claimed by two or three who had been drinking pretty freely, for it was sometime after supper, so I left them all swearing together, she as well as the rest, and went home. . . .

The only exception to Rogers' general dismissal of "the beauty and fashion" of Hannibal was a certain Kate Hayward whom he described as a "brilliant star in *our set.*" In fact he spoke with such familiarity of her that his mother became alarmed. Her words of caution elicited from John a description of conditions in Hannibal which displayed more than a little dissatisfaction with its social standards:

> I have never said anything that I know of & certainly never intended to that could lead you to suppose that Miss Heywood [sic] was at all exceptionable in any way. You need not feel at all alarmed that I may ever marry her. In the first place she is already married, but as she is separated from her husband she has resumed her maiden name & in the next place I would not marry her if I could. This assurance I hope will make you easy as far as it goes, but with regard to the standard of female society in Hannibal all I can do is to choose the best that there is. There are but two families that I call regularly at, one is Mr. Talcott's & the other Mr. Southack's. I should be very glad if there were more of the same class in town for I like refined society as much as you do, but I can't have everything that I want & I have made up my mind to be contented with what I have. As for getting married I must say the chances are rather *slim* here but I have faith in the future. "Patient waiters no losers" they say. I should be very much happier to be well married but I shall not act rashly about it.

Though his letters home, especially to his sisters, often betray this lingering feeling of caste, part of his Yankee heritage, Rogers moved about with less restraint in Hannibal than he had in Manchester. He might complain about the dearth of refined society, but he took part actively in whatever social life the Missouri village had to offer. This took a variety of forms, many of them entirely new to him, and he probably enjoyed himself more than he would admit. With his abhorrence of formal parties, he should have found Hannibal's informality refreshing. If he laughed at it, it was a kind laugh. His work, and the varied experiences of his life away from the limited circle of Roxbury and Boston, were beginning to break down his own provincial intolerance.

Picnics were the chief summer amusement in Hannibal. The novelty of the railroad adding to the local zest for this particular form of entertainment, a party of ladies and gentlemen was organized to ride to the end of the line — about 9 miles out — in May 1856, barely a month after John's arrival. "As we had to wait a couple of hours in the woods before the train returned," he wrote, "we passed it in picking flowers and setting round on the logs in the woods and having a general good time."

On his first Fourth of July in Hannibal, he was introduced to the "barbecue," which, he explained, "signifies nothing more than a great picnic where a dinner is furnished for everybody." He thought it "rather a stupid affair," since "they had nothing to eat but dry bread and meat and no music or anything going on but some speaking." The next year's celebration of the Fourth was held at Monroe City:

> The natives of the place had got up a large tent made of common sheeting. A floor was laid in the centre and seats round the sides raised like a circus and behind them the tables for dinner. The dinner was cooked in barbecue fashion by digging a long pit in the ground filled with fire and across the top of the pit laying sticks with sheep and whatever meat they had strung on. The most amusing sight was to see the dancing. The country girls were dressed to kill and danced away with the perspiration rolling off their faces. We finished the day with a few fireworks and a concert in the evening.

Other outdoor entertainments Rogers commented on included a fishing party across the river; a public tea-party for the benefit of a church, admission 50 cents; an organized walking party, which he declined to join because of the July heat; an excursion to the cave by chartered ferryboat; and a moonlight sail on the river also in the ferryboat. The last, Rogers concluded, "was a most sensible way to have a picnic for there was no fatigue and we could have all the other enjoyments that we could have at a common picnic." One of these "common enjoyments" was sparkling Catawba wine which, Roger noted, was drunk in quantities that "would astonish a Yankee picnic party."

Still another outdoor event was the camp meeting, that characteristic element of religious life on the frontier. Rogers attended one shortly before he left Hannibal, and described it to his mother:

> For the first time in my life I went to a camp meeting yesterday, or rather they did not call it a camp meeting but a *basket meeting*, the difference being that they did not have tents, but went home at night or stopped at houses in the neighbourhood. We got there just about dinner time when all the people were divided up into groups eating their dinners, which gives it the name of *basket*. We had brought ours in the same way so we ate ours & then walked round to see what could be seen. After dinner there was preaching & singing but I did not see any of that excitement which I supposed usually attended camp meeting. The negroes had a part of the woods to themselves & seemed to enjoy themselves highly, as I have always found they do on such gatherings. The meeting was broken up early & we came away to avoid the dust & crowd on the road. There is to be a *regular* camp meeting in the vicinity soon, which I mean to go to for curiosity.

When cold weather set in, Hannibal's social life moved indoors, where it was more restricted and, to Rogers, less novel. He attended his first dance in October 1856. He found that the black fiddler called only two figures all evening and all the dances were cotillions, which made the evening "very tedious, particularly when it got towards three o'clock." "The assemblage of beauty and fashion" at a later ball reminded him "very strongly" of Manchester, a remark not intended to be complimentary either to Hannibal or Manchester. Most of these dances were public affairs.

Entertainment of a more serious nature was scarce, Rogers found. In Hannibal he could expect to hear no lectures by Agassiz or Dana, as he had in Manchester's Lyceum. There was, however, a debating society, to which John was elected in January 1857. Not being a ready speaker, he was a bit nervous about his first appearance, but was consoled by the thought that, "as there are only about a dozen members in this society, who are smoking, chewing and spitting all round a little dark room lighted by a tallow candle," his diffidence would be little noticed. For the amusement of his family, he sent home a letter he received from one of his fellow-debaters:

March 26, 1857

Honored Sir

With Regard due and highest Respect I drop you these lines to inform you that on our last Friday night in our polimical Society yourself was chosen by me on the Affirmative of the question chosen for discussion on 3rd night in April

Question is this

Resolved that reading of the works of fiction has a tendency to injure both mind and morals.

D M White Affirmative

his first choice John Rodgers jur
second choice Frank Levering

P. S. pleas come and we will be certin to have Victory. the Truth is powerfull and must prevail.

I am Yours with Respect
Daniel M. White

If D. M. White had known that, not long before, Rogers had read and enjoyed Harriet Beecher Stowe's antislavery novel, *Dred,* he might have been less anxious for his support in this debate.

With the coming of spring Rogers put into operation several plans for his own comfort and enjoyment. One was to order from Pittsburgh a sailboat. "A finer place to sail," he wrote, "could scarcely be found. The river is about as wide as Jamaica Pond and any length you please. . . ." He had devised a boathouse to float on two rows of empty barrels and to make the boat perfectly safe he also planned to have airtight compartments at each end. Inventing these improvements was almost as much fun as sailing itself.

His other plan, now put into effect, was one he had tried once before in New York — taking an unfurnished flat and fixing up a bachelor apartment. Having found a pleasant room in the center of Hannibal, he proceeded to furnish it himself, with plenty of assistance and advice from his "lady friends," particularly Kate Hayward on whose taste he depended heavily, since he considered his own taste faulty, especially in regard to colors. The colorblindness to which he attributed his difficulty in choosing a handsome carpet was, perhaps, another reason why Rogers seems never to have been tempted to paint pictures rather than model them in clay.

In the furnishing of his apartment, Rogers once again indulged his fondness for experimentation:

> I suppose you can imagine [he wrote to his mother on March 15, 1857], that I could not furnish a room without having *some* novelty about it. I think I shall have one now that will be "some punkins." It is a *hydrostatic bed*. I recollect reading in Arnott's physics a description of one which was described as most delightfully easy. In the first place there is a water tight tank the size of a bed. This is filled with about six inches of water. Then a water tight cloth is spread over it loosely & fastened to the sides of the tank & on this a mattress is placed. You can't sink much because of the mattress & what can be a more perfect spring than water seeking its level. It will be so elastic as to fit every part of the body. My tank is already made & I shall set it up tomorrow. If it succeeds, I shall expect a great rush to my room to see the curiosity. . . .

After some trouble with leakage, John did finally get his hydrostatic bed to work and it did prove an attraction to the natives. The story of John Rogers' hydrostatic bed, in fact, is still current in Hannibal. He also stocked his room with engravings and current numbers of the *Boston Journal,* the *New York Tribune,* and the *Illustrated London News,* and kept on hand a supply of oranges "for bait to attract pleasant people in." His friends told him he would get so many comforts about him that he would never get married, but John wasn't convinced. "I imagine a pretty face would be the most charming ornament I could have about the room & a conversable mind the best library, but there is a very poor assortment of that kind of article on hand in the market now & I must be contented with what the market can supply, that is in the way of pictures, nightmare scenes, &c. . . ."

The nightmare scene he was referring to was one of two clay groups Rogers modelled while in Hannibal. He had found some "excellent clay" in the neighborhood in the fall and "could not resist working in it." His first figure was an "Old Bachelor," similar to one he had made earlier "but varied in the composition." This evidence of his talent in an unexpected line caused his stock of popularity, he wrote home, to go up about fifty per cent, but he thought he would attempt no more in Hannibal. He kept this resolution till the following April, when the need to ornament his new room inspired him to take up his modelling sticks again. The subject, a "nightmare scene," was one he had used before in a group for Oliver Bayley at Manchester, but the design was varied and "the Agony . . . piled up a little more":

> The victim is in bed and is being hugged by a skeleton from which he is *squirming* to get away. The old devil himself is leaning over the head board, quietly grinning and admiring the scene. Two little imps are sawing the man's legs off and a few small imps are scattered round engaged in various kinds of mischief. I have it understood as I think I told you that the poor fellow has been boarding lately at the same house where I board and the hard fare don't agree with him. My landlord was up here to see it a little while since but I concluded it was most too pointed a joke to tell him.

Unlike most of his other early clay models, the Hannibal "Nightmare" has not crumbled into dust. Preserved for many years by the family to which Rogers gave it when he left Hannibal, it is now owned by a private collector there. As one of the two known surviving works of the early period of Rogers' life, it would be of inestimable value even if it were not, as it is, a delightful example of Rogers' humorous, good-natured attitude toward the common lot.

"The Nightmare" was the last piece of modelling undertaken by Rogers during his eighteen-month stay in Hannibal. Once spring brought renewed life to Hannibal, he was too busy to afford time for a hobby that took concentrated effort.

In April work was started on the new machine shop and engine buildings he had been promised the previous fall. The old quarters, unheated in winter and subject to annual flooding, were to be replaced with brick structures built to the master mechanic's own specifications. At the same time he was extra busy getting up a lot of cars for the western end of the railroad where track was now being laid eastward from St. Joseph, in setting up a turntable in Hannibal, and in building handcars. "They tell me," he wrote with pride, "I have got up the best hand car in the country. It has certainly performed some astonishing feats. They use it on the prairie with a sail and go by the wind with the speed of a locomotive sometimes."

After a year on the job at Hannibal, Rogers felt more satisfied than ever that the decision to go West had been a wise one:

> I don't think you appreciate how contented I am here [he wrote his mother in July 1857]. I have a great many kind friends here and it would really require very strong inducements to make me leave. I am getting now about fifteen hundred dollars a

year, full confidence is placed in me, I am just moving into a fine new shop and it is but a short trip to St. Louis or Quincy whenever I wish to go. You know I am not of a particularly social disposition and the society of a large city is not of so much importance to me as it would be to many others. To tell the truth, if I were only well married, I should be as happy here as anywhere else I think. . . .

His prospects were so encouraging, in fact, that in May Rogers invested part of his savings in a lot in Hannibal, his first real estate investment. A few months later he built a small house on this lot at a cost of about $500, expecting to rent it for $125 a year. He was also speculating in shingles in a small way and hoped to invest more money in land.

At this point, just when he seemed to have found himself at last, the bottom dropped out of everything. The money panic of 1857, starting in the eastern centers of banking, gradually reached out to paralyze the whole country. Rogers first mentioned it on October 4, with the comment that "it does not affect Hannibal much." Two weeks later, however, hard times reached Missouri. On October 19, John reported to his father: "I received orders on Saturday to discharge all the hands & shut up shop which I did. I suppose the idea was that they wanted to reduce the force very much & so considered it expedient to discharge all hands & hire over again when they wished to resume work. . . . I had an excellent set of men, mostly prudent & saving & they all took their dismission very cheerfully." The following day the blow fell:

I have been notified that there will be nothing more for me to do as the shop has stopped. I hardly know what to do. I shall stay here for two or three weeks yet I presume, till I can finish my house & settle up some of my affairs here & then if I hear of nothing to do out here I shall probably go home for a while & make a little visit before starting fresh. I am sorry it has happened so, not so much that I regret leaving Hannibal, but I had got interested in my business & fairly started in as fine buildings as I could desire & had the confidence & good will of my employers here. But it can't be helped & I must make the best of it. You will probably see me in the course of a month from now.

VARIATIONS ON A THEME BY WILKIE

Above, left: "Game of Draughts," from a design by Sir David Wilkie, on a transfer-printed Staffordshire plate. *Above, right:* "Checker Players," clay, John Rogers' earliest surviving group, collection of the Society for the Preservation of New England Antiquities. *Below, left:* "Checker Players," plaster, 1860, collection of The New-York Historical Society. *Below, right:* "Checkers up at the Farm," bronze, 1876, collection of The New-York Historical Society.

CHAPTER V

European Studies

"NIGHTMARE" was not only the last group Rogers made before the panic of 1857 sent him jobless back to Roxbury; it was also the last he is known to have made as an untrained amateur. His next work was executed under the eye of a European master of quite another art tradition. The result of that encounter was to reveal just how far Rogers' personal style had matured during his eight years of experimentation in clay.

Because of the perishable medium in which he at first worked, only two of Rogers' clay groups have survived: "Checker Players," c. 1850 [3], and "Nightmare," 1857 [20]. Sixteen others are referred to by title or described in family letters: "Apple Woman," "Robinson Crusoe," "Dominie Samson," "Haymaker," "Old Bachelor" (two copies), "Nightmare," "Old Oaken Bucket" (two), "Black Knight and Friar Tuck in the Hermitage," "Santa Claus," "Little Nell in the Curiosity Shop," "Unprotected Female," "Irishman and Pig," "Little Thieves," and the unfinished bust of his mother.

In an undated pencilled list written by John Rogers, probably about 1857, he jotted down the titles of all his clay groups. It includes all those listed above, along with thirty-two others, as follows:

> "Dutchman," "Irishman," "Boys Fighting," "Gossips," "Saturday Night," "Victory," "Deserted Village" (two), "Dog and Cat," "Playing Marbles," "Girl and Kitten" (two), "Christmas," "Girl and Boy and Umbrella," "Man's Head," "Woman's Head," "Blind Man's Buff," "Young America," "Pocahontas," "Alarm of Fire," "Boys Fishing," "Boys Stealing," "Doctor," "Indian in Ambush," "Leisure Moments[?]," "Pedlar," "Return from the Fields," "Tangled Skein," "Waking Up the Doctor," "The Little Beggar," "Reading the News," and "Address to the Jury."

The last four are sketched on the sheet and may have been only ideas for groups. One other clay, "At the Confessional," was named in an 1895 newspaper article as having been made by Rogers in Manchester during the

1850s. In all, then, we have evidence for Rogers' having made or projected at least fifty groups, single figures, and heads during these eight years of spare-time modelling.

The most significant feature of this list is the overwhelming predominance of subjects drawn from everyday life and popular literature. In American sculpture this was a decided novelty. Portrait busts and statues and Neoclassically inspired ideal figures, of which Hiram Powers' "Greek Slave" was the best known example, had hitherto been almost its only interests.

A brief glance at the work being done between 1849 and 1857 by his American contemporaries, both at home and abroad, points up John Rogers' remarkable divergence from the accepted tradition. Among the better-known expatriates in Italy, Thomas Crawford was during these years engaged on a "Beethoven" for Boston's Music Hall, an idealized "Babes in the Wood," and the monumental "Armed Freedom" which was to top the Capitol dome in Washington. Hiram Powers was swamped with orders for busts and ideal statues, all more or less in the vein of the "Greek Slave." Michigan's young Randolph Rogers produced an ideal "Ruth" in the midst of his labor on the historical reliefs for the Capitol's bronze doors. The lady sculptors, like Harriet Hosmer with her "Aenone" and "Puck," and John Rogers' own cousin from Salem, Louisa Lander, with her idealized "Virginia Dare," were just as firmly committed to the prevailing modes of the Roman world in which they were so much at home.

Closer to home, Henry Kirke Brown of Brooklyn was at work on his "Washington," America's first important native equestrian statue. In Albany, Erastus Dow Palmer was turning out medallions and ideal figures, mostly in the vein of religious allegory, while William Rimmer was hewing a powerful head of St. Stephen out of granite at Quincy, Massachusetts. Although the work of these men showed a trend away from the Neoclassic style, in their choice of subjects they too stayed largely within the conventional bounds of sculpture.

In Boston, where John Rogers was most likely to pick up ideas on sculpture, the Neoclassic tradition was almost as firmly entrenched in the 'fifties as it was in Rome. The city which had nurtured the noble intentions of Horatio Greenough at this period boasted at least six professional sculptors, mostly now forgotten. John Crookshanks King, Edward Augustus Brackett, Henry Dexter, Margaret E. Foley, Peter Stephenson, and Thomas Ball made their livings primarily as portraitists, but they turned out ideal and monumental works also, such as Brackett's "Shipwrecked Mother" in Mount Auburn Cemetery and Stephenson's "Wounded Indian."

While Thomas R. Gould and William Wetmore Story were at this time still amateurs, both had produced portraits and would soon become famous for ideal statues. Boston's Athenaeum Gallery, with its fine collection of casts from the antique, along with some modern works, afforded the beginning sculptor further contact with the prevailing fashions.

Rogers was certainly aware of the sort of things a sculptor was expected to do. We know that he saw Powers' "Greek Slave" at the Boston Horticultural Hall in 1848, although we do not know what he thought of it at the time. He may well have visited the Athenaeum, of which his uncle Henry Bromfield Rogers was a trustee. Thomas Ball was a close friend of another uncle, George Derby.

In view of his nonclassical education and his essentially unromantic nature, Rogers' failure to respond to Neoclassicism is not too surprising. Although he read some novels and history, he was largely indifferent to literary culture and to abstract ideas and therefore not likely to be moved by the allegorical and pseudo-philosophical themes which preoccupied the sculptors of the "ideal." He was more wise than most of those who attempted such themes when he candidly confessed to his mother that he would surely get out of his depth if he attempted something "in the beautiful order."

More puzzling is his failure to take up portraiture. His initial efforts in this line, as we have seen, were not successful and it was not until ten years later, after he had made a name for himself as a modeller of genre groups, that he again turned, with better success, to taking likenesses. Lack of patience had a good bit to do with Rogers' difficulty in this type of work, as well as the habit he early developed of working, as he put it, "from *impression*." His peculiar forte, even at this early stage of his career, was in catching the characteristics of a pose or an expression, rather than the particular structure of a given body or face. In spite of the seemingly random elaboration of detail in much of his work, his groups, as Lorado Taft long ago pointed out, are summaries, not literal transcripts, of nature. Since he was, at this early period, modelling primarily for his own amusement, he did not take the trouble to study how to catch a likeness and concentrated on what came easily — impressionistic genre. It was not until later, however, that he was able to reassure himself, and then only with much wavering, that this interest was as respectable as the more traditional ones.

Though he evidently owed very little to the academic sculptors of his own time, it is quite possible that Rogers was influenced to some extent by more popular types of plastic art. Parlor statuary, in the form of small plaster, china, parian, wax, or, more rarely, bronze figurines and groups, was a familiar feature of the early Victorian middle-class home. Much of it was imported from England and the Continent, although Bennington and other American potteries turned out a good number of parian and china mantle ornaments. Domestic animals, busts of famous men, and figures from modern fiction vied for popularity with the more traditional shepherds, shepherdesses, Cupids, and chaste, though nude, females in this pre-Rogers Group age. Rogers' clay groups had little in common with most of it, however, aside from scale, and there is no evidence that he received from it any direct stylistic influence. He certainly later profited, however, from the taste this sort of work had created for small-scale sculpture.

If he was influenced by any plastic artist, it was probably by a transplanted Englishman, Robert Ball Hughes, who lived in or near Boston from about 1840 until his death in 1868. Hughes had a penchant for sculpture in little. Although best known for his full-size statues of Alexander Hamilton and Nathaniel Bowditch, he also produced in the eighteen thirties a popular statuette of Washington Irving. More significant, in relation to John Rogers, were three small clay groups by Hughes exhibited at the Boston Athenaeum between 1835 and 1860. All three illustrated familiar scenes from English novels: "Uncle Toby and the Widow Wadman" from Sterne's *Tristram Shandy,* "Little Nell" and "Oliver Twist Lying at Mrs. Maylie's Door" from Dickens. The scene from *Oliver Twist* was "a very clever performance," according to a contemporary critic who felt, however, that it was a subject "better for painting than for sculpture." Lorado Taft, the early historian of American sculpture, in 1904 characterized "Little Nell" as "mild." It is by no means certain that John Rogers knew these little works of his fellow Bostonian, although he may have seen them at the Athenaeum or even at the Roxbury home of Edward Brinley who reclaimed "Oliver Twist" from the Athenaeum in 1847 and "Uncle Toby" in 1860. From a letter of 1861, in which Rogers expressed pleasure on hearing of "Ball Hughes favorable remarks" on "The Picket Guard," it seems a reasonable inference that he had at least some prior acquaintaince with the older sculptor. The degree of Hughes's influence on Rogers, if indeed he had any, remains problematical.

The influence on Rogers of contemporary painting, chiefly through the medium of engravings, is more clearly demonstrable. In several early letters he referred to "cuts" which were or were not suitable to be copied in clay. His "Old Bachelor" originated in this way; so did "Checker Players," suggested by an engraving after the Scottish genre painter, Sir David Wilkie. Wilkie, in fact, was probably the artist who exerted the strongest influence on Rogers at this period. A collection of engravings after Wilkie's paintings, published as *The Wilkie Gallery,* was in Rogers' possession in 1854 and gave him endless delight. "I send down two more Wilkies for you to see," he wrote to Ellen in April; "I think that 'blind man's buff' is a fine study. You seem to find something new the longer you look at it." His own model of the same subject can safely be attributed to the influence of this print.

In Wilkie's life, too, as presented in the introduction to *The Wilkie Gallery,* there was inspiration. The youthful Wilkie had been held back by a father who found small attraction in an artist's career, had persevered, and in later life had ascribed his success "to this attribute of dogged perseverance, rather than to the original impulse of genius." Most important, Wilkie's career illustrated the value of an artist's "cultivating his own peculiar talent . . . instead of idly grasping at the shadow of past greatness" and of his making available at small expense good reproductions of his works. It is impossible to overestimate the influence of Wilkie on John Rogers, through this volume of engravings which came into his hands so early in his artistic development and taught him to portray, in Wilkie's own spirit, "the amenity of humble life, dashed with a proportion of comic pleasantry."

Rogers' debt to contemporary American painters of realistic and sentimental genre is less clear. One incidental reference in 1850 to "the boatmen" hanging over his mantelpiece in Manchester may well refer to a print of George Caleb Bingham's "Jolly Flatboatmen." This reference and a marked similarity between the central group in Bingham's "Raftsmen Playing Cards" and the handling of Rogers' "Checker Players" and "The Village Schoolmaster" (both 1861) suggest that Rogers was familiar with the Missourian's works. Although there is no evidence to link Rogers directly with any other individual of the genre school E. P. Richardson has denominated the "romantic realists," his work was clearly related in spirit to that of Bingham, William Sidney Mount, and Richard Caton Woodville, as it was later to that of Winslow Homer, Eastman Johnson, Thomas Waterman Wood, E. L. Henry, J. G. Brown, and Thomas Hovenden.

When the panic of 1857 interrupted his railroading career, Rogers' dormant ambition to be a professional artist came to life. From Hannibal he had, in fact, written in September 1856 that he sometimes felt provoked at himself that he should be plodding away his life when, as he put it, "if I only exerted what talent I am possessed of I might travel over the world." In the spring of 1858 he decided the time had come to exert his talent. Reluctantly, the family gave its support, moral and financial.

From the first it was apparent to Rogers that he needed technical training. Although he had shown native skill in modelling his small genre and literary groups, in the two traditional branches of the art — portraiture and the "ideal" — he had had no success at all. Since these were the staples of the professional's repertory, he felt the need of study under an experienced sculptor before he could hope to make his own way.

Like almost every American sculptor of his day, John Rogers decided to go to Europe for his training. Although Boston in 1858 had several resident sculptors who were turning out acceptable portrait busts and statues, cemetery sculpture, and some ideal figures, it was still generally felt that a young sculptor needed to go abroad, preferably to Italy, to study under the influence of the "antique" masters. For a sculptor, Europe also had practical advantages. Living costs were generally much lower than in America, good marble was more readily available, and so were the skilled stonecutters upon whom almost every sculptor then depended to put his ideas into marble. Most important of all, Europe had an atmosphere in which, most artists felt, the arts could flourish far more luxuriantly than in their own raw country.

Until about 1820 the great center for American art students had been London, where the American-born President of the Royal Academy, Benjamin West, so generously gave of his time and experience to help his young compatriots. In the 'twenties, however, the stream had begun to flow toward Italy, "that central clime," as Nathaniel Hawthorne put it, "whither the eyes and the heart of every artist turn as if pictures could not be made to glow in any other atmosphere, as if statues could not assume grace and expression save in that land of whitest marble." The pioneer in the new movement had been a Bostonian, the sculptor Horatio Greenough, who first went to Italy in 1824 and settled there permanently in 1829. Others had been quick to follow his lead, sculptors and landscape painters particularly, and by the mid-'fifties both Rome and Florence possessed distinct colonies of American artists. Other American colonies, it is true, had grown up at Düsseldorf, the great center of German genre and historical painting in the 'thirties and 'forties, and at Paris, where a few landscape and figure painters from America were beginning to gather in the 'fifties, but until after 1860 Italy was still the great magnet for American sculptors. In 1858 there were at least fifteen American sculptors resident in Rome or Florence and only one in Paris.

In the circumstances, we should naturally expect John Rogers to have turned to Italy when he decided to go abroad to study sculpture. Even before he thought seriously of going he had written: "How glorious a trip to Italy would be." He would have had the advantage of personal contacts, too, for his family knew William Wetmore Story, who had gone to Rome in

1856. Thomas Ball had been in Florence several years earlier and was to return there permanently in 1864. Rogers' cousin, Louisa Lander of Salem, had studied in Rome with Thomas Crawford and returned there only a few months after Rogers' departure for Europe in the fall of 1858.

It was neither to Rome nor to Florence, however, but to Paris that John Rogers decided to go for his training. We can only guess why, for his letters give no clue to his reasons. Although the Parisian schools were beginning to attract some American attention, there is no evidence that Rogers was drawn to them by any previous knowledge of French sculpture, with its growing Romantic emphasis on vigorous movement and naturalistic modelling. It seems more likely that Richard S. Greenough's presence in Paris prompted the decision. Though not so well known as his older brother, who had died some years before, the younger Greenough was highly regarded as a sculptor in his native Boston. A connection with him might have appealed to Rogers and his family, especially since Greenough had just completed a bust of Governor John Winthrop for the chapel of Mount Auburn Cemetery and was therefore well known to John Rogers' uncle-by-marriage, the Hon. Robert C. Winthrop.

His own savings supplemented by money advanced by his uncle Henry B. Rogers and his aunt Mrs. Winthrop, John Rogers was prepared to remain abroad for two or three years, long enough to secure a good technical training in modelling portraits and the human figure, as well as some understanding of marble carving and plaster casting. After that he planned to open a studio in Boston.

From the easy security of Roxbury, where he was surrounded by admiring relatives and friends, it all looked delightfully simple. But once alone, on board the ship which was to carry him to Europe, doubts began to cloud Rogers' enjoyment of his prospect. Shortly before the *Ariel* sailed from New York on September 4, 1858, he dashed off a rather blue note to his family: "I didn't know before that my eyes were so leaky as they were at parting from you all, but I had got nervous in anticipation & found it impossible to control myself, but," he added, not very convincingly, "I shall only look on the bright side & hope for the best."

John Rogers' first days in Paris, where he arrived on September 21, were not very encouraging. Bewilderment, rather than excitement, marked his initial reaction to the gaiety of the Imperial capital. Getting about was awkward enough, for he found his school-boy French scarcely more useful in Paris than his native tongue, but even more unsettling was the difficulty he had in finding out how to accomplish the object of his trip. "You probably expected," he wrote about two weeks after his arrival, "that I would be in a rather more ecstatic state in my first impressions of Paris. . . . To tell the truth I was rather too impatient to be settled and at work."

His original intention had been to enter the Academy, but this turned out to be impossible, for the fall term had already begun and the next would not commence until March. The principal of the Academy advised him to enter a private studio and study French in the meantime. By the first of October Rogers was accordingly enrolled as a pupil of Antoine Laurant Dantan, to whom he had been introduced by Greenough. Dantan was a former pupil of the French Neoclassicists Bosio and Brion and a winner of the Grand Prix de Rome in 1828 for a "Death of Hercules." Sixty years old in 1858, he belonged to the same generation as François Rude (1784–1855) and Antoine Louis Barye (1796–1875), the two great French exponents of the Romanticism which was gradually supplanting the Neoclassicism of Canova and his followers. Though more conservative and less gifted than these masters, Dantan apparently shared to some extent their reaction against the older style, judging by the titles of several known genre subjects from his hand: "Young Bather Playing with His Dog," "Neapolitan Girl Playing the Tambourine," and "The Happy Age." When Rogers arrived in Paris, Dantan had just given up his large studio and most of his pupils, but the American was permitted to join a small private class of "young gentlemen" the master continued to instruct in a smaller studio on the Rue de l'Oratoire. The fee was thirty francs a month, plus incidental studio expenses.

As soon as Rogers took up the familiar clay in his deft fingers his doubts disappeared, giving way to unbounded optimism. "I think I am lucky," he told his parents. "I have stepped right into a studio already furnished, I have the best master in Paris, I have a most *capital* French teacher, an excellent chamber & a chance of getting into the Academy." M. Dantan showed a flattering interest in his new pupil: "he has been in every day since I have been here," Rogers noted with pride, "when he usually comes only three times a week." With his first modelling assignment, an anatomical figure "to learn the muscles," he won a "très bien" from the master, and after only two weeks was allowed to work up an original composition. He chose the most American subject he could think of, an Indian with bow and arrow. Dantan "was mightily pleased with it & wants to have me cast it in plaster," Rogers triumphantly reported. "I suspect," he added, "they think I have lived amongst the Indians, I dressed mine up so readily & spoke so knowingly of what was right & wrong. It is just as well to appear wise when we can."

John Rogers' self-confidence soared as he watched his fellow-students at work.

> If I can't leave them out of sight before long, I can't do what I have done. They showed me some of their works today that they had received medals for at the Academy. They were about equal to mine after about two hours work. So rough I could scarcely make out what they were. . . . I have seen nothing remarkable yet that the artists have done here, and flatter myself that I stand a pretty good chance with them *now*. However, I won't brag yet.

After he got into the Academy the next spring, he felt, there was nothing he would not be able to do, even to winning the coveted Grand Prix de Rome: "as I am a foreigner I could not be sent to Rome but I could contend for the prize," he wrote, "and I mean to get it too if I get in."

With everything apparently going so well, it must have come as a shock to the family in Roxbury when their "young hopeful" suddenly announced in November his intention of leaving Paris. Rogers himself felt it necessary to justify his decision at some length in a letter to his mother, dated November 19, less than two months after his arrival in Paris and just a month after he had spoken so enthusiastically of his prospects. Anticipating the family protests he knew would come as a consequence of his abrupt change of plans, he catalogued some of his reasons:

> I have lost my faith in Mons. Dantin [*sic*], and now that I have seen his works, flatter myself that I could do "all the same as so." . . . The French style of sculpture has no sentiment in it at all. It is clear matter of fact and what I don't wish to copy. . . . One great thing I lack here is *sympathy*. Mr. Greenough is the only sculptor that I have to talk with and though he has very good ideas of art, and I like him exceedingly as a man, yet as a sculptor he does not come up to my notions at all. Now that I know him I see he is just the man to delight in making such work as the ruff collar of Gov. Winthrop. . . . In Rome the artists are clubbed together and I could see more good works and hear art talked of more in a day than I could here in a month I have no doubt.

With all this, however, Rogers might have been willing to stay on in Paris rather longer if he had not developed a hearty dislike for his studio-mates, whose fondness for talking, smoking, playing chess, "& most everything but working" distressed his industrious, conscientious Yankee soul. "I was dissatisfied in Paris," he wrote soon after leaving, "because I was in a studio with a number of French fellows whom I could not get along with comfortably. . . ." Their fumbling efforts at modelling had been as irritating as their habits:

> They have done nothing but copy the antiques ever since they began [Rogers wrote] and now they can do nothing else. They can't make anything from *impression* to save their lives. One of them commenced a little figure three days after I went into the studio which is now nearly two months ago, and although he has had a living model for a week and a plaster figure from which he has copied the drapery almost exactly yet it isn't finished yet. I am *sure* I could do what he has done in four days.

"So you can imagine," he concluded, "my surroundings are not very inspiring."

Though he left Paris in December 1858 with little regret and hoped to find in Rome a more congenial atmosphere, John Rogers' self-confidence was badly shaken. In leaving Paris so soon he had acted on impulse, however well grounded that impulse had seemed at the time, and he felt that in doing so he had shown a certain weakness. He dreaded the reaction of his family for this reason; "I am afraid," he wrote home, "you will come down on me in a pile — uncles & aunts and all." His greatest fault, he decided, was "want of patience" — patience to go through the drudgery of his apprenticeship and, perhaps more important, patience to stay away from home. The prospect of remaining abroad for three or even two years was just too disheartening. He had scarcely got settled in Paris when he wrote: "I look forward to the time when I shall feel prepared to go back and settle down in the good old City of Boston, for you need have no expectations that I am going to *live* abroad after I have acquired what I have come for." Once having mastered the techniques of bust-making and monumental work and plaster-casting, there would be nothing to hold him longer in Europe. "As far as mere study goes," he said, "I am convinced that Boston is just as good a place as Paris or Rome, for copies of all the antique statues can be had there." By December, his projected stay in Europe had dwindled from several years to less than a year and he announced that he hoped to be home by the summer of 1859. His artistic ambition had suffered a corresponding contraction:

> I think my best course is to pursue the path that I have begun, to improve my taste in that and make small figures in bronze or very nice plaster such as they have a way of making here and not attempt any *high art* for I shall certainly step out of my depth if I do. I think if I get my name up for that style and represent pure *human nature* I can make a living by it as well as enjoy it exceedingly. If I still adhere to this plan, which I thought of some time ago in Paris, I shall return home in the summer while I have money enough left to start on in Boston. . . . I hope my plan will succeed, for if it don't I shall have to be a machinist again and that will come hard —

Somewhat revived in spirit by the prospect of an early homecoming, Rogers determined to make good use of his remaining time in Rome. His first concern was to find a teacher. A letter provided by the helpful Mr. Greenough introduced him to Randolph Rogers, a promising sculptor from Ann Arbor, Michigan, who was only four years older than John Rogers, but he was too busy putting the finishing touches to his bronze doors for the Senate Wing of the United States Capitol to take on any pupils. John Rogers, during the next month, tried to ease a "perfect fever" of impatience by working in his own sunny room on the Pincian Hill. Idleness was unbearable: "I find the only way to keep my impatience down," he wrote, "is to keep busy. The harder I work the more contented I am."

With the beginning of the new year, the outlook brightened a bit. Randolph Rogers still being too busy, John Rogers applied in January 1859 for admission to the studio of the English sculptor Benjamin E. Spence. Through the influence of another American, the painter Luther Terry, Spence was persuaded to take the young American as a pupil. An "unassuming and pleasant" gentleman of about forty, Spence was one of a group of English sculptors who had settled in Rome in the shadow of the Welshman John Gibson, on whom had descended the Neoclassic mantle of Canova and Thorwaldsen. His best known work, one of Rogers' favorites, was a gently romantic "Highland Mary." Like most of the English School in Rome, he was thoroughly competent but not particularly distinguished.

To Rogers, Spence's studio was a delight. "The room I shall have," he wrote, "is one that he has used for modelling in himself. . . . It is on the second story, is full of casts from the antique, and a capital light. In fact," he exclaimed happily, "I don't think I could have done so well in any place in Rome." The mere fact of being once more at work gave a lift to his spirits. "There seems to be nothing in the way now of my going ahead. I expect to have to do a great deal of drudgery & tiresome work but I mean to start with good resolutions to go through with it all. . . . I only hope," he added, remembering past experience, "I shall have *spunk* enough to carry them through."

It was easy enough at first, for everything was much more pleasant than it had been in Paris. Language was no problem, since there were many American and English artists with whom he could talk; his studio was "the *nicest* place that could be conceived"; his master was "as attentive as if I were a customer with any quantity of orders for him." Through his connection with Spence, also, he expected to profit from the experience of the English artists, for whose thoroughness he had great respect, while the English

Academy, to which he had free access, offered additional advantages in its evening drawing classes, library, and reading room.

> Oh, if I had only gone to Italy ten years ago [Rogers lamented]. . . . The ten years I have spent in the wood . . . are the *middle ages* of my life. I have just got to about the time when printing was discovered & I hope soon to arrive to the discovery of *gunpowder* and then of *America*. I think Boston & Roxbury will be the first land I shall sight.

After three weeks under his new master, Rogers was still fairly cheerful about his progress, but there was a hint of trouble to come. Spence was a harder master than Dantan and worked according to rules his American pupil, with his style already well set in a different pattern, found difficult to follow. An original figure Spence had assigned gave him more trouble than he had anticipated and forced him, apparently for the first time, to consider the theory of sculpture:

> according to the classical ideas prevailing here, and no doubt they are the true principles, statuary should be as simple as possible, with very little drapery and no *accessories* as they call all the little odds and ends that I used to put round my groups to help tell the story.

Leaving out the accessories, the young sculptor felt, made it next to impossible to tell a story in marble or clay, and without a story, as far as he could see, any piece of sculpture was pointless.

> Look at Powers Greek Slave — there is nothing in the world that has made that so popular but that *chain*. The chain showed that she was a slave and the whole story was told at once. There are plenty of figures as graceful as that and it is only the effect of the chain that has made it so popular.

Although he felt that the prevailing theory was wrong, Rogers wrote that he was prepared to do as he was told as long as he was in Rome and hoped "to see things differently by and by." As for his immediate problem — finding a subject that was simple and scantily draped enough to meet Spence's criteria — he confidently expected to "get hold of something before long."

Rogers' optimism did not carry him far. Despite all his good resolutions to follow wherever his master led, he had come up against something in himself which made it impossible for him to go on. The more he saw of the theory and practice of sculpture in Rome, the more stubbornly he rebelled against them. No matter how hard he tried, he simply could not adapt himself to principles of art in which he did not altogether believe. It was this, in part at least, that had made him so dissatisfied in Paris. In Rome he had expected to find the inspiration his rather flagging spirits needed. The experiment was foredoomed, as Rogers realized almost immediately, though he tried to force himself into the mold. "I don't think I shall ever get into the classic style," he wrote after his first visit to the sculpture galleries of the Vatican; "I do not take to it." Only a few of the antique statues were "deserving of unlimited praise," he concluded. Most of them had grave faults and did not seem worthy of the great veneration in which they were held, except for their great age. "Very few *express* a great deal in the faces," he complained. "The grace of the figure seems to have been the chief object to attain."

Here was the great stumbling block. The ancients and their modern imitators looked upon the expression of form as the great end of sculpture. Rogers, on the other hand, regarded sculpture chiefly as a medium for storytelling and consequently judged a statue much as he judged a painting, more on its literary merits and its handling of character than on its aesthetic quality. It is not surprising that among the ancient works he saw in Rome the only one that drew his unstinted praise was the "Dying Gladiator," which combined naturalistic modelling with a subject that brought to his mind, as he said, all the stories he had read about gladiatorial combats in the ancient world.

The more he thought about it the more convinced Rogers became that he was right and the other artists were wrong.

> The success of a statue [he told his brother] depends more on the subject than anything else though it is strange that the artists here don't seem to appreciate it. It seems strange to go into the studios here and see so much labor spent on so little thought. In fact the *thought* is a very secondary consideration — they merely make a graceful figure and call it anything. To show you how it is done I will tell a little experience I had today. I was in an artist's studio today and he had just made a little group roughly in clay of two figures. He thought the legs and arms and general arrangement would make a good group to model. There was a good deal of doubt whether the figure had better have wings or not but it was a great question what to *call it*. One figure was a little drooping and the other was holding it up. Mythology was thought over to see if any coincidence happened like it — then characters in books were talked over — then it was thought it might be considered allegorically. I came away before the matter was decided on.

The whole process disgusted him. "Now that is not the way that *I* want to go to work. I want the idea first and then I will suit the statue to it."

The experience of the few American sculptors Rogers knew in Rome offered little inducement to perseverance, though in his general disappointment he may have exaggerated their troubles somewhat. The profit of the sculptor's trade, he wrote, was small, because marble and workmen to cut it were both "immensely expensive," so that unless an artist sold a number of copies of the same design he could hardly make up the expense of modelling, much less the costs of putting it into marble. It was, indeed, a depressing picture he drew of the difficulties under which his fellow countrymen and countrywomen labored. Louisa Lander's work was "all money out of pocket," Harriet Hosmer's was "about as valuable," and William Wetmore Story's brought in less than the rent of his studio. "There have been but *three* orders given this winter to American sculptors and those are the oldest ones," he reported gloomily. "Of course when the old ones can't pay their way what could *I* do."

Out of sympathy with Rome's aesthetic principles and convinced that he could not hope to earn his own way for years even if he did persevere in his studies, Rogers rapidly exhausted his small store of enthusiasm and confidence. By mid-February 1859 he had had enough. In what he called "professedly a *blue* letter," he admitted to his brother that he was about ready to give up and come home.

> Now will you write me [he wrote to Henry on February 13, 1859] what your advice is and Father's & Mother's but don't speak of it out of the house for it is rather mortifying to come down from my high horse without a *very* good cause for it, but I shall have the satisfaction of having seen something of Europe at a time when there was not much else for me to do at home and of having put at rest all the longings I have had at different times in my life to be a sculptor. . . . I suppose you will tell me that it is perfectly suicidal to think of giving up now — but its a great satisfaction to be able to *blow off* when we get up to bursting point, but I mean to tie the safety valve down till I hear from you & perhaps I shall be in a very different state of mind then. I think I had a presentiment of this which accounted for my not going off more pluckily from home. If I had a quarter of the pluck that our artistic cousin [Louisa Lander] has I should be all right.

Rogers did not wait for advice from home, after all. The very next day, in a postscript to the above letter, he briskly announced he had made up his mind:

> Dear Father. I will finish this letter to you. . . . I am quite sure I will come to it in the end and I might as well say at once that I shall give up sculpture as a *dependence* but shall improve myself as much as possible while I am here and keep it as an amusement as I have done heretofore. I wish I could have a good talk with you for it's a comfort to free one's mind when in doubt, but it depends so entirely on myself that after all I am the one to decide. I imagine that you are rather pleased than otherwise. Mother will be sorry that she can't speak of her son the *distinguished* artist and the rest will all say "D——h!" I am sorry to disappoint them all and myself, but I have seen what a hard time artists, till they become known, have when

> they depend on their profession for support, and as it would be several years before I could do much, I do not dare to trust myself to stand the discouragements — and I rather *desire* that you should explain it so to my friends. . . . I trust that you will all make the best of it and consider it as a fact and not indulge in too many useless regrets. As for making small work as I proposed once I don't think it would pay and it would not be satisfactory. I had better step right out than go through a retrograde movement and fail in the end.

Rogers was so relieved to have wakened from the dream which had turned into a nightmare that he scarcely felt apologetic for the disappointment his decision would cause among his Roxbury friends. He was convinced that he had been mistaken in his ambition and proud that he had had enough sense and honesty to admit it before it was too late. To his mother he wrote two weeks later:

> I suppose my last letter took you a little by surprise though by my previous letters you must have felt that I was not entirely satisfied. I had felt ever since I came to Paris that I had made a mistake in taking up sculpture as a profession but still I took hold energetically so as to give it a fair trial and conquer it if I could — but I found that I was constantly feeling *blue* and impatient and knowing that I should have to go through several years of such life before I could do anything of much credit, and in the meantime leading a miserably discouraged life & most likely obliged in the end to borrow money to live on, that I concluded as I wrote in my last letter to give it all up. Since then I have not regretted it a moment. I have talked with a number of my friends and they think that I have acted wisely. . . . I consider it an *impossibility* to have kept on for I never would have consented to borrow money with the poor chances of repaying it that this business offers. I hope you will look on it and speak of it in that *light*. I have enjoyed myself more since my mind has been at rest than at any time before.

Once having made up his mind to give up sculpture, Rogers could hardly restrain himself from leaving Rome at once. "I feel like a soda bottle," he wrote, "and am afraid my head will pop off my shoulders like a cork if I don't get to work at something. I find *loafing* don't agree with me. I must have some active life to be contented." Although he had no very clear idea what he wanted to do now that he had rejected an artistic career, he had no desire to return to a machine shop. If he could not get a job somewhere as a draftsman, he thought he might even take up farming. "It always used to be my hobby theoretically," he wrote to his mother, "& now I want to try it practically. I have a strong love of my *independence* and hate to be *under* anybody's direction."

Staying in Rome only long enough to see the Carnival, which he found rather distasteful, Rogers left the city on March 14 in company with three

American ladies, spent two days in Florence, then sped through Pisa, Genoa, and Turin, and across the Alps to Paris. After a few days in the French capital, he went on alone to London. On April 13 he sailed for New York on the *City of Washington* and two weeks later was reunited with his family in Roxbury.

Years later, in the autobiographical sketch dictated to one of his sons, the old sculptor passed over his European experience without a word. Possibly he felt it had been too unproductive a period in his life to merit mention in an account of his development as a sculptor. Certainly it was one of the unhappiest years of his life. It was not time wholly lost, however, for he learned in Europe the importance of salesmanship in art. "I find that the artist's business is a sort of trade," he wrote with some disdain, shortly before he left Italy. "It takes the same qualifications that a good salesman has." Some of the poorest sculptors, he noted, sold the most because they had a knack for showing off their works. "In fact it requires qualifications that I don't possess to *sell* statues," he concluded, ironically, in view of the exceptional gift for salesmanship Rogers was to show later in his career.

Even more important was the part his European experience played in confirming Rogers' native preference for unheroic realism and an unfettered style. Unlike so many sculptors who tended to be overawed by the fame of the classic masters and their modern imitators, this young American had found in Paris and Rome little to admire and nothing to imitate. For the Neoclassic style, to which he had been indifferent at home, he had now conceived a hearty distaste. In this there was nothing especially meritorious, for it betokened as much a lack of appreciation for beauty of form as it did a realistic temper. But Rogers' explicit rejection of the accepted style marked him as a truly independent spirit. In the spring of 1859, however, it seemed highly unlikely that John Rogers would ever cut much of a figure in the art world. At the time the trip to Europe seemed to have been an unmitigated failure, just one more false step in a discouragingly erratic career.

CHAPTER VI

John Rogers, Artist

PURGED FOREVER, as he thought, of his hankering for the artist's life, Rogers willingly exchanged Rome for Roxbury late in April 1859, and after five months of idleness he was even ready to try railroading again. In June he left for the West, hoping to pick up where he had left off, in Hannibal. The superintendent of the Hannibal and St. Joseph Rail Road had nothing better to offer, however, than a draftsman's job which, Rogers decided, was not tempting enough to induce him to remain in Missouri. Nothing loath, he set off for Chicago where, with the help of influential friends, he was sure he would "scare up something before long." Even in Chicago business proved to be "*excessively* dull" and Rogers found that his friends there were no more able to help him than Superintendent Hayward in Hannibal. After ten days of fruitless job hunting, he was thoroughly discouraged.

> If I had half the tact that most people have [he wrote home disconsolately] I should be able to keep out of idleness, but I suspect I was intended for a sort of outside passenger in this world, and so I have got to stay there. However, everybody finds a place somewhere on the great coach and, if I can't find a seat, I must "hang on behind."

As it turned out, the very next morning Rogers found "an inside seat at last" as draftsman in the office of the city surveyor, with whom he had worked on the Boston Water Works a decade before. "I expect to be very contented with the business," he wrote home, explaining that his job consisted of drawing land plans, at a salary of two dollars a day.

> I have enjoyed the novel situation of working steadily for several days past [he wrote a week later], and the satisfactory feeling at night of having accomplished something — which is no small thing — for when I pass a day in idleness the unsatisfied, discontented feeling destroys the enjoyment I should otherwise take in other things. But my employment now is light & agreeable, my companions pleasant and all as I could wish. I think if I keep along here, and get a good reputation and

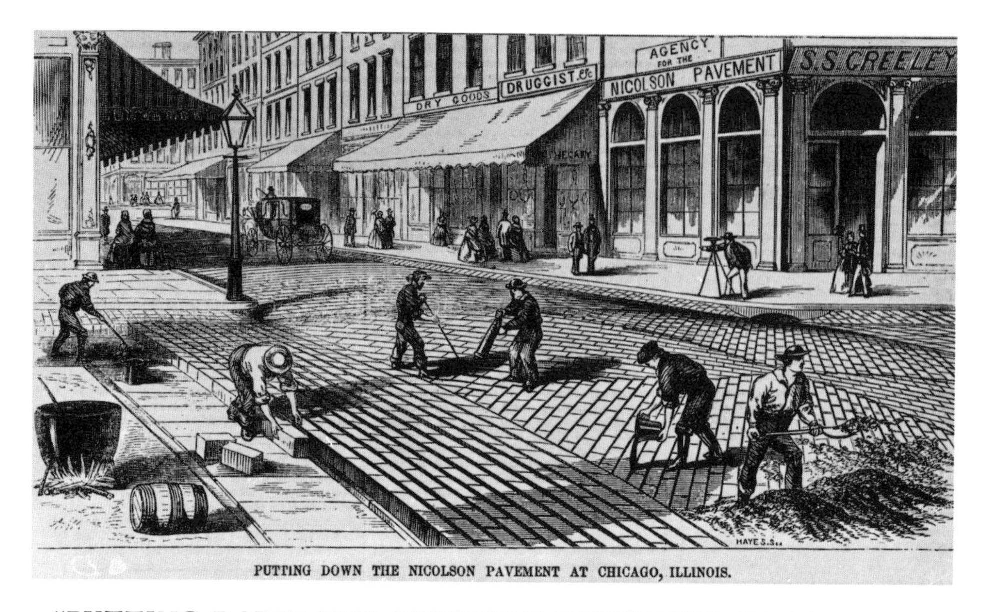

PUTTING DOWN THE NICOLSON PAVEMENT AT CHICAGO, ILLINOIS.

"PUTTING DOWN THE NICOLSON PAVEMENT AT CHICAGO"
From *Ballou's Pictorial Drawing Room Companion,* October 15, 1859, p. 253. Rogers made the original drawing of this street scene for his employer S. S. Greeley. It was sent to Boston to be engraved on wood by George D. Hayes, who left out, as Rogers had expected, the lager beer saloon on the corner which Rogers considered "quite characteristic of Chicago."

acquaintance, that I shall undoubtedly do well at something here eventually — at present I am perfectly satisfied & delighted with what I have to do.

Rogers' satisfaction with his job was equalled by his delight in the young city of Chicago. "I wish I could find some agreeable occupation to keep me here," he wrote while his future was still in doubt, "for I could enjoy living here very much." Although Chicago's fascination undoubtedly derived, in part, from the contrast between its "most princely residences" and the "shanties" of Missouri, there was also something about the spirit of the city that strongly appealed to a hitherto dormant quality in Rogers himself. "I tell you what," he told his mother in August, "Chicago is a wide-awake place. I have seen more originality here than Roxbury could exhibit in ten times the time." Underneath the reserve and sober attention to duty which his family had studiously bred into him there lay a more aggressive, imaginative quality closely akin to the spirit which had animated his Rogers and Derby merchant forebears. To the same quality in the flamboyant Chicago of the late 'fifties John Rogers responded with an enthusiasm strong enough to weaken his strong attachment to Boston and alter drastically the course of his life. "It would take very strong temptation to make me leave here," he informed his parents, "even for Boston."

Throwing off the shyness and aversion to polite society that had helped to spoil his sojourn in Rome, Rogers quickly made friends in Chicago, most of them transplanted New Englanders and parishioners of the recently organized Unity Church, where the Reverend Robert Collyer preached "without any clerical gloss" on "man acting his part in the theatre of the world." Collyer's insistence, as a contemporary put it, "upon the practical duties of life — upon purity and holiness of character," pleased the young mechanic from Massachusetts. Though never a pious churchman, Rogers did appreciate "practical, reasonable sermons" and admired Collyer's "uncommonly strong, practical sense." Their friendship, begun here in Chicago in 1859 and renewed twenty years later in New York, ended only with Rogers' death in 1904, when Collyer conducted the funeral service at his friend's grave.

It was Rogers' connection with Unity Church that led to his taking up again his old "resource and enjoyment." Two months after his arrival in Chicago the ladies of the church drew him into the whirlpool of activity attendant on organizing a citywide Charity Bazaar. Knowing of his talent for modelling (his "Old Bachelor" [21], owned by a former Hannibal acquaintance who had moved to Chicago, had been exhibited in Chicago's first art exhibition a few months before Rogers' arrival), the ladies prevailed on him to get up a clay group to be raffled off.

For his subject Rogers returned to an idea which had attracted him once before and which he was to use at least two more times in his career: a game of checkers [56]. Although the original clay group has disappeared, it was fully described in a contemporary newspaper article which the artist saved:

> The model represents two old-fashioned yeomen in rustic garb, seated on an old-fashioned wooden settee, and engaged in the old-fashioned game of checquers. The game has progressed to the close, each having but two Kings left on the board, and by the moves one player has *penned* the remaining forces. The winner leans back and enjoys his victory in a hearty haw-haw while the loser pinching his nether lip, appears to be both pleased at the adroitness of his adversary, yet puzzled to understand how it happened. The expression in the features of both is conveyed with wondrous faithfulness, and there is an ease and freedom in every line of this little clay model which indicates the maker as the possessor of no ordinary artistic skill.

"Checker Players" was an instantaneous success. The artist had it on view in his office in City Hall for two weeks before turning it over to the manager of the bazaar and was both flattered and amused by the attention it attracted. "I have been interrupted three or four times while I have been writing this letter," he wrote his mother one day at work, "by ladies & gentlemen, strangers to me, who have climbed up eighty two steps to see my checker players. I am in a fair way of being spoiled at last by flattering remarks. Rather a pity, isn't it?"

Despite competition from a trade fair which also opened the night of September 12, 1859, the eight-day Charity Bazaar was a "decided success," clearing nearly two thousand dollars. "Checker Players," its creator noted with pride, "attracted universal admiration" and was raffled off for seventy-five dollars (three hundred tickets at twenty-five cents each). What was more, two or three disappointed ticket-holders spoke to the artist about buying other groups. Suddenly the door of the future had opened just wide enough to reveal an alluring vista of pleasure and profit. This success, as Rogers put it many years later, set him thinking how he could turn it to account. Thought quickly matured into concrete plans.

> Business in the office will probably be dull soon [he told his father a few days after the bazaar closed], and I think Mr. Greeley will be glad to make an arrangement by which I can stay away part of the time and work on my groups. If I can sell them at a fair price as fast as I can make them ["Checker Players" had taken about a week], I will do pretty well at it — and now that I have got my name up so well I think there will be no difficulty.

Mr. Greeley consenting to the proposed arrangement, Rogers at once set to work in earnest on two subjects that had been in his mind since before the bazaar opened. "One is the same idea as Country Courtship though simpler," he wrote home, "& the other is a slave auction, which I think will be pretty good. The first one I want to make for Mrs. Greeley. The last I think I shall sell."

"Country Courtship" (soon renamed "The Town Pump") was begun late in September and completed by October 16, not without some difficulty [57]. "I had it all put together," he wrote on October 8, "but found it did not balance well & I was disgusted with it, but this morning I cut it to pieces & twisted it round & with a few additions it is quite satisfactory now." It was a decidedly more ambitious piece than "Checker Players," containing two human and two animal figures: a pretty village maid, with her dog at her feet, on one side of the town pump, a sturdy plowboy watering his horse on the other. One Chicago editor who saw it was much impressed with the natural and easy position of the figures and the lifelike expression of the faces, but his highest praise was reserved for the anatomy of the horse, which he thought "really wonderful" in its fidelity to nature. His review concluded with the pious hope that Rogers would soon turn his attention from such little works to "the sculptor's art."

Just at this point Rogers was not receptive to such suggestions. He was more interested in making a living than a reputation. "My great mistake when I went to Europe," he had just told his mother, "was in turning my attention to 'high art' instead of my particular *forte*. I have no doubt if I followed my specialty of treating *popular* subjects I could soon make it quite remunerative."

In this respect the fate of "The Town Pump" was hardly encouraging. After two weeks in a prominent downtown shop window, it remained unsold — he had given up the idea of presenting it to Mrs. Greeley because he needed money. Several out-of-state offers he had been obliged to turn down because he could not guarantee safe transportation of the fragile clay.

For his second group, however, Rogers had higher hopes. He began work on "The Slave Auction" [58] early in October, as soon as "The Town Pump" was out of the way, and was most enthusiastic about its possibilities. On October 8 he wrote home:

> The design is a man & his wife & two children who are standing before the desk of the auctioneer who is selling them. The sentiments expressed are the maternal affection of the mother and the sullen resignation of the man while the auctioneer is expressive of heartless calculation. The desk supports them all well and the group comes in very symmetrically. . . . I feel very much delighted with the design myself,

ROGERS' FIRST "PUBLISHED" WORK

"The Slave Auction," issued in December 1859. From an 1863 photograph by Moritz Stadtfeld.

and, if I finish it as I hope to, I think it will be far the most powerful group I ever made. Considering the subject & all, I think it will be very popular and I set my profits on it at five hundred dollars. I'm talking rather large I suppose you think but we shall see.

When the model was almost finished, Rogers called in a few of his friends to see it "in order to make any alterations that might strike them before it is too late." They were, he reported proudly, "unqualified in their praise." Rogers himself was quite carried away with his own handiwork:

I have got a magnificent negro on the stand. He fairly makes a chill run over me when I look at him. He would be a capital fellow in a Harpers ferry insurrection. The auctioneer I have rather idealized and made such a wicked face that Old Nick himself might be proud of it — two little quirks of hair give some impression of *horns*. The woman will be more nearly white & she & the children will come in very gracefully. I am entirely satisfied to stake my reputation on it & imagine the present excitement on the subject will give it great popularity.

The public soon had a chance to give its verdict. With an eye to publicity, the artist invited a journalist friend in to see the almost completed model. The next day appeared the following flattering notice, which Rogers sent home for the edification of his family:

A WORK OF GENIUS. — We have been permitted to see a group in clay, modelled by Mr. John Rogers, a young artist of this city, which, we predict, will give him a high and enduring reputation among the lovers of the beautiful in this country. The work is called the *Slave Mart;* and though the figures are minute, the story and the whole design of the artist are told by a glance at the group.

A detailed description of the group followed, concluding with a flourish that must have particularly delighted the artist:

But no words can convey to the reader's mind a sense of the exquisite fidelity with which these figures are wrought, nor the effect which they produce upon the sympathies of those who behold them. . . . He and his work will be heard of hereafter.

Warned by the fate of "The Town Pump" which had been standing in Cooke's shop window on Lake Street for almost a month, admired but unsold, Rogers decided on a different approach to marketing. His plan was ambitious but sounded sensible enough.

My plan is to get subscribers for it here [he wrote], and then take it to New York and get it cast. I shall then send copies to all the large cities and dispose of them at fair prices so as to become known & have them popular. If I succeed in this, you need not doubt but I shall follow it up. . . . If I don't succeed [he added in a later letter]

> no one will be to blame but myself. If the plan is not approved of at home please say nothing in your letters to discourage me, for I am acting according to my best judgement & that of friends *here*.

With this brusque declaration of independence and the statement that he was going to put all modesty in his pocket and make "a perfect balloon" of himself from that time on, John Rogers, at the age of thirty, set off for New York, even then the Mecca of aspiring American artists.

Arriving in New York on the "very raw, chilly, rueful" 27th of November 1859, the business-like artist allowed himself only a few days to get settled in a small room overlooking lower Broadway before setting in motion the plans he had outlined for himself in Chicago. His immediate problem, as he saw it, was a three-fold one: to get his "Slave Auction" cast and into the shops before Christmas, to get ready some new designs, and to "pump the bellows" of publicity by every possible means. His watchword, he decided, would be "large sales and small profits."

In the first part of his program Rogers was only partially successful. With the help of an old Italian image-maker to whom he had been recommended by the Reverend Robert Collyer of Chicago, Rogers did manage to get a few "Slave Auctions" out a week before Christmas, but getting them on the market proved impossible. "I find the times have quite headed me off," he wrote home in dismay on the eve of his first Christmas in New York, "for the *Slave Auction* tells such a strong story that none of the stores will receive it to sell for fear of offending their Southern customers."

Rogers' disappointment over the "Auction" group's chilly reception was mitigated somewhat by the warm commendation it received in the *National Anti-Slavery Standard.* In a highly appreciative review, published on December 30, the editor spoke in flattering terms of the artist's powers of execution, as well as his high moral purpose. From this, the first public notice of his work in New York, Rogers derived little more than personal satisfaction, however, for it brought to his studio only one visitor — a "dilapidated artist" asking for money.

Meanwhile, Rogers was busy with the second part of his program. Soon after his arrival he had begun modelling a group in quite a different vein, pure genre with no moral or political overtones. "The Farmer's Home," as he called it [59], portrayed a cheerful domestic scene, the happy young farmer at play with his children, the wife looking on with "a deeper, quiet, heartfelt sober delight." Rogers worked away at it in high spirits.

> You don't know how I enjoy myself now [Rogers wrote home]. . . . I have so much to do that I have no time to get discontented, and with a lump of clay before me I

> should not have a moment's lonely feeling if I did not speak to a human being for a week at a time. I get so absorbed in my groups that, for the time, I am connected with them and I have the same feeling that I am working out in the clay. All the figures in my last group are smiling or laughing and I have done the same thing from morning till night. My thoughts wander off to all the happy scenes of my life and I have caught myself repeatedly laughing out loud almost before I was conscious of it. . . . These home scenes really give me more enjoyment than anything and I think I shall confine myself mostly to them and not make any more political pieces.

As the year 1860 opened, Rogers was ready to attack the third problem on his original list, the matter of bringing his works into notice.

> In the first place [he informed his father], I shall put them into some of the best stores on Broadway. . . . Then another plan is one that I intended to start the *Slave Auction* with, but which I think is well to carry out with my other groups. It is to employ a good looking negro to carry them round on a sort of tray, with an appropriate notice printed on the front. There is no license required. The black man will be a distinguishing feature from the italien [*sic*] & it will bring them more into notice than any other way I think. . . . Then I shall try & get some of the hotels to accept of some to put in their sitting room with a notice stating where they can be had. It will attract the eyes of the country people who will want a copy to take home with them.

Reasonable though these plans sounded, only one produced any results during the first three months of the year. The hotel plan apparently never even got tried, and the three stores the sculptor approached refused to handle his wares, even the innocuous "Farmer's Home." Plaster, one dealer informed him, was "too cheap a material." He suggested that he would do better to offer them in bronze. This Rogers decided would only defeat the end he had in view. "As I want them *popular* they *must be put low,*" he declared, "or else nobody but the rich will buy them & they would not want them in their parlors. . . . Large sales & small profits," he repeated, "is the motto I must stick to."

Rogers' plan of hiring a Negro to hawk the groups about the streets proved, as he had anticipated, an excellent device for promoting public interest. On the very first day the sculptor's colored agent had the good fortune to cross the path of Lewis Tappan, a leading abolitionist. Buying a "Slave Auction" on the spot, Tappan gave the startled Negro a list of prospects and rushed over to Rogers' studio to meet the artist. Thanks to the interest aroused in anti-slavery circles, the vendor's sales thereafter averaged about two a day for two or three weeks and would have been even higher, Rogers complained, had the caster not fallen behind in his work.

More important than the slight stimulus it gave to sales was the notoriety Rogers' clever promotional device brought him. Toward the end of January callers began to appear daily at his fourth-floor studio. As far as Rogers was concerned the most important of these was the Reverend Doctor George B. Cheever, eloquent pastor of the Church of the Puritans and author of *God Against Slavery*. Cheever's first visit resulted in a long article in *The Independent,* New York's leading abolitionist organ, in which the "Farmer's Home" and "Slave Auction" were highly praised for their contrasting portrayals of "freedom and happiness on the one side, and of slavery and wretchedness on the other." Neither this "puff" in *The Independent* nor a brief notice in the *New York Tribune* a week later had any appreciable effect on sales, except perhaps to scare off a few prospects whose views on slavery were more moderate than Dr. Cheever's. They did, however, bring an influx of visitors to Rogers' studio at a time when the artist was glad of any attention. "It will be like the lawyer in one of Dickens works," he wrote, "who begged that someone would only *kick* him so as to make himself famous."

A large portion of Rogers' time during the early part of 1860 was taken up with experiments in plaster casting. His success, as he realized, depended not on publicity alone but even more on his ability to turn out casts of good quality at low cost and high speed. It had, therefore, been to him a matter of serious concern to find, as he did even before Christmas 1859, that the Italian image-makers upon whom he had to depend were slow, unreliable, and expensive. With characteristic confidence in his own ability to solve any merely mechanical problem, Rogers soon decided to undertake the casting himself right in his combination bedroom-studio at 599 Broadway. Economy was his principal motive — making his own casts was, he said, "like pulling teeth, pretty much all profit" — but he was also interested in improving the quality of the casts he intended to sell.

Although he fretted a good deal over the amount of time he had to spend in casting rather than modelling, events proved the value of the sacrifice. For one thing, the experience gave him valuable insight into the limitations of the medium. The "Slave Auction" and "Farmer's Home," for instance, as he discovered when he tried to make his own casts from them, were "too complicated and difficult" to reproduce profitably. It was a great help to know beforehand whether or not a design was going to be suitable for casting. Learning the caster's trade, furthermore, gave Rogers a decided advantage later in 1860 when he was again in a position to hire men to do the work for him. This was demonstrated when his very first employee "commenced apparently as if he knew all about the business & didn't like to be shown." Rogers shrewdly let him go his own way at first, but the next day, "as he had not made a single perfect cast, . . . took hold & made one for him." Thereafter, Rogers noted with satisfaction, the man was very deferential.

In April 1860 Rogers finally completed two new designs. One was a new version of "Checker Players" [61], little, if at all, different from the one which had been so well received in Chicago. The other, "The Village Schoolmaster" [63], was a new design illustrating a line from Goldsmith's *Deserted Village:* "For e'en though vanquished he could argue still." Both were finished in time for Rogers to enter them in the Spring Exhibition of the National Academy of Design. Although the artist reported that his were "the only works of the sort there [and] attracted as much attention as anything," his debut as an exhibitor at the Academy went completely unnoticed by the press.

More encouraging was the fact that the proprietor of Williams and Stevens, one of the best of the Broadway fancy goods shops, was sufficiently impressed with "Checker Players" to put it in his window. Against his better judgment, Rogers allowed him to price the group at five dollars rather than three and to take a 40 per cent commission.

> It seemed a very large commission [the artist explained to his mother], but he said they were not used to selling such small things, but if I could allow them a large commission so that they would feel it to be an object, it would be for the interest of all of them to *push* it. I saw at once the advantage of having them sold to the class of customers they have, so I agreed to the terms & they sold them quite readily, rough & poor as they were.

Popular interest in the group in Williams and Stevens' window soon wore off, however, and Rogers found himself in May 1860 faced with the unpleasant fact that six months of unremitting effort had brought him, not large sales and small profits, but small sales and no profits whatsoever.

There was no doubt in his mind, as there had been when he was in Rome, of his ability as a sculptor. His error, he decided, was in limiting himself to cheap plaster and scenes from everyday life. If he was ever to amount to anything, it seemed clear, he would have to aim higher. "I now see the necessity of finishing my works with more care & making more of a study of them," he explained to his mother in May 1860, "& I expect at the end of every six months to be ashamed of what I made in the six previous months." Rogers had not arrived at this point of departure from his original thinking without help from others. Williams and Stevens had been working on him for months to wean him away from what they considered his unfortunate addiction to realistic genre groups. In fact, as early as March they had almost persuaded him to do an "Evangeline" [64] based on a popular engraving, but "after a very precarious life of a few days," as the artist himself reported, "Evangeline" was "buried in the clay pail" and reborn as a "Fireman" [62].

Williams and Stevens were more successful in persuading Rogers to execute a pair of low-relief medallions copied from Thorwaldsen's famous "Night" and "Morning" [65, 66]. Although he still disclaimed any interest in the Neoclassic style, Rogers was pleased to find that he could copy it successfully, especially when the medallions, selling at fifteen dollars a pair unframed, turned out to be more saleable than anything else he had done.

When he was commissioned in June to make a small copy of William Randolph Barbee's Neoclassic nude "Fisher Girl" and executed the work with great credit to himself [68], Rogers' confidence in his powers soared to new heights. Already half-persuaded that plaster was beneath his dignity, he now turned on it almost savagely.

> I think I gave you warning some time since [he wrote to his mother on July 1, 1860] that I expected to improve in my style & would very likely soon be discontented with what I am doing. In my association with artists I have felt it coming over me for some time. They tell me that it is a pity to waste my time on plaster. I am good for something better — it is cheaper material & can never be made artistic. I have found this out by experience. The very name of plaster condemns any work of art.

The next step was almost inevitable. "Now I aspire to marble," he announced a fortnight later, "& next winter I expect to come out a full-fledged sculptor."

CHAPTER VII

Marble, Bronze, or Plaster?

FROM THE TIME he renounced plaster for higher things until he returned, much chastened, to the course he had originally laid out for himself, John Rogers was for three years in frequent danger of losing his artistic identity. Too easily influenced by those about him, he had forgotten the primary lessons of his European experience. In a vain effort to compass the whole range of traditional sculpture, he came close to smothering his genuine talent.

His first wasted efforts were directed toward the production of works of an "ideal" nature. Wisely, considering his inexperience in modelling the human figure, he attempted nothing more exacting at first than "The Fairy's Whisper" [71] (July–October 1860), "representing the lightsome figure of a fairy, rising out of a cluster of fern-leaves, and whispering in the ear of a child whose beautiful face is molded into a sweet and winning expression." Aside from the tiny fairy, there was nothing particularly "ideal" in the group, for the life-size child and the fern-leaves were rendered with Rogers' customary attention to realistic detail. Still the subject was somewhat remote from everyday life and thus met, in part at least, the requirements of idealism.

The artist himself seemed to feel a bit self-conscious about "The Fairy's Whisper," referring to it variously as "my Boy," "the Fairy in the bullrushes," or "something which the ladies would call a 'sweet thing' (emphasis on the *sweet*)," but the critics gave it fulsome praise when the clay model was revealed for their inspection. A work "of exquisite beauty and tenderness of feeling" the *New York Tribune* called it, while the *New York Times* singled out for special praise the modelling of the child's face, "whose expression, radiant with all the intensity of a rare poetic intelligence, still remains exquisitely childlike." Though noting that the work was not without faults of workmanship, *The Independent* considered it, on the whole, a "true conception of genius." Despite his recently professed aversion to plaster, Rogers reproduced "The Fairy's Whisper" in plaster rather than marble, for a very practical reason. If the group were to be put into marble, he found, he would have to sell it for six hundred dollars in order to make any profit. Plaster casts he could sell profitably at twenty-five dollars. With Christmas approaching and the critics' praises ringing in his ears, Rogers foresaw a better return with plaster and postpone to a later day his debut in marble. He still professed a strong distaste for small groups, however, and was more than ever determined to fulfill the prediction of Theodore Tilton, assistant editor of *The Independent,* that his destiny was "not for plaster but for marble."

With his sister Ellen, who had been after him for years to turn his talent to more elevated ends than merely tickling the popular fancy, Rogers at this point in his career shared the loftiest notions of what these ends should be.

> Your idea of what sculpture should express is exactly mine [he wrote to Ellen in October 1860, just after his thirty-first birthday]. I feel that it should be elevating in every way & be made to express pure & noble truths. I feel that the power is gradually developing in me to do it. I never had the implicit faith & reliance that you have — it was not born in me — but I have the most profound respect for all great moral truths & admire purity & goodness in every shape. For the same reason I feel that I could never be a minister but still could write my sermons in stone & be as impressive in that way as if I was eloquent in the pulpit.

The principal difficulty, he added, was "to think of designs that will convey all of such an idea where it is necessary to be so simple as in sculpture."

Under the spell of this almost religious mood, Rogers projected a design he called "Vesper Bells" representing "a peasant girl who hears the vesper bells and offers her devotions, half kneeling, with face upturned and her beads in her hand." Ten days later his mood had changed. Having "just tried something ideal," he decided that "it would be well to try another line which might be turned to better account." He had in mind a two-foot statue of Lafayette. Another change of mood brought him a month later back to the ideal and a design [72] somewhat similar to "The Fairy's Whisper" which he refused to describe at first, not wanting to give more "false alarms."

In mid-December 1860, six months after first voicing his aspiration to put something into marble, Rogers received a commission which made this possible. His unexpected patron was a cousin of his own age, Hattie Appleton of Boston, who had recently come into a legacy and wanted to spend about four hundred dollars on a small marble statue. Rogers viewed the commission with mixed feelings. "Of course I shall lay myself out on the occasion," he wrote home, "as it is a chance that I have been wanting . . .

but I feel more & more convinced that my style of modeling is better suited to bronze than marble."

Reassuring himself with the thought that it would be good to have some experience in cutting marble, Rogers attacked the problem of "Hattie's marble" with fair confidence and zest, but only a few weeks sufficed to dull his enthusiasm. By February 1861 he was ready to give the whole thing up as a mistake.

> I can't get interested in the fairy business [he wrote home on February 24]. I intend to make some alterations in Hattie's piece but if it does not come to suit me at once I shall pull it down.

He carried out his threat the following month and did not take up Hattie's project again until May, when he began a wholly different figure. The outbreak of civil war in April had temporarily drawn his attention away from his work, as had his move to a studio in the new Dodworth Building on Madison Square.

"Air Castles" [80], as he christened his new design, portrayed "a country girl who has gone to a spring for water & becomes absorbed in thought, building air castles," while her unheeded pail runs over. To the sculptor the idea seemed to meet all the requirements of high art. "She will have a pleased expression," he explained, "& as it is a single figure, simple & tells the story I flatter myself it is a good design." Even "Jemima," as he sometimes called the new figure, failed to hold Rogers' interest for more than a short time. "I still think it will be pretty," he wrote after about three weeks, "but it's not my style & don't interest me much." The encouraging words of artist friends who thought it better than "The Fairy's Whisper" made him persevere, however, and Rogers finally completed the clay model and cast it by the end of August 1861. During the next three months the marble was roughed out by a hired marble cutter. Finally, toward the end of November, Rogers reported that "Jemima" was back in his own hands.

> As I am used to tools [he announced a week later], I soon got into the way of working the marble & now cut away with much more confidence than I did at first. I suppose it will take two months to finish it. I don't know how my patience will hold out, for I long to get at the clay again.

His patience actually held out less than a month, for in mid-December he reported that he had turned over the job of finishing the marble to a professional marble cutter. "I am very glad it is out of my hands," he wrote. "I should certainly have spoilt it with my impatient way of going to work on it." Three months more brought the marble to completion just in time for the April opening of the National Academy exhibition, where Rogers showed it along with the clay model of "The Town Pump" [89], an updated version of the one he had made in Chicago, with a soldier replacing the original farmer boy.

The moral of this drawn-out effort was quite evident to Rogers when he noted that "The Town Pump," on which he had spent only a few weeks, "received much more notice" at the Academy than "Air Castles," which had taken almost a year to produce. "Visitors," he remarked to his father, "seem to be more attracted by the originality of my smaller works rather than the simplicity requisite for marble." Since the public's feeling coincided with his own, however he might try to conform to the standards set by the leaders of artistic fashion, he was only mildly, if at all, surprised by the popular verdict. He had, in fact, anticipated it in December of the preceding year when he announced to his family, as he had two years earlier from Rome, his intention of renouncing high art:

> I have got into such a nervous impatient state over my Air Castles [he wrote on December 8, 1861] that I fear I should get into the same state with any large figure which takes a long time to finish, so that I feel convinced that my temperament is not suited for such works. I am going to work now on small work & I hope I may have firmness enough not to be allured aside by any tempting offers of larger commissions which prove an expense instead of a profit in the end. . . . Why is it not better to do a thing one has a natural taste for well, than to try & force oneself into doing what *some* people consider of more importance. Benvenuto Cellini certainly gained more credit by his small work than his large. It is not so much what one does as his doing perfectly whatever he undertakes. . . . I have been so often shaken in my resolve by people asking me "Well, what are you doing of *more importance,*" as if large works *were* of more importance than small ones that convey the same idea, that I feel the need of some strong friend to say "stand firm."

Complaining that it would ruin him, mentally and financially, to get involved in another large statue, he concluded with the statement that "Air Castles" had at least served to make him satisfied with his groups.

He had good reason for satisfaction with his groups just at this moment. After two years they appeared at last to be really taking hold. Behind the growing interest in his smaller works was an unpretentious group Rogers had casually turned out in the early summer of 1861 to relieve the monotony of work on "Hattie's marble." Illustrating a familiar scene of the war which had begun less than three months before, "The Picket Guard" [83] had looked "bully" to the artist at the time, but he had not bothered to get any casts on the market before the end of August, because, he said, he didn't think he could sell enough to pay the expenses. To his surprise the group proved quite a hit wherever it was put on sale. In Williams and Stevens' Broadway window it attracted so much attention that Mr. Williams himself called Rogers in to ask if he had anything else to exhibit. "I told him of the Whisper," Rogers wrote home, "& he wanted me to send a copy right down to him & he would put it in the window." When Williams and Everett in Boston reported selling four copies of the groups and Williams and Stevens sold three in one day, Rogers was inspired to reintroduce two of his earlier works — "Checker Players" [61] and "The Slave Auction" [58] — and to bring out two that he had modelled in clay but never cast — "The Village Schoolmaster" [63] and "Shylock" [77]. So successful was the experiment that by the end of November 1861, for the first time since his arrival in New York, Rogers was selling enough groups to cover his weekly expenses. With fair prospects of at last achieving his goal of "large sales & small profits," it was with undisguised satisfaction that in December, for the second time in a year, he renounced his aspiration to the title of "sculptor" and demolished the life-size clay model of "The Flight of the Octoroon" [86], a design for marble over which he had been laboring for several months in the hope that it would be to him what the "Greek Slave" had been to Hiram Powers. "With this weight off my mind," he wrote as the year came to a close, "I have taken hold of my groups again & mean to stick to them. . . . I can consider that I have got a fair start & can go ahead."

The way ahead was not quite so clear, however, as Rogers anticipated. Although he brought out two more "scenes from camp life" early in 1862 ("Camp Life: The Card Players" [87] and "Camp Fire: Making Friends with the Cook" [88]), his late winter sales were disappointing. "I certainly get notices enough," he complained in March, "but people don't seem to buy as rapidly as I should think they would when the groups attract so much attention as they seem to." Between March and May, however, he added "The Town Pump" [89] and "Sharp Shooters" [90] to his growing inventory of war subjects in plaster.

In May 1862, after issuing four new groups in as many months, Rogers put down his modelling sticks and clay to devote his attention to business matters. Thanks largely to the generous notice given his latest works in the newspapers of New York and Boston, he had a fair reputation in those cities. He was also enjoying some sales in Philadelphia through the art dealer, James Earle. But Rogers was enough of a businessman to see that this market was too limited. He realized the need to reach out into the hinterland of America where, he reasoned, cheap art on popular themes would be even more saleable than it had proved in the more sophisticated cities of the Atlantic seaboard. His groups were, after all, as he said in

February 1860, "not intended for rich people's parlors but more for common houses & the country."

That Rogers did not know exactly how to proceed is not surprising, for he was attempting to do something comparatively few manufacturers of the time had done, to develop a national market for a product which could only be classed as a luxury. Certainly no artist, with the notable exception of the print-makers Currier and Ives, had made a similar attempt to reach so large and unpredictable an audience.

The success of Rogers' ambitious program depended on quantity production, consistently high quality, safe and cheap transportation, effective promotion, and close attention to the popular taste. By 1862 Rogers had most of these well in hand. He had struck a popular vein in his camp scenes, he had worked out by experiment a method of packing the groups in boxes filled with sawdust (later, barrels filled with wood shavings) which seemed to meet the challenge of the express company "baggage smashers," and he had mastered most of his casting difficulties. His chief remaining problem was to create a wider demand for his works.

Only lack of money held Rogers back at this apparently favorable moment. During the first six months of 1862 he had dipped into his small capital to get out casts of four small groups and to patent three of these and three earlier ones. Sales during the latter part of this period had been relatively good, but not good enough to give him a real profit. In June, however, the summer exodus from the city caused sales to drop alarmingly. "The plaster business is still wretchedly bad," Rogers wrote on July 6. "Another week has passed without a sale." With his income reduced to practically nothing and his reserve capital to about two hundred dollars, Rogers was forced in mid-summer to suspend casting operations and wait for a more propitious time to carry out his plans for expansion.

Money worries, renewal of the old trouble with his eyes, and plain boredom combined to make the summer of 1862 a frustrating one for the young artist. He toyed briefly with the idea of taking likenesses [91] in fashionable Newport but gave it up partly because he still lacked full self-confidence in this branch and partly because he wanted to rest his eyes. Most of the summer he simply puttered around making improvements in his studio. The one bright spot in his summer was a spur-of-the-moment trip to the White Mountains to spend a fortnight with his family, but even this was ruined, three days after his arrival at Conway, by the news of President Lincoln's draft order. Expecting an early call, Rogers rushed back to New York to put his business affairs in order. "The state of uncertainty I am in seems to make it impossible to apply my mind to any work so that I have accomplished nothing since I came back," Rogers complained on August 23. Although the draft threat did in the end prove abortive, thanks largely to the wave of enlistments it inspired, it left the sculptor with nerves rather on edge. And to make matters worse, fall brought no immediate financial relief. By mid-October his slim reserves were reduced to one hundred fifty dollars.

In these circumstances, the sculptor once again abandoned his plaster groups for what he hoped would be more profitable lines. First he thought of getting up a bronze illustrating some scene from Irving's "Legend of Sleepy Hollow," but he quickly dismissed the idea because of the capital outlay involved. Next he turned to portraiture, in which, after two years of intermittent practice, he was at last beginning to feel reasonably competent. By October 1862, as reported in at least two papers, Rogers was prepared to model twelve-inch plaster statuettes and six-inch busts [see 91–94] and cast them in any quantity desired, but a two-month trial sufficed to show that the market for such work was small. His only recorded sale, though he undoubtedly made others, was to his uncle, Robert C. Winthrop, who ordered "two groups" of his step-son George Welles [94]. "The ready money style of doing business," as he had called it, did not have the "great advantages over the groups" which the artist had hoped for.

November found Rogers near the end of his resources. With Christmas drawing near he needed to get out additional casts in order to meet the anticipated holiday demand for his groups. Into this effort he poured the last of his capital, only to have his caster walk off the job just when he was most needed. "If you were going to have a dinner party and your cook should suddenly leave," Rogers told his mother, "you could not feel in a more anxious state of mind than I do." Although Rogers would somehow have managed even at this crisis in his affairs, it was nonetheless important to his morale that at this low point in his fortunes as an artist words of encouragement and some solid financial help came to him from one of the family in Roxbury.

> I think if you had seen the stream of sunshine which came into my room when I read your letter [John wrote to his sister Ellen on November 21, 1862], you would have been gratified. I had been all the morning down town & had just drawn out my *last* fifty dollars & came back tired & wet & low spirited. I had been turning over in my mind how long I could keep on at my present rate of expenditure, for I had nothing left but a share in the Worcester R. R. and my watch, which I would not part with till the last extremity, but when I found your letter awaiting me with such a generous present, I felt sure that my good angel, that I have always thought watched over me in my most desponding moods, had not forsaken me — even if I lost every-

> thing else I should never lack a word of sympathy from home. . . . I am determined to be no more disheartened, feeling sure, after my experience today, that there is a silver lining to every cloud.

With Ellen's money in his pocket and two new casters at work in his plaster shop, Rogers hurriedly completed a new work, rather more pretentious in scale and theme than any he had previously produced, a statuette of Edwin Booth as Hamlet in the first-act ghost scene [97]. In spite of Booth's cooperation — he helped choose the subject and pose, lent the artist his costume, gave him at least one sitting, and allowed a mask to be made of his features — the piece did not turn out nearly so well as Rogers had hoped. "In trying for the expression," he complained, "I have not secured a very strong likeness." The few casts he could get out before Christmas were priced at ten dollars. "I don't expect to sell many of them," the artist explained, "but, under the circumstances, I prefer to sell fewer & make more." Of the handful of casts of "Hamlet" Rogers published at this time (there was no second casting), at least two were sold, but none is known to have survived. Luckily, the other groups, familiar though they were, sold well during the holidays, at a clear profit of three hundred dollars.

Despite the evidence of growing popular interest in the small groups, particularly those dealing with the war, as 1862 ended Rogers was still looking for a medium which would give him greater prestige as an artist and at the same time a comfortable margin of profit. For some time past he had felt that bronze might be the answer. Early in December he finally broached the subject to the family, a necessary preliminary since such a venture required a capital investment beyond his own means. Both his father and his younger brother Henry, now established in New York City as a tobacco merchant, offered to advance whatever money was needed, and John accordingly set to work, as he said, "with renewed heart," feeling confident that at last he had found his "true course."

All risk in the bronze venture was removed when the sculptor received from his uncle, Henry Bromfield Rogers, a New Year's gift of five hundred dollars.

> This generous present relieves me from all anxiety [he wrote home exultantly], & with over three hundred dollars from my Christmas sales, I find myself a capitalist of nearly a thousand dollars — quite enough to put all my plans through. Hoping the New Year opens as pleasantly for you is the wish of
>
> Yr. Affec'te Son, John

By mid-January 1863 the artist's design for his first bronze was far enough advanced in the clay to be exhibited at the season's first Artists' Reception in the Dodworth Building. "Union Refugees," as he called it, depicted a Union family in flight from their Southern home [98]. Standing over twenty-two inches high, compared with the nine to slightly over fourteen inches of his previous works, the group was more carefully modelled than the earlier ones and decidedly more effective artistically. "I consider it a design with more character & sentiment," Rogers wrote, "& that it will do me more credit than anything I have done." The critics of five New York papers agreed wholeheartedly and Rogers exulted that with such an endorsement he felt quite secure in his bronze project.

After the actual modelling was completed and the plaster cast made from it late in February, Rogers began to lose some of his enthusiasm for this new project, just as he had for his earlier ventures in marble. For one thing, he was not yet inured to investing a large sum of money in one work. For another, he found it annoying to have to depend on outside help in getting out the bronze casts. For a third, he found it irksome to have one job drag on for months while he was itching to get to work on something new. Finally, he could not quite shake off his early conviction that "large sales & small profits" were a surer road to financial success than smaller sales and larger profits. Consequently, when the bronze (really spelter, or zinc bronze) "Refugees" at last appeared in August 1863, Rogers was firmly convinced that he had been on the wrong track after all.

> I have at last got over my perplexities about my casting & have come back to plaster again [he announced on August 30, 1863]. . . . The bronze had been a sort of hobby with me & it came hard to give it up — but I intend to start on a new system with my new plaster designs which I hope will be more satisfactory & quite as profitable as the bronze.

Unlike the other turnings Rogers had taken during the preceding three years of erratic wandering through the maze of indecision, this one led straight to where he wanted to go. Although he did not know how near he was to the realization of the ambition that had brought him to New York in 1859, he at least sensed that he was once more headed in the right direction. "I assure you," he told his father, "it is a weight off my mind &, in spite of all the trouble I have had with plaster, I feel as I should on coming home from a long, tiresome journey."

"THE WOUNDED SCOUT: A FRIEND IN THE SWAMP," 1864
This eloquent sermon in plaster was praised by President Lincoln as "very pretty and suggestive." "It is a significant lesson of human brotherhood for all the coming ages," wrote another admirer. From an 1864 photograph by J. F. Aitken.

CHAPTER VIII

Scenes of Camp Life

JOHN ROGERS' final decision in August 1863 to concentrate on producing cheap statuary for the average home marked the real beginning of his phenomenally successful career. From that point his rise was swift and sure, as before it had been slow and uncertain. The rapidity with which Rogers won the favor of the American people and the strength of his hold on their affections over a period of almost thirty years stemmed from his perfect sympathy with the feelings of the common man and from his perfect sense of timing. Both these qualities showed themselves for the first time in full strength in the works which brought him into the public eye during the Civil War.

As we have seen in the preceding chapter, the attack on Fort Sumter in April 1861 had little immediate effect on Rogers or his work. This did not mean that he was indifferent to the country's perilous situation, for he had been following and commenting on the drift toward war for months before it came. His views were staunchly Unionist, antislavery, and pro-Lincoln. "I have every confidence in Lincoln," he wrote shortly before the inauguration, "& think he is the right man for the time." When war actually came he was so excited, as he said, that for several days he could not work. "I hope the government will not flinch now," was his reaction to the news from Charleston on April 13. "I feel very warlike & want to thrash the traitors." Barely two weeks later, ensconced in his new studio away from the noise and excitement of Broadway, with its marching soldiers, bands, and cheering crowds, Rogers calmly began work on "Air Castles."

During the ensuing months and years of war Rogers followed the battle news in the daily papers and continued to support Lincoln in hot arguments with a brother-in-law who belonged to what Rogers called the "craven spirited" opposition. "For all that can be said against Lincoln," he wrote soon after the 1864 convention, "he stands head & shoulders in dignity and manhood above McClellan with his shuffling letter of acceptance and Fremont with his spiteful letter of resignation."

The sculptor's strong Union sympathies did not, however, divert him more than momentarily from the pursuit of business as usual. He made no move to enlist in the spring of 1861 or later. He did volunteer in the summer of 1862 to make one trip to the James River as a nurse on a military transport, but his offer was turned down because the Sanitary Commission had suddenly decided to accept no more such casual volunteers. As we have seen, President Lincoln's draft order later the same summer, which was not immediately put into effect because it produced the desired spurt in enlistments, had no other effect on Rogers than to put him into a state of uncertainty that interfered with his work the rest of the summer. The draft did eventually reach him early in April 1865, when he was notified that he had been called up for one year's service, but Lee's surrender a few days later cancelled his call.

Rogers' attitude toward military service was very clearly expressed in letters to his family at the time of the first draft call in 1862. Making "no pretence to any military enthusiasm at all," he told his mother that he would not go to war unless he was drafted and then "only from a combined feeling of compulsion and duty."

> If I am drafted, I shall have to go, but it will be very much against my inclinations, as it will so completely break up my arrangements here & put an end to the plans I was in hopes to carry out. . . . But I won't be more selfish than I can help & will take my fate with as good a grace as I can.

Since the public opinion of the time did not demand military service of every able-bodied man, Rogers' failure to enlist excited no adverse comment at the time or later. On the contrary, he was praised for contributing, through his plaster groups, to the immortalization of "the scenes of civil war engaged in by a government to defend and support the purest principles of constitutional liberty." John Rogers, as an admirer wrote after the war, performed his wartime task "as nobly in plaster and clay as [Thomas] Nast [artist-correspondent of *Harper's Weekly*] performed his with the pencil, or [Henry J.] Raymond [editor of the *New York Times*] his with the pen."

When he modelled "The Picket Guard" in June 1861, just two months after the outbreak of war, Rogers apparently had no idea how well it would be received, for he let two months pass before deciding to have it cast. Something of the eager delight with which the civilian gazed on this evocation of one of the characteristic activities of camp life is conveyed in these words of a correspondent of the *Springfield Republican:*

> ["The Picket Guard"] is composed of three figures, the central one a little in advance, each peering out, as if into the darkness, with attitude so tense and expression

so intense, you involuntarily hold your breath, and lean, and look out, and listen with them.

An obviously stolen chicken, hurriedly stuffed into one private's knapsack, provided a characteristically humorous note lacking in Ethel Lynn Beers's popular pathetic poem, "The Picket Guard," which was first published only a month or so after Rogers' little group appeared on the market.

A similar light touch characterized Rogers' other "scenes of camp life" which followed during the next two years. "Camp Life: The Card Players," two Zouaves playing cards on a drumhead, and "Camp Fire: Making Friends with the Cook," a soldier reading the news to a Negro "contraband" cook, were both pure fun. "Sharp Shooters," on the other hand, portrayed the more grim humor of the front lines, one soldier drawing fire with a dummy while the other draws a bead on the unsuspecting enemy. This group, understandably, was less popular than the others though equally praised for its realism. One other group which appeared at this time pictured a home-front scene, a mild flirtation between a country lass and a soldier boy at "The Town Pump." Critics particularly admired the artist's ability to make even a pump poetic. The story pleased too. It was, wrote one admirer, "no Isaac and Rebecca at the well affair, but an out and out *flirtation.*"

By August 1863, when "Union Refugees" introduced to the public a Rogers Group of a more finished quality and larger scale, the sculptor's reputation was solidly established. Partly because of the clever workmanship and cheapness of his early groups, even more because he had been one of the few artists in the country, aside from the artist-correspondents of the illustrated papers, to seek his subjects in the great war for the Union, John Rogers had been well noticed in the press, at least in New York and Boston. What was more, his work had been acclaimed by the artists themselves, who in May 1863, less than four years after his unnoticed arrival in New York, awarded him their highest accolade, full membership in the National Academy of Design.

Rogers was reaping his reward, "Periwinkle" observed in the *Springfield Republican* in December 1863, not only in "golden opinions," but in "golden greenbacks" as well. Actually his income was very uncertain before the fall of 1863, frequently falling below his shop expenses, but that winter and the succeeding year were marked by a sustained increase in sales that by October 1864, was to put him, in his own words, "beyond all pecuniary troubles."

The sudden rise in sales, beginning late in 1863, Rogers credited principally to the marked improvement in the quality of his latest groups. The praise accorded "Union Refugees," which won him election to the Academy, led him to adopt its larger scale and more careful modelling for all his new works. Three of these were available to the public at Christmas 1863: "Union Refugees" (both in spelter and in plaster), "Country Post Office" [99], and "Mail Day" [101]. Just as the sculptor had anticipated, these larger works were called for more than the early ones. Since he was able to sell more of these groups at fifteen dollars than he could of the others at five and derived more profit from each sale besides, Rogers had good reason for optimism as the year 1864 opened.

Another advantage the larger groups had over the smaller, though not mentioned by the sculptor, was readily apparent in "Country Post Office" and his first group of 1864, "The Returned Volunteer: How the Fort Was Taken." Both offered Rogers an opportunity, which he obviously relished, to throw in a multitude of accessories which helped tell the story and faithfully reproduced familiar everyday scenes, a cobbler's shop and smithy, respectively. He thereafter made free use of such homely, always relevant details with joyous disregard for the rule of simplicity he had learned in Rome. The public, of course, enjoyed this sort of thing as much as he did. "The literal truthfulness of Mr. Rogers's creations, in all the pretty and homely details," one writer observed in 1864, "is their greatest charm."

Above all, the larger scale of the new groups gave Rogers a greater range of expression. With the small groups it had been hard to avoid an impression of cuteness, which was acceptable for humorous subjects, but less happy in a work of serious nature like the "Slave Auction." "Union Refugees," his first essay in the new style, showed a notable improvement in this respect, but with "The Wounded Scout: A Friend in the Swamp" [103], which he brought out in the spring of 1864, Rogers for the first time produced a work which went beyond the conventional in feeling. The story it told was a simple one:

> A Union scout has been shot through the arm, round which he has twisted a tourniquet. He is weak and faint from loss of blood, but an escaped slave is conducting him to his home in the swamp. A copperhead snake is raising its head to strike the negro while he is doing this friendly act.

In this almost monumental group Rogers actually approached far closer to the "ideal" than he had done in the naive "Fairy's Whisper" and "Air Castles." It was an allegory couched in modern, realistic terms, voicing quietly but with compelling force the faith in universal brotherhood which gave dignity and meaning to the nation's agony. The only jarring note was the rather crude allusion to the "Copperheads" whom Rogers and many others regarded as an enemy scarcely less vile than the Southern slaveholders. Beside this powerful group "Slave Auction" seems little more than an antislavery cartoon and "Union Refugees" a rather sentimentalized illustration for *Parson Brownlow's Book*.

Highly praised, according to Rogers, by "all the strong thinkers, who pronounced it far ahead in its meaning" of anything he had previously done, "The Wounded Scout" was especially admired by Jessie Benton Fremont. Rogers noted in a letter to his mother, February 28, 1864, that "Mrs. Fremont staid round it long after most everybody else had gone & the next morning early sent the cards for her reception." She asked permission, he added, to bring in "the General." A week earlier Mrs. McClellan had also been in his studio and had likewise asked permission to bring in her general. President Lincoln, to whom the artist sent a copy as a gift, praised it as "pretty and suggestive."

Rogers' next group was a tribute to the common soldier, whose courage and self-reliance had been so often displayed on the battlefields of the war that was at last drawing to an end. "Wounded to the Rear: One More Shot" [105] (October 1864) portrayed with impressive simplicity two wounded Union soldiers, one seated, bandaging a leg wound, the other standing, one arm in a sling, preparing to load up with his free hand for a parting shot at the enemy before he is retired from the scene of battle. Rogers achieved in this group a monumental quality lacking in most of his work. Epitomizing far more eloquently than words could do the dogged spirit which had carried the Union through its darkest days, "One More Shot" had an instant and long-lasting appeal.

The plaster business was particularly helped in 1864 by the Sanitary Fairs held in New York, Philadelphia, Boston, Albany, and other cities for the benefit of the United States Sanitary Commission, forerunner of the American Red Cross. To each of these fairs Rogers donated some of his groups, anticipating a flood of additional orders from which both the artist and charity would profit. The investment paid notable dividends, the plaster shop being kept busy well into the normally dull summer season.

In August 1864 Rogers took his first real vacation in five years, a week's excursion to Mount Desert Island, and on his return started preparing for the usual Christmas rush. "My expenses in connection with my work shop & studio are now about $700 a month," he noted at this time, "so you see I must sell a good many casts [over five hundred] in the course of the year to lay by anything over eight thousand dollars, but they are getting a good start now and will sell well, particularly if Grant puts an extinguisher on the rebellion."

In October 1864 John Rogers celebrated his thirty-fifth birthday and a month later the fifth anniversary of his decision to make sculpture his profession. Reviewing the course of his life during those five years, he indulged in a little self-congratulation.

> I always used to feel that I was getting old without having accomplished anything in the world [he told his mother], as it seemed as if I was always beginning in some new business. It certainly seemed late in life to throw up all my former pursuits and commence an artist's life at 30 years of age, but I can safely say that I have never from the first regretted it and that the last two years have been the happiest of my life. I now feel that I have attained quite an enviable reputation and sufficient success to put me beyond all pecuniary troubles. So, if I *am* 35 years old, I can look back on the last *five* years, at least, with some satisfaction.

To crown his happiness, just at this moment John Rogers fell in love with Harriet Moore Francis of New York. Besides being "the dearest girl in the world & one whom you will love I *am sure* as fondly as I do," as John wrote to his mother, Hattie taught music at Miss Haines' Gramercy Park Boarding School for Young Ladies where she had been a pupil before her father, Charles S. Francis, failed in the book publishing business. Not the least of Hattie's virtues was the fact that she had "had the independence . . . to support herself." "Her duties have no doubt formed a good training for her character," Rogers wrote to his sister Ellen, "& I feel proud of her that she has gone through with them so nobly." Practical, efficient, and high-spirited, Hattie Francis was an ideal mate for John Rogers, who was inclined to depend rather heavily on the support and encouragement of his women folk. "I feel more & more every day that Hattie & I are perfectly suited for each other," John told his mother shortly before the wedding.

> It is so delightful to love & feel that one is loved in return — & to feel that not only we ourselves, but all mutual friends seem struck with the excellence of the match. I feel sure [he added] that when you come to know her more intimately you will find that you have gained a most affectionate daughter.

Hattie at this time was twenty-four, about eleven years younger than John Rogers. She outlived him by almost twenty-three years, dying in 1927 at the age of eighty-six. One who knew her in later life described her as "unassuming in manner, delighted in bringing help and happiness to others, gifted with bright mentality and a strong sense of right and wrong. . . ."

The wedding took place in New York on April 26, 1865, and was followed by a brief wedding journey to Niagara Falls and a visit to the Francis home at Milton, New York. In mid-May, the newlyweds sailed on a three month business and pleasure trip to England, France, and Switzerland.

"TAKING THE OATH AND DRAWING RATIONS," 1865
Rogers regarded this as his best work, an opinion shared by most subsequent critics.

After making arrangements for the sale of his groups in London and Paris, Rogers treated Hattie and himself to a bit of sightseeing there and in the Alps. They got back to New York early in September, feeling, as Hattie put it, that home was the best place in the world, "especially when it is in America."

Leaving Hattie, already pregnant, with her parents in Ulster County, Rogers returned to his studio in New York mentally refreshed and eager to get back to work. In the months just before the wedding he had hurriedly brought out two groups — "The Home Guard: Midnight on the Border" [106] and "The Bushwhacker: The Wife's Appeal for Peace" [107] — which he rightly felt were not up to his standard. He was therefore anxious that his next work should be particularly good. Ideas came hard at first, for this first separation from Hattie brought on what he called "a sort of dyspepsia of the brain," but after two days he had a flash of inspiration.

> Eureka!, Hattie, Eureka!! I have got a wrinkle which I think is going to make a good group. . . . It is the same idea that your Uncle told of seeing in Charleston, with a difference. A proud southern woman taking the oath and drawing rations. There is a chance to make a magnificent woman — something of the style of Marie Antoinette in the trial scene. I have been sketching it out but have not got the arrangement to suit me exactly yet — but feel that I am all right on the main idea and there is a chance to make a splendid group. So now I am happy — & then tomorrow! Oh Golly! I shall be with you — thirty two hours from this time.

"Taking the Oath" did indeed turn out to be "a splendid group." The subject was a particularly timely one, for the victorious North was bitterly divided over the course Reconstruction of the South should take, the way of reconciliation or the way of vindictive punishment. In a letter to Hattie at this time, Rogers stated his own feeling that "the conciliatory course is the right one now," and this conviction was implicit in his new group. "Taking the Oath" voiced, as had Lincoln's moving Second Inaugural Address six months before, the hope of moderates on both sides that the restoration of the Union would be accomplished "with malice toward none, with charity for all."

But "Taking the Oath" had more than a strong message to recommend it. Into its composition went more thought and into the modelling and characterization more subtlety than is to be found in any of his earlier works and, indeed, in most of those which came after. Inspired by a theme which enlisted his deepest feelings and by the joy he had found in his marriage, Rogers gave to this work the very best that was in him, as an artist and as a sensitive interpreter of the Civil War experience.

"Taking the Oath" was John Rogers' masterpiece and when it appeared, in the fall of 1865, its creator was unquestionably one of the most vital artists at work in America. As a recorder of the spirit of the common man in his heroic hour he had few peers. As the pioneer of a realism in sculpture which took as its peculiar province the actions and thoughts of ordinary men and women, he had no important rivals. As a champion of popular art, good in quality but cheap in price, he was beginning to make his influence felt throughout the country to an extent unmatched by any other serious artist of his time, except perhaps Louis Prang with his chromolithographic reproductions of Old Master paintings. It is no wonder that James Jackson Jarves singled out John Rogers for praise when he withheld it from almost all other American sculptors. It was "Union Refugees," "The Returned Volunteer" and "The Wounded Scout," not the later Rogers Groups like "Parting Promise" and "Phrenology at the Fancy Ball," that Jarves had before his eyes in 1864 when he wrote of Rogers' work:

> Although diminutive, they possess real elements of greatness. In their execution there is no littleness, artifice, or affectation. . . . His is not high art, but it is genuine art of a high naturalistic order, based on true feeling and a right appreciation of humanity. It is a healthful work and endears itself by its mute speech to all classes.

"THE PHOTOGRAPHER," 1878

On rare occasions Rogers abandoned story-telling for pure genre, with such delightful results as this single figure from "The Photograph."

CHAPTER IX

"Rogers' Celebrated Groups of Statuary"

HAD ROGERS died in 1865, just after he completed "Taking the Oath," his name would probably be held in considerably higher esteem today than it is. During the almost thirty years he continued to turn out about two groups each year, he never again equalled this early achievement and all too frequently fell far below it. Like the painter J. G. Brown, with his endless parade of New York bootblacks and newsboys, John Rogers became a prisoner of his popularity. Deprived of the emotional stimulus of the war and forced by the requirements of a seasonal trade to produce new works almost on a fixed schedule year after year, he tended more and more to lose his keen sense of "the true poetry of every-day life." To a large extent, of course, this failure to develop beyond the point he reached in 1864–65 must be blamed on Rogers' creed of "large sales and small profits." Popularity was, for an artist, a dangerous goal in an age of which Ulysses S. Grant was the most potent political symbol and the Centennial Exposition the measure of its taste. It is to Rogers' credit, and to the credit of his mass audience, that he managed to maintain his wide appeal for so long without sinking to the level of much of the popular sculpture of the Gilded Age, with its "Iolanthe" in butter, its mawkish "Forced Prayer," and its pseudo-Rococo bisque figurines. Whatever they might lack in force and aesthetic distinction, even the least of the Rogers Groups of the 'seventies and 'eighties were characterized by good workmanship and "warm human sympathy," and it was this latter quality, as a newspaperman pointed out in 1877, which "assured him so much success among the masses, and won for him the enviable title, 'the artist of the Common People.' "

Between 1859 and 1893 there appeared on the market eighty-eight works in plaster or artificial stone by John Rogers. By far the greater number of them, more than two-thirds, illustrated scenes from everyday life. Of the remainder, seventeen drew their inspiration from literature and five from history. Only five — "The Fairy's Whisper" [71], "Night" [65], "Morning" [66], "The Fisher Girl" [68] (1860), and "St. Catherine"

[79] (1861) — can be classified as "ideal," and of these all but "The Fairy's Whisper" were commissioned.

In an article entitled "The Artist as Historian," published in 1872, the popular historian Benson J. Lossing bestowed upon John Rogers high praise for his "faithful chronicles" of the Civil War and Reconstruction and his "accurate pictures of the costumes of the actors in them." This praise was well deserved, to be sure, but in making those groups Rogers had been motivated not by any interest in history as such, but rather by an interest in the life of his own people and his own time. For history as a record of past events he had little feeling. Of the five essentially historical groups that appeared after 1866 three were designed to memorialize leaders in the war to preserve the Union and free the slaves. "The Council of War" [112] (1868) showed Lincoln, Grant, and Stanton conferring on military plans. "The Fugitive's Story" [116] (1869) portrayed three of the great spokesmen of abolitionism — Garrison, Whittier, and Beecher — listening to the sad tale of an escaped slave mother. The "Beecher" statuette of 1887 [176] was a straightforward portrait occasioned by the great preacher's death. The other two historical works Rogers produced were commemoratives: a full-length statuette of Washington [144] (1875), issued at the start of the Revolutionary centennial, and "The Watch on the Santa Maria" [204] (1892), Rogers' contribution to the quadricentennial of the discovery of the New World.

Of these five groups the most successful artistically was the simple Beecher statuette, inspired as it was by affection and long acquaintance with the subject. Far more popular, however, was "The Council of War," with its realistic, if somewhat stiffly posed, portraits of Lincoln, Grant, and Stanton. Though modelled from photographs, the Lincoln portrait in particular was highly praised both by the President's family and by Secretary of War Stanton, who wrote of it: "In form and feature it surpasses any effort to embody the expression of that great man which I have seen." "The Fugitive's Story," though it too contained good portraits, suffered even more from the stiffness that marred "The Council of War." Though Rogers tried to adapt the genre technique to history in these two groups, it required a self-conscious effort which was only too apparent. His talent required a free play of the imagination which history did not permit.

If the Rogers Group mirrored the middle-class taste of the day, as its great popularity would suggest, the Gilded Age much preferred literature to history. As against five historical groups, Rogers published between 1860 and 1893 seventeen groups illustrating scenes from plays, poetry, and prose fiction popular in his generation.

Judging from the number of copies that have survived, which in the absence of sales figures is now the only possible test, the most popular of these literary groups were " 'Why Don't You Speak For Yourself, John?' " [168], from Longfellow's poem "The Courtship of Miles Standish"; " 'Is It So Nominated in the Bond?' " [160], from *The Merchant of Venice;* and "Rip Van Winkle at Home" [122], the first of three groups from Joseph Jefferson's dramatization of Irving's story. In descending order of popularity, using the same measure, Rogers' other literary subjects were " 'Ha! I Like Not That' " [165], the handkerchief scene from *Othello;* "Rip Van Winkle on the Mountain" [123]; "Courtship in Sleepy Hollow" [113], after Irving; "The Shaughraun and Tatters" [143] representing actor-author Dion Boucicault and his dog in his popular play *The Shaughraun;* " 'Madam, Your Mother Craves a Word With You' " [170], from *Romeo and Juliet;* " 'You are a Spirit I Know, When Did You Die?' " [169], from *King Lear;* "Rip Van Winkle Returned" [124]; "Faust and Marguerite, Their First Meeting" [193], and "Faust and Marguerite Leaving the Garden" [195], both from Gounod's operatic version of Goethe's drama; "Fighting Bob" [183], Joseph Jefferson in the role of Bob Acres in Sheridan's *The Rivals;* "The Wrestlers" [162] from *As You Like It;* "The Village Schoolmaster" [63], from Goldsmith's poem, *The Deserted Village;* "Marguerite and Martha, Trying on the Jewels" [194], from *Faust;* and Booth as "Hamlet" [97].

Of the authors Rogers drew upon, three were American by birth (Irving, Jefferson, and Longfellow), one an American by adoption (Boucicault), three English or Anglo-Irish (Shakespeare, Goldsmith, and Sheridan), and one French (Gounod). Eleven of the groups were based on scenes from nine plays, three on scenes from a single popular opera. " 'Why Don't You Speak For Yourself, John?' " and "The Village Schoolmaster" were the only ones derived from poems. Prose fiction was drawn on directly only for "Courtship in Sleepy Hollow," although the three "Rip Van Winkle" groups owed as much to Irving's story as they did to Jefferson's play. Oddly, the novel, popular though it was in the nineteenth century, was not represented in Rogers' published work.

There were good reasons why Rogers should have drawn so heavily from the literature of the stage. "My forte lies more in spirit and action," he once wrote, and the same qualities in the drama attracted him to the theater. Of all literary forms the drama was the one which lent itself most easily to realistic sculpture, both depending to a large extent on gesture and facial expression, costumes, and accessories to convey action and character. The theater, too, was enjoying its heyday as a popular art in America, which

"'IS IT SO NOMINATED IN THE BOND?'" 1880
Typical of Rogers' literary groups, this scene from Shakespeare's *Merchant of Venice* was highly praised for its intricate detail.

meant that scenes from popular plays had the attraction of familiarity on which his success depended. Theatrical subjects had another, highly practical advantage in that they permitted the artist to combine familiar subject matter with portraits of well-known actors. Of his ten dramatic groups eight included portraits of such famous stars as Edwin Booth, Joseph Jefferson, and Dion Boucicault and thus were doubly interesting to a theater-conscious public. "Rip Van Winkle at Home," an enthusiastic reviewer predicted in 1871, "will be prized as a memorial of a charming bit of American Literature, and of the most delightful actor in the American drama."

The best of the literary groups were those derived from the tales of Washington Irving. A passage from one of his letters helps to explain why Rogers portrayed Irving's most famous character so successfully:

> I went to see Jefferson in Rip v. Winkle last night [he wrote on August 31, 1869, while his family were visiting in Roxbury] and I had an awfully sympathetic feeling come over me when the poor fellow bemoaned his fate while away from his wife & children. . . .

Not surprisingly, Rogers was, in the words of a generally friendly critic, "not as felicitous in his Shakespearean groups as in the lighter phases of comedy." In attempting Shakespeare, as in "The Council of War" and "The Fugitive's Story," he was forcing his talents into an uncongenial mold, and the result was somewhat similar. In an effort to achieve historical accuracy and good likenesses of the well-known models (Edwin Booth appeared in at least three of them), he overloaded the Shakespearean groups with detail and thereby sacrificed both clarity and strength of expression. The public was nonetheless impressed and the sculptor's popular reputation was enhanced, as he had hoped it would be, by his adoption of what was considered a higher order of subject matter.

Before 1880 John Rogers' use of literary subjects was incidental to his major concern with genre. Between 1860 and 1880 only seven of his groups depicted scenes from books and plays, as against forty-three portraying incidents of everyday life. Six of the seven were humorous. Between 1881 and 1894, on the other hand, Rogers' output was divided almost equally between ten literary and twelve genre scenes. Eight of these later literary groups were serious in tone.

This sudden change of emphasis, from genre to literary illustration and from comedy to more sober themes, probably reflected an opportunistic desire on the sculptor's part to profit from the "artistic" craze which followed the Centennial. Certainly, from the number of surviving copies it appears that the public responded well to his versions of Shakespeare and

Longfellow. Shylock and John Alden enjoyed greater popularity, in fact, than any genre group after "Checkers Up at the Farm" [145] (1875). But there was another motive besides profit behind the shift. As he grew older, John Rogers became less satisfied with mere popularity and material success and more concerned about his future reputation as an artist. As in 1860 he had sought respectability in marble and bronze, so in 1880 he turned from "Polo" [158] to "The Merchant of Venice" [160] in the hope that more elevated subjects would enhance his prestige among the sophisticated. Thereafter, in effect, he matched each homely piece produced in response to popular demand with one of a "higher" order, better calculated, as he thought, to satisfy the critics. "Taking my designs from Shakespeare," he had written in 1861, "will give them a dignity that everyday subjects don't have." The same thought was undoubtedly in his mind in 1880.

Despite his early and late attempts to dissociate himself from it, the genre group was the foundation both of John Rogers' immediate success and of his enduring fame. During the greater part of his long career this was what the public wanted most — simple, heart-warming, familiar scenes which expressed "the true poetry of everyday life." At a time when most American sculptors had for years been hopelessly wedded to a style which had long since lost what vitality it once possessed, Rogers brought the modeller's art into direct relation to the experience of the average American and gave sculpture an honored place in the American home, earning for himself in the process a comfortable living and the affectionate title of "the people's sculptor."

Rogers' success was based on his recognition, early in his career, of two simple facts of life: "Home scenes interest *everybody*" and "By taking a subject on which there is a divided opinion I lose half my customers." There was more than a little opportunism in this, of course, but not so much, perhaps, as his words might seem to indicate. In his concentration on "the more smiling aspects" of life in an era that had its full share of meanness, corruption, and violence, John Rogers reflected as much his own tastes as those of his public. "These home scenes really give me more enjoyment than anything," he had said in 1859, when he turned from the somber "Slave Auction" to the light-hearted "Farmer's Home." "My thoughts wander off to all the happy scenes of my life & I have caught myself repeatedly laughing out loud almost before I was conscious of it." Although he showed in such works of the late 'sixties as "The Charity Patient" [110] and "The Foundling" [121] that he was aware of certain social problems, the mood that inspired even these halting comments on the social order passed soon after the war's end.

THE ROGERS HOUSE, NEW CANAAN

Built in 1877–78, this house stood on Oenoke Ridge, just beyond the Silliman house, until torn down in 1960. *Above:* The house as it appeared about 1880. *Below:* The parlor, about 1887.

After 1870 John Rogers, along with most of his generation, was content to take things pretty much as they came.

> John Rogers [wrote William Ordway Partridge in 1896] is not one of the men who start out upon the ocean of life giving every sail to the wind and crying out to the elements, "Carry me safe over to the haven of my desire, or drown me!" His temperament is a more conservative one.

Only at the very end of his career did he show once more, in his life-size seated "Lincoln" [203], something of the depth of feeling which had appeared in his work of the war and immediate postwar period.

As a sculptor of true genre, Rogers' favorite themes were home and rural life, with special emphasis on the pleasures of childhood. In handling these subjects he felt completely at home, for they mirrored his own abiding interests. That they were also the most popular was his good fortune.

In spite of his largely urban upbringing, John Rogers always looked back on the six years he spent as a child in the little town of Northampton, Massachusetts, as the happiest of his young life. "Everything stands before me in the brightest colors," he wrote of those years in 1857, "the rides we used to take with Grandma . . . down by the river & the chestnuts we used to go after on Round Hill, . . . the cows I used to milk, the hop vines on the barn." It was memories such as these that led him, as soon as he had a family of his own, to spend his summers at New Canaan, Connecticut, just beginning to be discovered by doctors and other professional people from New York. After 1877, when he built an all-season house on Oenoke Ridge, just above the town green, Rogers and his family looked on New Canaan rather than New York as home and left it only in the depth of winter, sometimes not even then. "There is a feeling of freedom here, with so much more light & room than we had been having," he wrote in April 1883:

> New Canaan may be lonely in winter, but it is delightful & healthy from now till winter & even on a stormy day like this the children do not find any time hang heavily on their hands. The school room is turned into a carpenter's shop and the turning lathe & hammering that is going on would shock a strict presbyterian.

The quiet pleasures of life in New Canaan left their impress on the sculptor's work. Much of his modelling after 1868 was done there, at first in a room in the old St. John place, later in the little vine-covered studio he built a little apart from the house on Oenoke Ridge. Here he found inspiration for such characteristic studies of village life as "Coming to the Parson" [120], "Going for the Cows" [138], and "Neighboring Pews" [166], as well as authentic models for "We Boys" [130], "Hide and Seek" [139, 141], "A Frolic at the Old Homestead" [174] and other groups.

JOHN ROGERS' STUDIO, NEW CANAAN
The studio stood a little apart from the house on Oenoke Ridge. It has been moved a short distance to the grounds of the New Canaan Historical Society and has been designated a National Historic Landmark by the U.S. Department of the Interior.

Even more persistent in Rogers' genre work was the theme of love, in its most innocent and touching manifestations, from the healing love of the kindly old doctor in "The Charity Patient" [110] and the fearful love of the young mother in "The Foundling" [121] to the flirtation of "Neighboring Pews" [166]. Of course, this high frequency of love interest was partly dictated by public taste, but here again the artist was naturally in tune with his public. Rogers had an almost feminine sensibility. "Everything seemed so charming, that I felt almost as much like crying as laughing, from pure happiness," he wrote to his mother the Christmas after his marriage. "You know," he added, "I have a weakness of long standing in that direction." Allied to this, perhaps, was his rather dependent relationship to the three most important women in his life: his mother, beautiful, reserved, and long-suffering; his unmarried older sister Ellen, the chief playmate and confidante of his early years; and Hattie, his very capable and spirited wife. Upon Hattie, after 1865, fell the burden, frequently heavy, of keeping John Rogers' spirits from drooping under real and imagined pressures.

> It is certainly one of my best good fortunes [Rogers wrote to Ellen in 1876] to have a wife who is always so bright & cheerful, for I am so easily influenced by my surroundings that I don't know what would become of me if she were the other way and if I had not been married at all, I imagine my reserve would have grown upon me so that I should have shut myself out from everybody. It is a great effort for me to overcome it now even — for though I like to be where people *are,* yet I never feel easy with anybody out of my own household. . . .

Much of his love and deep respect for Hattie found expression in the women Rogers put into his postwar groups. In "Checkers up at the Farm" [145], "Weighing the Baby" [150], "The Photograph" [156] and "The First Ride" [178] she actually served as a model, while in the moving dignity of the Southern lady in "Taking the Oath" [108], produced soon after their marriage, there is something of the independence and strength that had attracted Rogers to Hattie Francis. In "The School Examination" [111], too, with its sympathetic portrayal of a young lady schoolteacher, Rogers paid tribute to the profession Hattie had followed before her marriage. The most significant thing about Rogers' women, however, is their freshness. They are idealized, of course, but Rogers' ideal was far removed from the pallid sweetness of the Neoclassic female. The Rogers type is heartier and healthier, spirited and serenely confident of her equal partnership in the life of the home. Like the women and girls of Howells' novels, she reflects the changing status of women in the second half of the nineteenth century. Her presence in so many of the groups undoubtedly helped foster their popularity among the ladies, on whose favor his success largely rested.

In his handling of children, especially boys, Rogers was equally successful. Derived largely from observation of his own children, five boys and two girls, and their New Canaan friends, his scenes of childhood were well calculated to stimulate nostalgia. By associating childhood with rural life, Rogers also appealed to the memories of the farm and village which he shared with most of his generation. The distinctive quality of these groups lay not in their sentiment, however, but in their freshness of observation. Nostalgia may have guided his thoughts but a realistic eye guided his hands as he portrayed his own Johnny, Katy, Charlie, Derby, Alex, David, and Laura playing doctor, blowing bubbles, taking their first ride, and frolicking at the old homestead.

Rogers' men are generally less noteworthy than his women and children, perhaps because he viewed his own sex with less reverence. In the humorous groups it is almost always a man or boy, seldom a women or girl, who is portrayed in a comic role. In more serious works, with notable exceptions such as "One More Shot" [105] and "Taking the Oath" [108], the men tend to be stiff rather than strong. He was at his best when he was portraying men at work, like the blacksmith in "The Returned Volunteer" [102], the old doctor in "The Charity Patient" [110], and the organ grinder in "School Days" [152]. In such sympathetic studies he gave expression to his own democratic convictions. "I have no patience with the feeling that *appearances* should be kept up and that to work is derogatory," he told Ellen in 1882. "I have been with mechanics and that class so much during my life that I have a great respect for honest labor."

Rogers' "right appreciation of humanity" and his technical skill were nowhere more apparent than in his expressive modelling of the human face. The subtle blending of pride, maternal tenderness, and resignation he put into the features of the central figure in "Taking the Oath" shows him at his best as a master of expression. He rarely reached such heights, but even in his least significant pieces he marked each figure with the stamp of individuality. Although his emotional range was limited, "lingering longest on the middle notes of humor and pathos," as one reviewer put it, within those limits he revealed himself an observant student of human nature.

In his handling of animals Rogers showed the same fidelity to nature. Though often intended merely as accessories in the composition, each animal was individualized with scrupulous care. In "Going for the Cows" [138] and "The Balcony" [159], for instance, he used live models. His favorite animal subject was the horse. "Rogers dotes on equines," wrote a

THE ROGERS FAMILY, 1876

John and Hattie with (left to right) Charlie, Alex, Derby, Katie, and Johnny. Two more children, David and Laura, were born after this picture was taken.

lady admirer in 1889, "and is never so happy in his work as when modelling them." This interest dated back to the early days of his career. His Chicago version of "The Town Pump" [57] had included a horse which was highly praised and in 1860 he wrote that he wanted to make studies "of animals & horses particularly" in order to improve the quality of his work. He did, in fact, give quite a bit of time to such studies. He carefully noted down detailed measurements of a number of racing, riding, and carriage horses, made careful anatomical casts from specimens at the New York College of Veterinary Medicine (three of which he subsequently reproduced and sold at five dollars each, see Cat. Nos. 126–128), and studied Eadweard Muybridge's pioneer high-speed photographs of the horse in motion. After he moved to 14 West Twelfth Street in 1889, his ground-floor studio was especially designed so that he could bring horses into it directly from the street.

The fruits of all this effort — far more, apparently, than he put into formal study of the human body — were seven published plaster groups ("We Boys" [130], "Going for the Cows" [138], "Peddler at the Fair" [157], "Polo" [158], "Fetching the Doctor" [163], "Elder's Daughter" [173], and "The First Ride" [178]), one large bronze ("Ichabod Crane and the Headless Horseman" [175]), an heroic equestrian statue of General John F. Reynolds [164], at least eight groups and equestrian studies which never were completed [125, 172, 181, 182, 185, 186, 188, 192], and the three anatomical casts [126–128]. At first, in works like "We Boys" and "Going for the Cows," Rogers was content to show the horse in quiet attitudes, almost as a decorative background to the human action. Beginning with "Polo" in 1879 he essayed the more difficult task of depicting the horse in motion, running or, as in the more ambitious equestrian portraits, rearing back on his hind legs.

Despite their dramatic naturalism, the more spirited of these works were not so well received by the public as the more passive ones. There was general agreement that the artist had a thorough knowledge of equine anatomy. At least one critic felt, however, that in his equestrian statue of General Reynolds [164] and his model for "The Bugle Call" [172] (exhibited at the National Academy in 1886 but never released for sale) he had given an impression of instability to the whole work by throwing the horse off balance. It was also objected, with perfect truth, that Reynolds' magnificent steed made the general himself look dwarfish and insignificant. On the whole Rogers' "hobby" brought him more personal satisfaction than either popularity or prestige as an artist. It also brought him, according to his daughter, his only pupil, Alexander Phimister Proctor, a young Canadian who received informal instruction in the 'eighties from John Rogers and subsequently achieved some note as a sculptor of animals.

Looking over the long list of his creations, some deriving their immediate inspiration from history, some from literature, the bulk of them from everyday life, one fact is clear. It was his affectionate interest in people that distinguished John Rogers from most of the sculptors of his day. This affection, which his shyness made it difficult for him to express in terms of personal friendships outside his own family, he put into the plaster groups which won him the love of thousands.

> He is pre-eminently the sculptor of the people [Earl Marble wrote in 1876 for *The Cottage Hearth*]. He has taken the simple themes of life, that the unpretending people are interested in, and endowed them with a grace that is natural, a feeling that is profound, and intelligence that is not too far in the clouds to be appreciated by the humblest, and a depth that is of the heart and soul, so to speak, rather than of the head.

In his humor, he might have added, there was no cruelty, in his charity no condescension, and in all a "warm human sympathy."

CHAPTER X

John Rogers and the Realists

"THE MIDDLE RANGE of the nineteenth century in the New World" was, as Walt Whitman once wrote, "a strange unloosen'd, wondrous time." Among its minor wonders was the chance that brought Whitman and Rogers together at the Fair of New York City's American Institute in September 1871, the poet to read at the opening his "Song of the Exposition," the sculptor to exhibit more than twenty of his popular plaster groups. Whether the poet and the sculptor actually met or not on this occasion is unimportant; there is little reason to suppose that they would have taken to each other. But it is significant that these two artists, superficially so unlike, should have appeared, in effect, on the same platform. Even more noteworthy is the fact that they both presented essentially the same message of faith in the current and the average which marked them as members of the Realist school.

Defined by its chief literary spokesman, William Dean Howells, as "nothing more and nothing less than the truthful treatment of materials," American Realism was a bridge between the Romanticism of the pre-Civil War generation and the Naturalism of the nineties and after. Because he dealt with contemporary life in its normal aspects, the Realist considered himself more truthful than the Romantic, with his fondness for exotic scenes and high flights of emotion and imagination. Because he tended to emphasize the lights rather than the shadows of American life, he was in turn criticized by the Naturalist as a teller of only half the truth.

It was the historic function of the Realists to fix the image of America in the moment of transition from a predominantly agricultural society to an industrial society. Their art was largely documentary, concerned with capturing the appearance, speech, and customs of every section and class. It was marked by wide-ranging curiosity, keen observation of character and the minutiae of daily life, and sympathy for the common man. It was not, as a rule, heavily charged with emotion nor was it a school of reformers. When it was criticized for ignoring the darker side of life, William Dean Howells

DETAILS FROM FOUR ROGERS GROUPS

Illustrating the artist's use of "little odds and ends . . . to help tell the story."

a. Detail from "Neighboring Pews"

b. Detail from "The Travelling Magician" (from the back)

c. Detail from "Country Post Office"

d. Detail from "Coming to the Parson"

defended the school with the observation that, while sin, disease, and death were universal, America's "large, cheerful average of health and success and happy life" was "peculiarly American." A realism thus tempered was bound to find favor with a generation which had exhausted itself in civil war and was not ready to take up new causes.

Realism had many exponents in the field of literature — novelists like Howells, Mark Twain, and Edward Eggleston, poets as varied in character as Whittier, Whitman, and James Whitcomb Riley — and among the painters too, most notably Winslow Homer, Eastman Johnson, and Thomas Eakins. But in the field of sculpture its adherents were few. Most sculptors felt with William Wetmore Story that sculpture "really has nothing to do with the trivial things of common life," and that "when it enters the field of *genre*, it abdicates its highest office." There were, indeed, a number of monumental sculptors who adopted a more realistic technique and devoted themselves mainly to American subjects — John Quincy Adams Ward, Henry Kirke Brown, and Thomas Ball being the best of them — but even they showed no disposition to join with the literary and pictorial Realists in portraying the American scene. John Rogers alone among the major sculptors of the period was a Realist in the same sense as Howells and Homer. As James Jackson Jarves pointed out in 1864, he stood alone in his chosen field.

Rogers was well prepared for membership in the Realistic school by early experience of rural life at Northampton, by his practical education, by his work as a mechanic and draftsman in the Midwest, and by his early acquaintance with the works of proto-Realists like George Caleb Bingham and Sir David Wilkie. His natural affinity for Realism showed itself in his very earliest efforts at modelling, was strengthened by his contact with Romantic sculpture in Europe, and was fixed by the popular success of the camp scenes which won him fame during the Civil War.

Although he was not much given to theorizing about art, Rogers early worked out, in self-defense against the traditionalists who beset him in Italy and occasionally in New York, a philosophy that clearly aligned him with other Realists of the 'sixties. The cornerstone of this philosophy was a rejection of traditional European models and the adoption of the familiar as his standard. "I have taken everyday, natural subjects as my specialty," he wrote in 1863, "& have cut adrift entirely from the old school of allegory and mythology." Rogers cut adrift also from the old school's preoccupation with form. The forms in his works were determined by the function of each figure in its particular story. When he modelled his father's bust, "common sense" led him to reject "a bare neck like a Roman gladiator," and he rejected the use of the nude in sculpture for the same reason. "He saw no use in depicting the nude in art," a friend reported, "because we do not see it in actual life as in the days of Greece or Rome."

Like other Realists Rogers chose his subjects from actual life. In his choice of subjects, however, he displayed a catholicity which made him something more than a local-colorist. He could do this, although his roots were in New England, because he had spent seven of his first thirty years in the West (in Cincinnati as a child, in Hannibal and Chicago as a young workingman), and from 1860 on divided his time about equally between New York City and the little town of New Canaan. This varied experience of American life — embracing the East, the Middle West, and one of the Slave States, as well as the farm, the village, the summer place, the suburb, and the city — saved Rogers from some of the narrowness of the local-colorists and helped make possible his popularity outside the northeastern corner of the country where he happened to live.

As he drew on several sections of the country for his subjects, so also did Rogers portray in his groups a variety of occupations and levels of society. Besides the citizen soldier who appeared in most of the war groups, he presented the Negro, the preacher, the doctor, the blacksmith, the shoemaker, the peddler, the organ grinder, the school girl and boy, the old maid, the mother, the farmer, the villager, the city gentleman and the ladies of his family, and many others. With few exceptions, his characters were such as the average man might meet in his daily round.

Rogers' characters, whatever their station, are rarely shown engaged in action which might be termed heroic or even unusual. In this too he was animated by the spirit of Realism. Howells put the case for the unheroic very clearly:

> As in literature the true artist will shun the use even of real events if they are of an improbable character, so the sincere observer of man will not desire to look upon his heroic or occasional phases, but will see him in his habitual moods of vacancy and tiresomeness.

Like several other members of the school, John Rogers had an unusually sympathetic appreciation of feminine character, especially after his marriage. Beginning with his sensitive portrait of a Southern matron in "Taking the Oath and Drawing Rations," the sculptor produced a succession of female figures notable for their poise and assurance. Not fragile emblems of purity, but equal participants in the world's work, they are true sisters to Howells' Isabel March and Winslow Homer's healthy croquet-players.

Rogers' sentimentality, for which he has often been condemned, was as natural to him as it was to the common man who so greatly enjoyed his work. In this respect, as much as in any other, he was a faithful recorder of the mood of his time. Nostalgia for the carefree days of childhood and for the simple pleasures of rustic life was characteristic of the rapidly increasing urban population whose minds were haunted, in the midst of a feverish getting and spending, by an image of "an Eden from which they were forever debarred." Rogers' pathetic groups, like "The Charity Patient" [110] and "The Foundling" [121], likewise reflected a sentimental attitude toward poverty in an age which was usually more touched than aroused by the condition of the poor. It must be admitted, however, that Rogers leaned on pathetic effects more than the strictest Realism countenanced. It is this element in his work that perhaps most sharply separates Rogers from more objective Realists like Homer, Eakins, and Howells.

Humor was an important element in Rogers' popularity and his use of it also was in the true Realist tradition. A stolen chicken bulging from a soldier's pack, a cat-and-dog fight hinting at the spats of married life, schoolboy pranks, the flirtation of "Neighboring Pews" [166] — all are within the bounds of probability and the common experience. There is almost nothing of Dickensian exaggeration in it, and nothing of the strong flavor of Western humor. Nor does it have the delicate wit of Howells. It is essentially schoolboy humor, drawn from experience, obvious enough for all to understand, and innocent enough for all to enjoy.

In summary, John Rogers conformed to almost every standard of post-Civil War Realism. He turned his back on classical and European models, he was more concerned with character than form, he devoted himself almost exclusively to delineating American life and American character, he believed in the worth of the common man and everyday life, he upheld the dignity of labor and the equality of women, he acquiesced in the moral ideals of the middle class, and he largely ignored the darker aspects of life. He fell short of the standard principally in a sweet sentimentality which showed itself particularly in such works as "The Parting Promise" [117] and "The Favored Scholar" [135].

Rogers had few direct contacts, as far as we know, with other members of the Realist school, for he was little inclined to seek his friends among artists and literary men. Never much of a reader, he tended to shy away from intellectual company. "If I went to Mr. Gray's," he once complained early in his New York career, "Mr. Willis and Mr. Bryant might ask me to dinner & then they would get to talking poetry & I couldn't stand that nohow."

He was, however, familiar with the works of Whittier and paid the poet at least one visit in 1869, in connection with the group "The Fugitive's Story" [116]. Whittier wrote Rogers after receiving a copy of the group and expressed "great respect and admiration" for his work. This tribute from "the poet of the people" to "the sculptor of the people" was peculiarly fitting, for the two men, as artists, had much in common, as was noted by some critics of the day.

> *The Whittier of Sculptors* seems to us [said a reviewer in the *Boston Evening Transcript* that same year] not an inappropriate title for one who has so successfully applied his genius to the awakening of a permanent interest in whatever concerns the life of the obscure and lowly.

On the whole this judgment still seems just. While Rogers had much in common with the early Howells and Homer, particularly in his choice of material, there was a certain sophistication in the one and a quality of detachment in the other which separates them in spirit from the sculptor of the Rogers Groups. Nor was there in Rogers that strong element of folksiness which marked the work of James Whitcomb Riley and many other writers of the local-color school. The Rogers Groups are, in a sense, poems of the people, but they do not usually give the feeling that they are written in dialect. Whittier, in describing his own simple verse, came closest to expressing the spirit of Rogers' work:

> Of mystic beauty, dreamy grace,
> No rounded art the lack supplies;
> Unskilled the subtle lines to trace,
> Or softer shades of Nature's face,
> I view her common forms with unanointed eyes.

William Dean Howells did not take advantage of a good opportunity to comment on Rogers' work in his *Atlantic Monthly* article on the 1876 Centennial Exposition, at which Rogers exhibited many groups. That Howells was aware of Rogers' work is evident, however, from a passage in *Their Wedding Journey,* some four years earlier. Describing a wife's efforts to revive her sunstruck husband in a drug store by rubbing his head with an ice-filled handkerchief, Howells commented:

> Basil drank his soda and paused to look upon this group, which he felt would commend itself to realistic sculpture as eminently characteristic of the local life, and as "The Sunstroke" would sell enormously in the hot season.

It is impossible to tell from this single, humorous allusion to the realistic sculpture for which Rogers was so well known whether Howells took his work seriously or not. Howells' own early work, particularly *Suburban Sketches,* contained other scenes which Rogers might well have rendered in plaster. If he didn't admire Rogers, he should have.

Rogers' most earnest admirer among the Realists appears to have been, rather surprisingly, Hamlin Garland, who was advancing in the 'nineties a variant of Realism which he called Veritism. In *Crumbling Idols,* published in 1894, the year after Rogers retired, Garland devoted a page to the question of realistic sculpture. "Whatever the sculptor loves and desires to fashion that is his best subject," he proclaimed. To him logic pointed toward genre sculpture as the natural culmination of the art's development, the embodying in stone and bronze of "the scenes we all love in American life." "John Rogers, in his timid way," Garland concluded, "pointed the way after all."

That Garland really meant what he said in 1894 is confirmed by a warm letter he addressed to the aging sculptor in 1898 when the Rogers Group had few friends left to defend it:

> Seeing your name and address in a recent paper, I am moved to pay you the respect I have long felt for you and your work. I am a young man and associate with the younger artists, but I recognize and have always recognized the force and character of your work. . . . They are all full of character and individuality and are spontaneously American and so I am found upholding them. . . . The time will come when they will stand for much more than the highly finished figures copied from old world sculptors which are at present ranked above "The Checker Players" and "John Alden."

Perhaps because he came along late enough to see Rogers in perspective, Garland seems to have been the only Realist writer who clearly recognized the sculptor's contribution to the cause of artistic Realism.

Realism had a less pervasive effect on sculpture than it had on the other arts, although Rogers' success in the early 'sixties did lead to a mild flurry of imitation among some of the younger sculptors. A young artist named Deacon, for instance, exhibited baseball groups and an "Ichabod Crane" in 1868–69. Samuel Conkey (1830–1904) produced at least two genre groups about the same time: "In the Wilderness," a war scene, and "Trout Fishers," a genre piece quite in Rogers' vein. The latter has been misattributed to Rogers for the past thirty years owing to a nineteenth-century stereograph publisher's error in labelling (see page 278). Two sculptors who won fame for work of a quite different character — Daniel Chester French and George Gray Barnard — also directly imitated Rogers in their very earliest productions.

Rogers' influence is apparent, too, though less obviously, in the work of a small group of sculptors of the 'nineties and early twentieth century who specialized in small impressionistic genre and animal studies. A. Phimister Proctor, Bessie Potter Vonnoh, Abastenia St. Leger Eberle, Solon Borglum, Mahonri Young, and Frederic Remington adapted the scale of the Rogers Group to freer techniques, in which plastic qualities received greater attention and anecdote was less emphasized than in Rogers' works.

The school of realistic genre sculpture never assumed the dominance Hamlin Garland predicted for it in 1894. It did, however, constitute a vital and popular element in American sculpture until well into the present century. As its pioneer, Rogers exerted more influence on the development of American sculpture than has generally been recognized.

CHAPTER XI

"A Large Meed of Praise"

As one turns the pages of the four scrapbooks in which Rogers kept his press clippings, nothing is more striking than the near unanimity of contemporary popular opinion in respect to the Rogers Groups. Until the tide of fashion turned near the end of his long career, Rogers seemingly could do almost no wrong. Here and there one does come across a reviewer who felt that Rogers had faltered in this or that particular or who regretted that he did not undertake works of a more ambitious nature, but the boldest critic went no further, before the 'nineties, than to suggest that there was "a good deal of inequality both in conception and execution of his groups." In attempting to account for the universal appeal of the Rogers Groups, the historian is faced with an almost limitless number of qualities and combinations of qualities to which the artist's contemporaries pointed in their own similar attempts. The ones which have been selected for illustration here are those which contemporary reviewers mentioned most frequently and can, therefore, be assumed to be most representative of the public's reaction to the works of its favorite artist.

A Maryland editor pointed out in 1880 with honest bluntness that, although it might not be the highest taste, "average people like the imitative rather than the creative in art." Recognition of this fact was one of the key elements in John Rogers' success, for no feature of his work was more frequently singled out for praise than his realism. "The literal truthfulness of Mr. Rogers' creations in all the pretty and homely details," one critic wrote in 1864, "is their greatest charm." "Mr. Rogers is an artist of wonderful skill," wrote another in 1869. "He invests his figures almost with life itself; and one almost forgets, when looking at them, that they are only clay and not real flesh and blood." Literally hundreds of comments like these are scattered through the reviews, but the ultimate in praise on this point came from a reviewer of "Hide and Seek, Whoop!" (1874), who wrote that the girl was "too realistic to stand out in the rain, without making one feel like holding an umbrella over her."

More impressive to many than his skill in modelling human figures, animals, and inanimate accessories was Rogers' skill in delineating character. James Jackson Jarves spoke in 1864 of Rogers' "power over human expression" as the chief feature of his art and praised him for "bestowing upon plastic material a capacity and variety of soul action, which, according to the canons of some critics, it was useless for sculpture to attempt." A similar note was struck by J. H. Elliott, New York correspondent of the *New Orleans Picayune* who wrote in 1882 of Rogers' group from *Othello* [165]: "As for the expression of the faces, it is simply impossible for a tyro to comprehend how the stubborn clay can be moulded so eloquently in miniature." "There are few living artists," concluded another notice, "who have been able to individualize, as faithfully as he has done, human character in the faces of his subjects."

While his fidelity to nature undoubtedly held first place among the qualities which made Rogers a popular artist, his artistry in design and composition also came in for a high degree of praise. The public to which his work was addressed was no more sympathetic to "the canons of high art" by which he was later condemned than was the artist himself. None of his critics concerned themselves with questions of planes and textures, lights and shadows, and form in the abstract. If he handled his modelling tools, as one critic wrote, "with the plastic feeling of a painter," this was no matter, as long as his pictures in plaster were harmonious in grouping, correctly proportioned, and faithful to nature in every detail. Since Rogers was generally regarded as faultless on these points, it was as generally admitted that his groups were beautiful and artistic. "His fancy statuary are simply so refined and delicate in conception and execution," a Kentucky admirer wrote in 1873, "that any one possessing a love for the beautiful will secure them." A Hoosier editor was even more emphatic: "The peculiarity which above all else distinguishes them is their real artistic merit. Every curve is true to nature, and every posture to art." It remained for a later generation to discover, in the 'nineties, that the Rogers Group was of a piece with "haircloth furniture, wax flowers, plush albums and old-fashioned parlor furniture," truthful perhaps, but woefully inartistic. When a critic scornfully remarked in 1898 that there was nothing in the Rogers Groups by which they might be compared with the Greek masters or the works of the Renaissance, he was unconsciously underscoring one of the very qualities that had given the groups their unique hold on the American public.

Up to and even after 1860, the dominant features of American sculpture, outside of portraiture, had been its slavish adherence to a moribund Neoclassicism and its almost complete neglect of American themes.

> Let us run over the list of American sculptors and see how utterly non-American they are [wrote James Redpath in 1870]. Augur culminated in "Jephthah and his daughter." Hart's "Woman Triumphant" is a classical allegory. Brown's best ideal works are scriptural subjects. Story, like Anthony before him, fell down before "Cleopatra." He then relapsed into Judaism, in his "Judith" and "Saul," and paid homage to ancient Greece in his "Sappho." Ball's ideal pieces are chiefly classical, — as his "Pandora" and "Truth;" he must even portray Bowery-boy Forrest as Roman "Coriolanus." Ward is an American, and we thank God for *him*. Ives devotes his talent to "Pandora," "Rebeccas" and "Bacchantes." . . .

On and on went the list, through Joseph Mosier, Randolph Rogers, William Henry Rinehart, John Adams Jackson, Harriet Hosmer, Edward Sheffield Bartholomew, and Benjamin Paul Akers, all of whom, in Redpath's words, "trod the same broad road that leadeth to classicism." "Weary, weary of this eternal repetition of the eternal city's art, and twice ten thousand times told Grecian stories," Redpath often used to wonder, he said, whether sculpture was a dead art, as Latin was a dead language, but when John Rogers burst on the scene with "Slave Auction," "The Picket Guard," and other works breathing the life of his time and country, all doubt was dispelled. "I thanked God," Redpath wrote, "that we had got a sculptor at last, and saw that the plaster [plastic?] art, once so powerful, had not been dead, but sleeping only, and was now aroused to life."

James Redpath was better known as a promoter of literary culture than as an art critic, but his feelings were shared by many mid-century Americans. Reviewer after reviewer, through the 'sixties and well into the 'seventies, drew the contrast between the imitative productions of Americans who went to Italy and ancient Greece for inspiration and the thoroughly American, modern, and unconventional works that came from the hand of John Rogers.

> The genius of Powers, or Story, or Palmer, or Crawford is lifeless, lusterless and cold [the *New York Evening Mail* put it in 1868] beside the living fire which has animated the faces of the little statuettes in the studio of John Rogers. . . . Talk to us of "classical" art, and "purity of form" and "repose" — we would give more for one plaster statuette from the hand of John Rogers, were its duplication impossible, than for a whole gallery of faultlessly accurate forms in marble.

Although the originality and American flavor of his work gradually ceased to exert so strong an appeal after Augustus St. Gaudens and other students in the Beaux-Arts tradition had introduced new life into American ideal and monumental sculpture, even toward the end of Rogers' life a few critics still found in these qualities the essence of his artistic significance. Typical of latter-day feeling toward the Rogers Group, however, was the lukewarm comment of an anonymous writer at the time of the artist's death in 1904:

> As to the "masterly handling," the knowledge of anatomy, the genius, found by the enthusiastic Jarves [in 1864], we now shrug our shoulders and smile, remembering that the back garret holds what was once the cherished ornament of the front parlor; but we are grateful to Rogers for the modest part he took in the artistic development of the nation at a time when most of the sculpture produced by Americans was not American sculpture at all, but a vapid foreign echo of an echo.

The impact of John Rogers' private rebellion against the tyranny of Neoclassicism was greatly strengthened by his use of distinctively native themes drawn from the experience of ordinary people. "John Rogers creates and fixes a new era in Sculpture," Mrs. Freeman told the readers of the *Springfield Republican* in 1863, "the American, the popular, the democratic," and she was right. No American sculptor before him had turned more than a cursory glance toward the life of his own times and his own country. Except in portraiture, sculpture stood aloof from the people. John Rogers' little plaster statuettes, at once physically, emotionally, and intellectually accessible to the average middle-class household, bridged the gap between art and life and gently led thousands to a new appreciation of sculpture.

> His art is for the people [wrote the Rev. Octavius Brooks Frothingham in 1869]; it is domestic; all can understand it; all can appreciate its meaning; all can perceive its truth, and respond to its feeling.

> His art is of that class which is so real and so true that it is from the first popular [said the Pottsville, Pennsylvania, *Daily Miner's Journal* in 1875, in an article headed "Sculpture for the People"]. It pleases the people — his subjects touch their hearts, enlist their sympathies, stir memories, recall the past, take hold upon the popular heart in various ways which not only increase the far-spreading fame of Mr. Rogers, but does something for the beautiful and true in the heart of every observer.

In short, as more than one reviewer pointed out over the years, John Rogers was without a peer in giving to the products of his hand that "one touch of nature that makes the whole world kin."

"One of the greatest merits of our famous sculptor, Mr. John Rogers," noted an anonymous journalist in 1879, "is that his subjects are so widely different," ranging, as another writer put it in 1890, "from the free and easy treatment of 'We boys' . . . to the statues of men prominent in the history of our country, and groups from the celebrated plays of Shakespeare." "They cover such a variety of subjects," explained a third in 1885, "that he must indeed be hard to please, if one or more does not strike the critic's fancy." It was almost inevitable that someone should say, "when in doubt, give a Rogers group," and Howard W. Sexton did so, in the Bordentown, New Jersey, *Christmas Greeting* for December 14, 1885.

> You have succeeded in a higher degree than almost any artist of any age [William Cullen Bryant told John Rogers in 1869], in making sculpture a narrative art, and giving to motionless and speechless figures the power to relate their own adventures.

To Rogers, who had always believed that nothing was so important to the success of a piece of sculpture as a clearly told story, this was welcome praise. That the general public shared the poet-editor's admiration for Rogers' story-telling skill is evidenced by many comments in the newspapers. "A young artist" writing under the pen-name "Atticus" in the *New York Leader* in 1862, noted with approval that the stories in Rogers' little groups were "completely told" and that it was not necessary to label them. The same idea was expressed in 1872 by a contributor to *Scribner's Monthly,* who wrote that "we are left no need to clamber up to the ideas of the artist, for they flash upon us electrically."

How important the story could be as a stimulus to enjoyment of the typical Rogers Group is illustrated in a letter received by the *Brick, Pottery, and Glass Journal* in 1879 from a lady who had recently visited the sculptor's studio:

> The objects composing a given group are necessarily few; and yet, by their combination, the effect of a great deal more than is portrayed is suggested. The story is told in such a way that the imagination of the spectator is appealed to, and itself becomes actively engaged in fashioning and prolonging the narration. . . . A healthful, bright young girl accompanied me on my first visit, and our ride home in the cars was enlivened by the relation of a great many incidents in the history of the various objects we had seen, and which had only been hinted at by the artist.

This lady and her healthful, bright young friend were, perhaps, unusually imaginative, but there is no doubt that Rogers owed a good part of his success to his skill in telling a simple story.

"The faculty of combining pathos and humor in a manner at once genial, delicate and forcible," according to one writer, constituted the main secret of John Rogers' popularity. Other commentators did not give this faculty quite such prominence, but most of them expressed approval, in one way or another, of the sentiments embodied in the Rogers Groups. If he eschewed the tragic, this was considered no fault, but a positive virtue for, as "Vidette" wrote in the *New Orleans Picayune,* "the tragedies of humanity are its exaggerations." Likewise his avoidance of the grotesque and the sharply satiric helped, rather than hindered, his popularity. "A large-hearted humorist, and apostle of the warm and loving tenderness that underlies the minor chords of every day life," John Rogers moved cautiously among the emotions and was rewarded with the approbation of even the most fastidious. "Full of benevolence himself, ordering his life on most exalted principles," as the Rev. Thomas Street told the readers of the *Illustrated Christian Weekly* in 1871, Rogers addressed himself to "the emotions which yield the greatest delight while educating the most refined taste."

A generation which saw in didacticism not a flaw but a virtue naturally accepted John Rogers as "one of the greatest — because of his evident didactic object — of living sculptors." Contemporary criticism of his work is thoroughly imbued with the conviction that, as Henry Ward Beecher wrote to the sculptor in 1866, "Art has a nobler mission than merely to tickle the fancy or amuse our elegant leisure," or as another writer put it, that "a work of art without a thought in it, and a thought worth entertaining, is as impertinent as a preacher with nothing to say, or a banquet with the edibles left out."

Rogers himself felt that sculpture ought to be elevating in every way and expressive of pure and noble truths, but not all his groups could by any stretch of the imagination be classed as intentionally didactic. Those that were, "Slave Auction" and "The Wounded Scout," for instance, appeared mainly during the earnest decade of the war. After about 1870 his mood was generally less grave and toward the end of his career, when the serious side of his nature found an outlet chiefly in scenes from Shakespeare and heroic portraiture, his genre groups were often little more than gentle jokes. The serious-minded, however, could find food for thought even in such a bit of rustic comedy as "The Peddler at the Fair" [157]. One minister actually used this comic group as his text for a Christmas homily: "Men who are Stingy with their wives," drawing from it the moral that every true husband should give his wife a nice Christmas present and a monthly allowance. Less strained were the lessons other writers drew from "Taking the Oath" [108] — "a perpetual reminder of chivalric honor to woman *because she is a woman*" — and from "The Foundling" [121] — "an illustration whose force we cannot resist, and whose teachings [that even the abandonment of a child may be an act of love] we may not disregard if we would seek to relieve the poor and rescue the unfortunate."

Besides their occasional didacticism, the Rogers Groups also had the more passive virtue of absolute wholesomeness. Although several of Rogars' admirers commented approvingly on this fact, none did it with more pointed delicacy than the editor of the *Christian Advocate:*

> One of the greatest charms of his works is *purity*. We have never seen a single figure of his that could cause averted eyes or bring a blush to the cheek of a modest maiden, or too curious questions to the lips of an innocent child. His statuettes are especially adapted to the home circle.

By inspiring many a noble impulse in the breast of youth and tempering many a passion in older breasts, as *The Educational Weekly* put it, and by banishing "the gloom of the misanthrope" and introducing "sunbeams into the domestic circle," in the words of the *Itinerant and Evangelist,* John Rogers fully justified the hope that Henry Ward Beecher had expressed for him in 1865, that he would be a true artist, one

> who, either purposely or unconsciously, employs form & colors, to express some worthy thought or emotion, & so allies art directly with the soul & makes it the tongue of the heart, & not merely the nurse of the senses.

The historical value of John Rogers' statuettes was early recognized by his contemporaries. "Aside from their artistic value," wrote the columnist Barry Gray in November 1862, "they possess another purely historical in its nature," which he thought would "hereafter cause them to be regarded with much interest, as truthful memorials of the present war." As such memorials, some of Rogers' war-inspired groups, notably "One More Shot" and "The Council of War," continued to enjoy great popularity long after the war was over, being considered particularly appropriate presents for veterans.

> Each one [it was said of the series which began with "Slave Auction" and ended with "The Fugitive's Story"] a sybilline leaf, containing rolled up a tale of doing, daring, suffering, which was written over those four years . . . shedding the light of a pure genius over the roughest path a nation ever trod, but transfiguring, by its shining rays, sorrow, suffering, even cruel war, till the terrible holocaust seems only a burnt offering of mercy, from whose ashes will rise the phoenix of a redeemed nation.

"The series should be kept in every reading room and public library," the same writer concluded, "that the memory of those five years may be kept green in the hearts of the young," and this thought was echoed by a number of other contemporaries.

Admired and honored as he was for his influence in stimulating pure and patriotic thought, John Rogers was even more enthusiastically praised for his part in raising the cultural level of the average American home. An age hungry for self-improvement saw in the Rogers Group, as it did in Louis Prang's chromolithographic reproductions of Old Master paintings, a potent force for making "popular synonymous with fine art." Rogers' influence as a taste-maker was solidly founded on the intensely practical consideration that the Rogers Groups were "marvels of cheapness," the average group selling for under fifteen dollars and only the lawn groups for more than twenty-five. As *The Cottage Hearth* pointed out in 1877, such prices brought "these love-inspiring, liberty-preaching, patriot-making, mirth-provoking, health-creating groups . . . within the reach of almost every household in the land."

In this matter of price, of course, John Rogers was not moved by generosity alone. Even at an average price of less than fifteen dollars he made a profit of over five dollars, or about 37 per cent. This profit, multiplied by large sales, gave him an income which many a less popular artist might have envied. At the same time Rogers did have a certain feeling for the man of limited means. To a dealer who called him foolish for pricing his works so low he said in 1860, "I prefer to put them at a price that no one who likes them need hesitate to buy." There was true democratic feeling in this as well as sound business sense.

> Mr. Rogers was the first man in this country [recalled a New Hampshire editor] to bring within the reach of persons of ordinary means anything that could reasonably be called statuary. Until his groups came into the market, there was hardly any statuary that was purchaseable except with hundred dollar bills. Those were the days of plaster-paris images and gilded vases, which people got in exchange for discarded coats and trousers. The Rogers Groups, when they came, were god-sends to many a household, the inmates of which were of artistic tastes, but were not overblessed with the wherewithal to gratify them.

More important than preaching to the artistically converted, the Rogers Groups, by their cheapness and popular appeal, were also "missionaries for art" and their creator, in the words of a Missouri editor, "the great pioneer in the scheme of educating a continent in the poetry of art." Along with Eastlake and Ruskin, John Rogers held an exalted place among the heroes of household taste. Not only did the Rogers Group do much "to brighten a happy home, or to bring sunshine into one which is not so happy as it might be"; it also exercised "an educating and elevating influence" on the whole household.

> In a family of growing children, one of these groups of statuary is of especial value: its daily presence will call into exercise the observing faculties, will cultivate the senses, will train the powers of perception, and above all will incite and strengthen a love of the beautiful that will afford an innocent and lasting source of pleasure while life exists.

After 1893, though few critics felt that they could conscientiously praise his works for their artistry, general recognition of the fact that John Rogers had been "the first American to show his countrymen that sculpture was a living art" ensured him at least honorable mention in the histories of American art. The public as a whole was less kind.

> In these days it is rare to see "The Charity Patient" proudly displayed in the front bay window to be gazed upon and envied by the wayfarer [a New England editor commented, on hearing of the sculptor's death in 1904]. It has disappeared . . . and in its place reigns an elongated blue and green vase, resting upon a standard which simulates beaten gold. No more do we read in the newspapers of vociferous surprise parties to popular Sunday School Superintendents or genial bookkeepers, where "Going for the Cows" was the visible token of appreciation, presented with a few well chosen words, and received with a modest and touching response. Nowadays it is a roll top desk, or if the givers have drunk deeply from any of the modern reservoirs of artistic lore, it may be one of Mr. Caproni's reproductions of the Olympian Hermes. . . .

"Satisfying as all this may be," the same writer concluded nostalgically, with a matchless understanding of what "The People's Sculptor" had meant to his generation, "it can never equal the joy which came with the ownership of the Rogers group in that unsuspicious day when the Rogers group was new."

HOUSEHOLD GODS

Lt. Col. George A. Custer relaxes in his study at Fort Abraham Lincoln, Dakota Territory, about 1873. Of the difficulties they encountered in transporting the two Rogers Groups from fort to fort, Mrs. Custer wrote at some length in her book, *Boots and Saddles* (pp. 177–78).

CHAPTER XII

"Large Sales and Small Profits"

When he was in Rome in 1859, Rogers had observed with some distaste the lengths to which certain artists went to bring their productions before the public. "I find that the artist's business is a sort of trade," he wrote. "It takes the same qualifications that a good salesman has." He rather prided himself then that he was totally lacking in those qualifications, but a few months in aggressive Chicago and a small taste of success there with his "Checker Players" caused a change of heart. On the eve of his departure for New York City in November 1859, he announced that he was going to put all modesty in his pocket and make "a perfect balloon" of himself from then on. "I think," he wrote, "a little brass and gas will carry me through." In spite of his genuine personal diffidence and modesty, Rogers displayed in his career a remarkable talent for self-advertisement which made his name, for three decades, a household word. Part of his success, of course, stemmed from the high quality and low prices of his productions, but without well-planned promotion his achievement would have been less impressive. Rogers proved to be as skilled a salesman as he was a sculptor.

An important element in Rogers' success was his early recognition of the principle of "large sales and small profits." At a time when sculptors normally worked in marble and sold few works at high prices, Rogers aimed at quantity production and a mass market. From the first, therefore, he was concerned with bringing his works before as wide a public as possible. The devices he used to this end were not new, but he worked them with great skill. Essentially there were four of them: the widespread display of samples; organized publicity in newspapers and magazines, local as well as national; the wide distribution of illustrated catalogues; and the release of photographic reproductions for albums, stereopticons, and magic lanterns.

The most obvious way to bring his works to public notice was to get them displayed in shop windows. At the very first, as we have seen, Rogers had some difficulty persuading dealers in New York to handle his low-priced wares, but after the appearance of the popular "Picket Guard" in the summer of 1861 this was never again a problem. Williams and Stevens in New York and Williams and Everett in Boston were the first dealers to exhibit and sell the new sculptor's works in this fashion. Soon Rogers' groups appeared in shops in Philadelphia, Providence, and Albany. By 1863 dealers in St. Louis, Baltimore, and Cincinnati were asking for samples, and by 1866 Hubert Howe Bancroft was displaying them in his San Francisco book store. Through the 'seventies and 'eighties Rogers Groups could be seen in the windows of hundreds of fancy goods shops and newspaper offices in cities and towns throughout the East and Middle West and, occasionally, even in the Far West, the South, and Canada.

Another opportunity for showing off his productions was afforded, particularly in New York, by art exhibitions. The most important of these was the annual spring exhibition at the National Academy of Design, where Rogers exhibited many of his statuettes between 1860 and 1893. Then there were the "artists' receptions" which the artists held two or three times a year in the Dodworth Building in the early 'sixties. The informality of these receptions and the opportunity they offered of seeing artists in their studios made them quite an attraction to art-lovers. "My room was crowded & I could not but feel flattered at the interest with which people looked at things," Rogers wrote after one of these receptions. "I made several sales ... & I have no doubt it was a capital advertisement for me."

During the Civil War, Rogers took advantage of the opportunity to show his groups at a number of fairs held to raise money for the United States Sanitary Commission. By sending samples to these fairs he won for himself both valuable publicity and additional orders. After the war he continued to enter his groups in fairs and expositions in the United States and abroad (Paris, 1867 and 1878; Santiago, Chile, 1875; and Melbourne, 1877). Among the medals he earned were three from the American Institute, three from the Massachusetts Charitable Mechanic Association, and bronze medals from both the Centennial and World's Columbian Expositions.

In his search for publicity Rogers even went so far as to link forces for a time with the great showman P. T. Barnum. During the 1873 season, Barnum's great Travelling World's Fair advertised as one of its chief attractions "Prof. Rogers' Group of Classic and Historic Statuary," drawn in procession on "12 Georgeous [*sic*] Statuary Chariots." Barnum had been after him for three months, Rogers explained to his mother apologetically, "till I was finally compelled to let him have them. . . . If he succeeds in moving them it will be a great advertisement for me," he added, "though the company is not altogether so exclusive as I could wish!"

As Rogers' business grew, his New York studio became something of a showplace in itself. Gradually the showroom aspect came to overshadow the workroom and in 1873 Rogers transferred his modelling activities to a studio on the top floor of his home on West Forty-third Street. In 1876 what he called the "lower Studio" or showroom at 1155 Broadway was a sunny, flower-filled room, where the groups were exhibited on large revolving stands in the center of the room, with "a wide stair carpet laid all round instead of in mats, and the rest of the floor varnished." Three years later Rogers moved into even more elegant quarters on Union Square.

> One of the pleasantest places for lovers of art to visit in New York at present [wrote the *New York Mail* in May 1879] are the Rooms that Mr. John Rogers has lately opened at No. 23 Union Square. . . . On the west side of the Square, with the wide street before it — here truly a broad way — looking out on the green trees and the fountain beyond, the situation is one of the most delightful in the city. In the long and broad front room — the first floor above the street — painted in delicate and subdued colors, with soft carpet and rich hangings, stand copies of the works which have given Mr. Rogers such an affectionate place in the hearts of his countrymen. . . .

> The new studio in Union Square [added *The World* on June 5] is not only more central, but in all other respects is more conveniently arranged for the exhibition of his works than the old quarters at Broadway and Twenty-Seventh Street were. About the walls and in the centre of the room the statuettes are arranged upon stands of ebonized wood and relieved by a background of dead maroon hangings against which the light-colored plaster shows most effectively. . . .

Visitors were always welcome in Rogers' studio, whether they came to buy or merely to look, and during the week before Christmas the room was open evenings.

Important as the widespread display of his groups was, even more important to the growth of Rogers' reputation was the publicity he received (gratis and otherwise) from newspapers, magazines, and trade journals. Through legitimate reviews of his works, direct advertisements, and "reading notices" (advertisements disguised as editorial matter), Rogers' name was spread far and wide.

One of Rogers' first actions on his arrival in New York was to take a copy of "Slave Auction" to the office of the *National Anti-Slavery Standard*. The result was a highly favorable notice which appeared at the very close of the year 1859. During the following year Rogers clipped ten notices, nine from New York papers and one from the *Boston Transcript*. For the most part these were written after Rogers had presented a group to the editor, but a few editors and critics actually came to see the young artist in his studio and gave him more than perfunctory praise. One of these was Theodore Tilton of *The Independent* who wrote an article on Rogers entitled "A New and True Artist." It concluded with this statement:

> These commendatory lines are written without the artist's knowledge of the writer, and are here printed solely from a conviction that the public will be glad of this hint that the fourth story of No. 599 Broadway is the hiding-place of a man of genius, who, though unrecognized and unrewarded, is yet brave enough to work in patience, to feed on faith, and to live for an idea.

Although he was willing enough to seek publicity Rogers was particularly pleased to have it come unsought. "It is very gratifying," he told his parents in February 1862, "to have so many newspaper writers anxious to write notices of my works without any solicitation on my part." So fulsome indeed were some of the praises heaped upon him that Rogers became almost embarrassed.

> A literary friend has just been in to get a *sketch of my life* for the Evening Post! [Rogers wrote home in September 1862] I gave him an outline rather reluctantly for though all these newspaper articles are very flattering, I feel as if I had hardly done enough to make a foundation for them. . . . It is at least satisfactory to know that none of them have been written at my request & many by personal strangers. So I must content myself with not being too modest and try to have my works keep up with my reputation.

As it had always been Rogers' plan to tap a wider market than New York and Boston, he was particularly eager to have his work publicized in other places. This did not begin until late 1861 when Mrs. Freeman published in the influential *Springfield Republican* of Springfield, Massachusetts, an account of a visit to his studio. Two more articles by Mrs. Freeman, under the name "Periwinkle," appeared in the same paper in 1862 and four in 1863. His first Chicago notice (not counting those which appeared in 1859 when he was living there) appeared in December 1862, and there was one in the *Hartford Courant* in April 1863. The year 1864 brought three notices from New York, two from Boston, two from Albany, one from Chicago, and three from Detroit. More important, in 1864 appeared James Jackson Jarves' book, *The Art Idea,* in which John Rogers received high praise from one of the most influential of American art critics. In 1865 Rogers clipped sixteen notices, including four from New York, four from Boston, and one each from Worcester and New Bedford, Massachusetts; Brooklyn, New York; Lafayette, Indiana; Wilkes-Barre, Pennsylvania;

and London, England; besides a long account of "The Way Rogers' Statuary Is Made" in April's *Scientific American.* In 1866 his works reached the conquered South (Nashville) and the West Coast (San Francisco).

Although Rogers' few surviving business records tell us nothing about his advertising campaign, the over nine hundred clippings in his scrapbooks give what must be a fairly complete record of where and how he sought to publicize his works through the press. From these clippings several conclusions can be drawn: (1) that close to a third of Rogers' publicity emanated from New York City and close to half from New York City and State together; (2) that almost half of his notices appeared in the three cities of New York, Boston, and Chicago; (3) that about half of the notices were published in the Middle Atlantic states, about a fifth each in New England and the Middle West, about 6 per cent in the South, and about one per cent each in the West and abroad; and (4) that Rogers' advertising reached a peak during 1874–78, the exact mid-point of his career.

It is also apparent that Rogers depended more on local newspapers than on any other single type of periodical, but that their share of his advertising gradually decreased until in his last decade he seems to have divided his advertising about equally between local papers and special interest periodicals. Of the latter, religious newspapers and magazines were favored by Rogers up to 1878, trade and professional publications after that year.

Most of his early publicity cost Rogers nothing. The notices in the *Springfield Republican* appeared in Mrs. Freeman's regular column of news from New York. Many of those which appeared in New York, Boston, and other papers referred to groups on sale in local stores and probably were paid for by the proprietors of the stores. But at least as early as 1865 Rogers began to send free samples of his work to out-of-town editors. The earliest evidence of this is in an article on "Rogers Groups" published in the Wilkes-Barre, Pennsylvania, *Record of the Times* in December 1865. "Several of these groups may be seen in our office," this article concludes, "all equally spirited and truthful." What sort of arrangement existed between artist and editor is not known. It is possible that Rogers sent the groups to Wilkes-Barre on his own initiative and it is equally possible that the editor, on a visit to New York, obtained the privilege of introducing them in Wilkes-Barre. In either case the notice was probably paid for in kind, not in cash.

As Rogers' business expanded he became less dependent on this rather hit-or-miss style of publicity. In 1877, fortunately, he began to record in his scrapbook just what he paid for each notice. In most cases the exchange was a simple one, one group for one notice. On a notice clipped from the *Ameri-*

can Christian Review (Cincinnati), November 19, 1878, for example, Rogers noted tersely: "Notice rec'd. Group P. T. ["Private Theatricals"] sent." For a very brief notice in the *New York Graphic,* December 3, 1878, Rogers sent only a bracket, worth considerably less than a group. In another case, where the original article was written especially for the *Daily Republican* (Attica, Indiana, February 28, 1878), Rogers apparently had to pay nothing, but to get the same article copied into the *Richmond Telegram* (Richmond, Indiana) he had to give away a copy of "The Charity Patient."

Cash payment was almost certainly involved in a few cases where Rogers employed the services of an advertising agency. The earliest instance of this occurred in December 1878, when Dodd's Newspaper Advertising Agency (Boston) placed an article entitled "The Right Use of Statuary" in three newspapers. The fee is not recorded.

Other notations, some of which are listed below, indicate a great variety of terms under which Rogers obtained his later publicity:

"Gratis" — *Christmas Greeting* (Bordentown, New Jersey), December 14, 1885.

"Notice with adv't for $50 trade" — *Manufacturer and Builder* (New York), December 17, 1885.

"Gratis, sent letter of thanks" — *American Bookseller* (New York), September 15, 1886.

"Trade $15" — *Gospel Age* (New York), November, 1886.

"Cash $40" — *Observer* (New York), December 16, 1886.

"Notice & 1 page adv. cash $100" — *Christian at Work* (New York), December 15, 1887.

"Shylock, for this & other following notice" — *Daily Democrat* (Emporia, Kansas), December 8, 1888.

"$10 allowed on any group" — *Hanover Herald* (Hanover, Pennsylvania), December 15, 1888.

"Group Othello to be given for this (No. 1) also for No. 2 notice" — *Bay City Tribune* (Bay City, Michigan), May 12, 1888.

"This & many others gratis, also adv. for cash $11" — *Clearfield Republican* (Clearfield, Pennsylvania), December 24, 1890.

"For different groups amounting $77" — Mrs. J. D. Moore Brinton, for notices in *The Baptist* (Baltimore), January 13, 1892, and fourteen other papers.

The use of illustrations in connection with Rogers' press releases began in May 1871 with the publication in the *Lyons* (New York) *Republican* of a very small, crude wood engraving of "Rip Van Winkle at Home." These cuts were probably supplied by the sculptor, who was already using them in advertisements and illustrated catalogues. Use of these woodcuts did not become common, however, until about 1879.

ROGERS' GROUPS OF SCULPTURE.

Taking the Oath, ...	$15.00
One More Shot, . . .	15.00
Wounded Scout, . . .	15.00
Union Refugees, . . .	15.00
Country Post Office, . .	15.00
Home Guard, ...	15.00
Bushwhacker, . . .	15.00
Charity Patient, . . .	15.00
Uncle Ned's School, . .	15.00
Returned Volunteer, . .	15.00
Mail Day, ...	10.00
Town Pump, ...	6.00
Camp Fire, ...	6.00
Picket Guard, . . .	6.00
Village Schoolmaster, . .	6.00
Checker Players, . . .	6.00

Any of these will be sent, securely packed in sawdust, on receipt of the price addressed to

JOHN ROGERS,

212 Fifth Avenue, New York.

Remit, for safety, in draft or check, payable to order.

*** In unpacking these Groups, the sawdust should be carefully removed, as much as possible, from the top of the Group, and then, by reversing the box, it can be assisted to slide out gently with the remainder of the sawdust.

TAKING THE OATH.—A Southern lady, with her little boy, compelled by hunger, is reluctantly taking the oath of allegiance from a Union officer, in order to draw rations. The young negro is watching the proceedings, while he waits to have the basket filled for his mistress.

CATALOGUE ADVERTISING

Two pages from the earliest catalogue of Rogers Groups, published in 1866.

Although he apparently preferred the informal "notice" which looked like a news item, even though it was often paid for, Rogers also bought space on the advertising pages of various periodicals. His earliest known advertisements appeared in 1870 in three magazines with wide circulation, *Godey's Lady's Book* (Philadelphia), *Every Saturday* (Boston), and *Scribner's Monthly* (New York). In January 1872 there was a full page advertisement in *Scribner's* and in October 1873 the same magazine ran a seven-page critical review of Rogers' entire output, plus another page announcing a plan for awarding Rogers Groups as premiums to subscribers to the new magazine, *Saint Nicholas*.

Rogers went in for advertising most actively during the 'eighties when his business reached its peak. Every month from November 1881 to January 1888 he had a quarter-page advertisement, with cut, in the *Century Magazine* (New York) which had a circulation in 1885 of about 200,000. From 1888 to 1890 he advertised in the *Century* only in December of each year and after 1890 not at all. During the 'seventies and 'eighties he also advertised in *The Continent* (Philadelphia), *Youth's Companion* (Boston), *American Art Journal* (New York), *Appleton's Journal* (New York), *Saint Nicholas* (New York), *Harper's Monthly* (New York), and a number of trade and religious journals. Most of these advertisements appeared between October and January, when sales were heaviest.

The earliest known catalogue of "Rogers' Groups of Sculpture" was published late in 1866 probably by John Rogers himself, although there is a possibility that it may have been issued by one of his agents. The little booklet contained a list of sixteen groups with prices, woodcut illustrations of all the groups, accompanied by descriptive text, and miscellaneous information on how to order, unpack, clean, and repair the groups. This was pretty much the pattern followed in the other catalogues which issued from Rogers' studio annually until the end of his career.

These catalogues Rogers at first distributed free to all applicants either directly from his studio or through his various agents. The *Lyons Republican*, for instance, told its readers in December 1872; "We have at our office a few of the catalogues, and will cheerfully supply them to such as may call for them, as long as they last." In 1876 Rogers began charging ten cents for the catalogues to cover mailing. In 1877 he introduced a more elaborate catalogue with illustrations from photographs printed by the "Albertype process," an early form of photolithography. For this catalogue he charged two dollars, promising to forward prints of each new design as it came out. Upon his catalogues Rogers built the mail-order business which contributed so greatly to his success during the 'seventies and 'eighties.

JEWELRY: PRECIOUS: STONES: &c. 12

THEODORE B. STARR,

206 Fifth Avenue (Madison Square), New-York,

Through to 1126 Broadway.

IMPORTER AND MANUFACTURER.

Choice DIAMONDS, Rare Pearls, Rubies, Sapphires, Emeralds, DIAMOND JEWELRY, Gold Jewelry, Stone Cameos, Fine Watches, SOLID SILVERWARE, Traveling Clocks, Chime Clocks, Mantel Sets, Candelabra, Artistic Bronzes, Glass Pungents, Decorative Porcelain,

of "Royal Worcester," "Minton," "Doulton," "Crown Derby," etc.

CAMEO GLASS In VASES of exquisite workmanship; the largest and finest collection in this country of this elegant and comparatively new production. Novelties, etc.

NEIGHBORING PEWS. Price, $15.00.

These groups are packed, without extra charge, to go with safety to any part of the world. If intended for Wedding Presents, they will be forwarded promptly as directed. An Illustrated Catalogue of all the groups, varying in price from $10 to $25, and pedestals (in mahogany and ebony finish), can be had on application, or will be mailed by inclosing 10 cents to

JOHN ROGERS,

860 Broadway, corner of 17th St. New-York.

Take the Elevator.

Wonder increases to astonishment that there is any intelligent man, not decrepit or indigent, who does not own and ride a bicycle. —*A writer in The Century Magazine.*

COLUMBIA BICYCLES and TRICYCLES.

Prices Reduced and many Improvements.

Spring Catalogue Sent Free.

THE POPE MFG. COMPANY,

597 WASHINGTON STREET, - - - BOSTON.

Branch Houses: { 12 Warren St. New-York. 115 Wabash Ave. Chicago.

"I am of the opinion that no exercise for women has been discovered that is to them so really useful."—*B. W. Richardson, M. D., F. R. S., on the Tricycle.*

MAGAZINE ADVERTISING

From *The Century,* April 1886.

One other medium by which Rogers advertised his groups was photography. This was the more important because his early popularity coincided with that of two early photographic fads, the album and the stereopticon. In July 1863 Rogers had seven of his groups photographed by J. F. Aitken and M. Stadtfeld and published by Aitken. Done in the currently popular carte-de-visite size (approximately 2½ x 4 inches), they were designed for mounting in albums. This series included "Slave Auction," "Checker Players," "The Village Schoolmaster," "Sharp Shooters," "Picket Guard," "Town Pump," and "Camp Fire." By June of 1864 the following had been added to complete the series: "Camp Life," "Union Refugees," "Country Post Office," "Mail Day," and "Wounded Scout." Stadtfeld also photographed and published for Rogers in 1864–66 the "Returned Volunteer," "The Bushwhacker," "One More Shot," "The Home Guard," and "Taking the Oath." These were published in two sizes — carte-de-viste and cabinet (7 x 9 inches). Similar sets were published in 1864–65 by J. H. Williams, of Williams and Stevens, Rogers' first New York agents, and in 1868 by Hamilton Wood, Jr., photographer, book, and print seller. Wood's set of twenty-three pictures, photographed by Soule and published by permission of John Rogers, was available in three sizes — carte, cabinet, and medium size (11 x 14 inches). Wood also offered a set of twenty-three stereographs, including two separate views of "Council of War."

The same year that Wood's set came out, an almost identical set was published in Boston, again with Rogers' permission, by A. A. Childs. The Boston set numbered twenty-three pictures, as did Wood's, but it substituted for the "Council of War" (in profile) "The Fairy's Whisper," which Wood had omitted. Sets exactly like that published by Childs were also issued in Boston by Joseph L. Bates, D. B. Brooks and Brother, and Dodge, Collier, and Perkins. They were also sold by local dealers in Amherst, Lynn, New Bedford, Worcester, and other Massachusetts towns. Entirely different sets, chiefly stereoscopic, were published in the 'sixties and 'seventies by E. and H. T. Anthony of New York, James Cremer of Philadelphia, C. Bierstadt of Niagara Falls, and J. W. and J. S. Moulton of Salem, Massachusetts. For a more complete listing see Appendix: "Notes for Collectors," Part D.

In view of the great popularity of albums and stereopticons in the 'sixties and 'seventies Rogers undoubtedly benefited from the publicity these various sets of photographs gave him, but it is not known whether he profited directly, through sale of rights or collection of royalties. Probably he did not, which might explain why he stated in his 1872 catalogue, that, while he had heretofore permitted photographs to be taken of his works, he had withdrawn permission and would secure his legal rights in the future. After 1872 five firms are known to have continued publishing stereographs of Rogers Groups, including C. Bierstadt and the Moultons. The last Rogers Group known to have been photographed as a stereograph was "School Days" (1877).

During the Rogers Group era the magic lantern also became widely popular, and in at least one contemporary catalogue of lantern slides, Rogers Groups were much in evidence. Thomas Hall, "philosophical instrument maker" of Boston, in his 1890 catalogue of slides listed no less than fifty of the groups, including every group Rogers had published from 1861 to 1882 except "Camp Life," "Camp Fire," "Bubbles," and the two "Hide and Seek" figures. No group published after 1882 was included, although the catalogue appeared in 1890.

In 1877 Rogers himself undertook the publication of photographs of his groups.

> As many inquiries come to Mr. Rogers from people living at a distance, who wish to see something better than a woodcut to enable them to make a selection of a group [it was reported in the *Lyons Republican* of November 29, 1877], Mr. Rogers has taken advantage of the process of printing photographs with printer's ink, called the Albertype Process, to reproduce his designs. These are collected in book form, and contain nearly all he has published, except some of the earlier ones, and will be mailed to any address, on receipt of $2.00. Mr. Rogers purposes to make separate prints when new designs are published, and these will be forwarded to anyone owning the book, and can be attached to the stubs left in it for the purpose.

This was apparently not a very successful venture, for no mention of it has been found after February 1879. Rogers' late annual catalogues were printed by the same process, though less elaborately bound, and sold for the normal ten cents.

From the time he made his first sale in 1860 until his retirement early in 1893 John Rogers probably sold somewhere between seventy and eighty thousand of his plaster groups. Advertising played an important part in this astonishing achievement, but even more important was Rogers' unwavering adherence to the principle of "large sales and small profits."

Rogers recognized from the first that success in his specialty depended not upon Fifth Avenue but upon Main Street. His little plaster groups were, as he readily admitted, "not intended for rich people's parlors but more for common houses & the country." This meant that he would have to "put them at a price that no one who likes them need hesitate to buy."

There were those who thought the young artist was foolish to cast his works in plaster and sell them for as little as five dollars. His sister Ellen, for instance, urged him to put his groups into bronze. "I think it wiser," he replied, "to bring them within the means of everybody & make them popular." "$5 is quite enough for my works," he wrote at about the same time. "It don't pay me much profit but it answers my purpose of an advertisement by scattering them round."

In 1863 Rogers introduced a new line of plaster groups, larger than the earlier ones and much more carefully finished. For these he charged fifteen dollars. Later, more elaborate groups, such as "The Council of War" [112] and "The Fugitive's Story" [116], were priced at twenty-five dollars. For a few years in the 'seventies he offered life-size outdoor figures at thirty-five and fifty dollars but these did not enjoy much success. The most popular groups, "Coming to the Parson" [120] and "Checkers Up at the Farm" [145], were in the fifteen-dollar class. For the thirty-year period from 1863 to 1892, the average cost of a Rogers Group was fourteen dollars and twenty-five cents.

Anxious to keep his stock moving, Rogers did not hesitate to raise or lower prices on individual subjects as demand suggested. "Checker Players" [61], for instance, was priced at five dollars when it first appeared in the spring of 1860, at three in November of the same year, and at six in 1866. "Union Refugees" [98] sold at fifteen from 1866 to 1878, for ten in 1882, and for eight in 1888. The "Hide and Seek" pair [139, 141], originally priced at fifty dollars each, were reduced to thirty dollars after about seven years.

Poor sellers were eventually withdrawn. Of eight early wartime subjects three were withdrawn before Rogers' first catalogue appeared in 1866 and three more were dropped by 1871, leaving "The Picket Guard" [83] and "The Town Pump" [89] as sole survivors until they too were dropped about 1880. Some of the later groups also fell by the wayside before 1893, including "Polo" [158], "Parting Promise" [117], and all three of the lawn figures [136, 139, 141].

To avoid competition between himself and his agents, as well as between agents, Rogers insisted from the first that the groups should be sold everywhere at the same prices, even though this meant that he had to absorb the cost of transportation as well as the agents' commissions, Rogers felt that the "one price only" principle would inspire public confidence and help to broaden his market.

Developing his mail order business, this matter of free delivery was of particular importance. By 1870 Rogers offered free delivery to any express station east of the Mississippi. After 1870 this service was extended to the whole United States. There is no doubt that Rogers' free delivery policy, made possible by the rapid growth of the railways and express networks after the war, helped to foster the popularity of the Rogers Group in the Midwest. "Any of these statuettes are now delivered free of extra charge in any part of the West," it was reported in January 1871, "and this offer will do still more toward placing them within the reach of all who have houses to embellish."

There is now no way of knowing just what proportion of Rogers' sales were made in his New York showroom, through his numerous agents throughout the country, and through mail orders. Over-the-counter sales in New York must always have been of considerable importance, since Rogers went to a great deal of trouble to make his showroom attractive to visitors. During the early part of his career, at least until the mid-'seventies, commissioned agents were also of great importance, since they were his chief means of reaching the out-of-town market. After his catalogues began to appear in the late 'sixties, however, Rogers presumably became more and more independent of his agents. From about 1869 most newspaper notices and advertisements urged prospective customers to write directly to John Rogers in New York for illustrated catalogues from which to order. It was characteristic of Rogers to avoid as much as possible the use of middlemen. At the height of his career, therefore, studio and mail-order sales probably greatly overshadowed agency sales.

Practically all of Rogers' business records have unfortunately been lost. There remains, however, one personal account book in which he recorded a few statistics on his income and expenses, both business and personal, for the years 1867–74, 1878–79, and 1886. From these figures it is possible to draw the following conclusions regarding the sculptor's business affairs during the middle years of his career. Sales tended to be the highest in the spring (April–June), fall, and early winter (September–January), with August the slowest month. On the basis of this pattern, Rogers usually brought out at least two new groups each year, one in the spring and one in the fall. His business showed a fairly steady rise to about 1874, dropped sharply in the late 'seventies (probably because of the severe depression which had begun in 1873), and rose again in the 'eighties. Although the incomplete records show 1874 to have been Rogers' peak year both for gross and net income from sales, Alexander P. Rogers, the sculptor's son, claimed that his best year was 1887. From about 1889 sales seem to have declined steadily until the sculptor's retirement early in 1893.

These same figures show that what Rogers called "shop expenses" or

IN THE SHOWROOM
Inside Rogers' last New York showroom-studio, 14 West 12th Street, about 1890.

"general expenses" (distinguished from personal or household expenses) increased at a faster rate than his sales income. Between 1867 and 1874 shop expenses averaged 55½ per cent of sales income; in 1878 and 1886 the ratio was 88 per cent and 76 per cent respectively. This sharp rise in production costs is not readily explainable in the absence of detailed business records. Some of it can, perhaps, be attributed to the cost of the successively more elaborate showrooms Rogers moved into in 1876, 1880, and 1885, and some, perhaps, to his increasing use of paid advertising in popular magazines. His labor costs, too, may have risen, although there is no information on this aspect of the business. Whatever the reason, the rise in costs cut heavily into profits and probably was a factor in Rogers' decision to curtail his plaster business after 1888.

From records covering approximately one-third of Rogers' whole career, it is possible to make at least a rough estimate of how many groups he sold between 1860 and 1893 and of his total and average annual net income from these sales. On the basis of the records for these ten years, Rogers sold an average of 1,700 groups each year at an average price of $14.25. By the same reckoning, his total sales over the entire thirty-three years of his career would have amounted to only about 56,000 groups. This figure is a good bit short of Rogers' own claim of 80,000, based on more complete figures no longer available. This probably means that a majority of the groups sold were in the $6–$15 class, which would substantially lower the average price per group and increase the number of groups accounted for by known and estimated income. The actual number of groups sold was probably between seventy and eighty thousand.

Contrary to popular belief, John Rogers did not amass a fortune from the sale of his plaster groups. At best he enjoyed for perhaps twenty years a very comfortable income averaging about $9,500 a year. On this he was able to buy a house in New York and build a substantial summer home in New Canaan, send his seven children to private schools and four of the boys through Yale, and indulge in such occasional extravagances as a trip to Europe in 1888. As soon as he was able he began to invest his savings in mortgages, stocks, and bonds. By 1873 his investments amounted to $14,000, and by 1878 to $16,400, and by 1886 to $77,000, plus $45,000 in his two houses. In the last year his income from these investments amounted to $6,848.50.

By 1894, however, soon after his retirement, the number and value of Rogers' investments had dwindled, and his income had dropped to $5,434, of which more than half came from renting his New York house in summer and the New Canaan house in winter. What happened to his savings is not clear. Undoubtedly part was eaten up by the college expenses of the sons at Yale in the late 'eighties and early 'nineties and some by his own illness. Some investments may have been wiped out in the panic of 1893. In any case, Rogers in the last years had comparatively little to show financially for the profitable labors of thirty-three years.

CHAPTER XIII

The End of the Vogue

"FOR OVER THIRTY YEARS," John Rogers told a newspaper reporter in 1890, "I have been engaged almost exclusively in modelling miniature groups of figures and I begin to think that the public is tiring of this style of art. Accordingly I have turned my attention to more important work." Behind this statement, in all likelihood, was a significant slackening in sales of the long-popular Rogers Groups. Although no statistics are now available to confirm this, certain other indications suggest strongly that business began to drop off sharply about 1888. From 1882 to 1887, for instance, Rogers had advertised every month in *The Century*. In 1888 he advertised only in January and December, in 1889 and 1890 only in December, and after 1890 not at all. A similar trend is noticeable in newspaper advertising, as reflected in Rogers' scrapbook of clippings. In 1887 he clipped thirty-two paid notices and advertisements; in 1888, twenty-six; in 1889, sixteen; in 1890, thirteen; in 1891, thirteen; and in 1892, when his last group was published, only ten.

The year 1888 also saw a substantial reduction in the price of many of the groups. His catalogue for that year, issued just before Christmas when sales would be heaviest, listed reduced prices on nineteen of the forty-seven groups and announced that some of the older groups would be withdrawn as soon as the existing stocks were exhausted. By 1890 nine of the groups, dating mostly from the 'sixties, had accordingly been withdrawn, and by 1892 five more had been dropped.

Also suggestive of declining sales and profits are Rogers' failure to take out patents on the seven new designs he published after 1888 and the fact that he did not have bronze master models made for these same seven groups. The last group for which a bronze was made and the last patented was "Politics," published in the fall of 1888.

Still another indication of retrenchment was Rogers' decision at the end of 1888 to close his Union Square showroom. After February 1, 1889, the groups were displayed and sold in his newly-acquired residence at 14 West

THE SCULPTOR IN HIS LAST STUDIO

Taken about 1893, this photograph shows Rogers at the age of 64, after his health had begun to fail. The bust of William Cullen Bryant was one of his last works.

Twelfth Street. Although the new salon may have been, as the New York correspondent of the *New Orleans Picayune* declared, "one of the most attractive art resorts in the city," it was certainly less elaborate and spacious than the rented rooms he had previously occupied, as well as much less expensive to operate.

What caused this comparatively sudden and rapid end to the vogue of the Rogers Group? Essentially it was the fact, as Rogers himself expressed it, that people were growing tired of a type of art which had been popular for a full generation. The Rogers Group no longer had the merit of novelty and, in fact, was becoming old-fashioned. By 1890 "haircloth furniture, wax flowers, plush albums, and old-fashioned parlor furniture" were being banished from the tastefully decorated home. In the general reaction against things "Victorian" the Rogers Group could hardly be expected to survive, for even if the original purchasers of these once-cherished symbols of culture clung to them with affection, the new generation of householders would be likely to dismiss them as "inartistic," send them to the attic, or simply throw them out.

The influence of fashion, however, would be most strongly felt in the East, especially in the larger towns and cities. In the country areas of New England and the Middle West, from which Rogers derived a substantial, if not the greatest, share of his business, the declining appeal of the Rogers Group may have been a direct result of the great depression which began in the Prairie States in the mid-'eighties, slowly spread and deepened, and culminated in the Wall Street crash of 1893. Because of this depression the demand for such a luxury item as the Rogers Group must have dropped considerably by 1888 just in the areas where it was otherwise least likely to be affected by changing fashions. Caught between these two forces, the Rogers Group was doomed.

Fortunately, John Rogers was prepared — at least he thought he was prepared — for this eventuality. If the public was tired of parlor groups, he would give them something more sophisticated. Even at the height of his success as a maker of popular statuary, he had cherished the hope that one day he would win equal acclaim as a monumental sculptor. Despite all the financial rewards and even critical approval that accrued to him as the modeller of America's "household gods," he was never quite able to dismiss from his mind the feeling that he was capable of what he called "more important work." Now, it seemed to him, was the time to prove it.

Early in his career this feeling, stimulated by the proddings of his sister Ellen, certain of his artistic and dealer friends, and a few newspaper critics, had led him into such ill-advised efforts as "The Fairy's Whisper," "Air

Castles," and the unfinished "Flight of the Octoroon." After his plaster groups began to take hold about 1863, Rogers' suppressed ambition lay dormant for almost two decades, except for a brief upsurge in 1873 when he submitted, in competition, a design for a Freedmen's Memorial [137]. Rogers did not win the competition and accepted his defeat with good grace.

> After all [he wrote home], I am quite thankful that the temptation of this commission is taken away from me, for it would have been difficult to keep up my present business at the same time, and that is so much more profitable & independent than any commission I could get, that I would do wrong to lose the advantage I have in it.

When a monument to John Eliot came up for discussion in February 1881, Rogers showed little interest. "I mean to devote myself to my groups and not be drawn off by statues unless they *come to me,*" he told Ellen.

That same year a statue [164] did come to Rogers. On July 1, 1881, an association was formed in Philadelphia to secure the erection in the city of a memorial to Major-General John F. Reynolds of Pennsylvania who had fallen on the battlefield of Gettysburg. "The difficulties in selecting a sculptor were obviated," reported a New York newspaper, "by the unanimous opinion of those most interested in the scheme that it should be placed in the hands of Mr. John Rogers of this city, whose name is known to every household in the land. Mr. Rogers," the account continued, "was loth to undertake a work of such magnitude, and, had it not been pressed upon him in the most complimentary manner, would modestly have refused the undertaking." After several months of negotiations Rogers finally submitted a design for an equestrian statue and a contract was signed on February 18, 1882. Rogers' fee was set at $25,000. "As this is the first important large work Mr. Rogers has attempted," the *New York Times* commented, "there is much interest felt as to its success."

Feeling his task "a peculiarly difficult one," Rogers gave it "the most attentive study," according to the New York *World,* which went on:

> That he had thoroughly studied the anatomy of the horse numerous plaster casts and portions of horses' frames which surround the walls of the studio amply testify. He first made an exhaustive examination of the different positions of the horse in action, from living models brought in the studio and from those in the town. . . . Then he turned to a study of the rider. He was unable to procure as satisfactory photographs of General Reynolds as he desired, and those from which he worked and which are now in his studio give evidence how much the art of photography has advanced in twenty years. Not alone was a faithful likeness to be procured but every detail of dress and accoutrement demanded equal attention.

The modelling of the full-size statue, twelve feet in height, was done on a large turntable in a studio erected for the purpose in Stamford, Connecticut. The final model, because of its size, was constructed of plaster rather than clay, and one contemporary account noted with awe that fifty barrels of plaster went into its construction. With characteristic ingenuity, Rogers worked out some improvements on a file invented by Hiram Powers and found that with this instrument he could work on the large plaster surfaces more easily than if they had been in clay. General Reynolds occupied most of Rogers' time for about eighteen months before it was shipped off to Philadelphia to be cast in bronze by Bureau Brothers and it was not until September 18, 1884, that the completed statue was finally unveiled near the north entrance of the unfinished Philadelphia City Hall.

Recognizing that there were, as he said, "many faults" in the work, Rogers was greatly relieved to find that the statue was "fairly well liked," and that, on the whole, the critics of the day approved of his first essay as a monumental sculptor. Certain obvious defects in the work, notably the insecurity of the horse's stance and the insignificance of the general's figure compared with that of his steed, were universally noted, but there was also general agreement that the sculptor had achieved a good likeness of General Reynolds and that he had rendered the spirited action of the horse with remarkable fidelity to nature. "While there are statues prettier than this," commented one critic, "I have my doubts whether there are more than one or two of as much common sense and archaeological value." "He has not mastered at one bound the secrets of grand sculpture," said another, "but is, nevertheless, to be congratulated for a signal advance in his art."

"If any more commissions come along," Rogers wrote home after it was all over, "I will try & do better." He was not very sanguine of getting others, though. "They do not often drop into my lap as this one did and I am not fitted to do much wire pulling, so I expect to stick to my small work and be contented with the spurt I have made."

Whether it was because he foresaw that the vogue of the Rogers Group was nearing an end or because he felt within himself at last the need and power to express himself on a grander scale than hitherto, in the late 'eighties Rogers began to devote more of his time to larger works. The first result was a double equestrian group in bronze, one-third life size, "Ichabod Crane and the Headless Horseman" (1887) [175]. Intended not as a parlor ornament, but rather for "large vestibules and public buildings," this work was not listed in any of Rogers' catalogues and no copies are known to have been sold.

Also in 1887 Rogers began an ambitious project which was to almost monopolize his attention for five years, end in bitter disappointment, and cast a shadow over his last years — a statue honoring John Eliot, celebrated Puritan missionary to the Indians [177]. Some Massachusetts friends urged John Rogers to prepare a design, presumably assuring him that the residents of Roxbury, where Eliot preached and where the sculptor himself had grown up, would jump at the chance to subscribe to a fund for its erection.

As usual, Rogers went to some pains to assure the accuracy of the likeness, the costume, and the various accessories. Justin Winsor, noted historian and librarian of Harvard College, provided the sculptor with information on Eliot's personal appearance and costume, as did Dr. Ellsworth Eliot of New York, a direct descendant of the subject. There being no authentic extant likeness, however, he had to improvise the face. Since Eliot was known to have preached against long hair and shaven chins, Rogers represented him with a full beard and short hair. For the Indians he placed at the preacher's feet, Rogers sought the advice of the Smithsonian Institution and the secretary of the Massachusetts Historical Society.

Between the spring of 1888 and January 1890, Rogers turned out at least six models for the Eliot monument, each one differing in some details from its predecessor, but all basically similar in design. His first conception, now in the First Church, Roxbury, was the strongest. It showed Eliot as a vigorous, middle-aged man, bare-headed and clothed in a short, practical jacket, standing on a rock, with one hand raised in a gesture of reverence, the other resting on a Bible, and his face lifted toward Heaven. At the foot of the rock were a young Indian woman and man in attitudes suggesting faith and doubt, respectively, and, between them — a typically Rogers touch — a small child playing with a dead turkey.

In the five succeeding versions, known through four photographs and one plaster model, Rogers made various alterations in the pose and costume of the principal figure and experimented with the foreground, eventually eliminating the child entirely and the foliage which at one stage hid the base of the rock on which Eliot stood. Most of these changes were made at the suggestion of the sculptor's noted uncle, Robert C. Winthrop, then well on in his eighties. "All my historical associations with Eliot would call for a more reverent & venerable figure, & for a costume more in keeping with a missionary preacher," Winthrop commented on seeing Rogers' first treatment of the subject. "If your figure could be modified so as to convey more of the idea of an Apostle, as he was always called, it would suit me better." The second model, in which Eliot appeared in a flowing "Geneva" gown, seemed to Winthrop "a great improvement," though he felt that the head was thrown too far back and the figure too long in the leg and short in the waist. "I remember that I was consulted by Greenough about the Franklin Statue, more than thirty years ago," the old man wrote, "he urged the importance of bending the neck & head so that spectators should look into the face of the figure." A week later Rogers submitted still another design, incorporating his uncle's suggestions. "I think it decidedly improved," Mr. Winthrop responded. "The elaboration of the grapevine had not struck me as excessive, but perhaps it might be slightly diminished. The bunch immediately before Eliot's right foot looks in danger of being crushed. The lowering of the head, & the introduction of the *jerkin,* are very successful."

On January 16, 1890, Rogers' final, nine-foot model, completed to his own and Mr. Winthrop's satisfaction, was exhibited to "the Artists and Members of the Press," at a private reception in the studio at 14 West Twelfth Street. Its reception was highly flattering to the artist. "Mr. Rogers' work is well conceived, interesting and impressive," wrote the *New York Herald,* while the *Boston Transcript* called it "a meritorious piece of heroic and picturesque composition." The New York correspondent of the *New Orleans Picayune,* long an admirer of Rogers' work, hailed the new work as "the crowning triumph of Rogers' artistic career and a work illumined in every detail by genius of a high order." Although a few critics objected to certain details of costume and pose, the most serious charge levelled against the statue was that it could be viewed only from the front and sides and would therefore be difficult to place suitably. All were agreed, however, that the work was an important one and eminently worthy to be set in bronze in Roxbury.

To the artist, who had put so much time and hard work into the Eliot project without even the promise of a commission, it came as a bitter disappointment when the expected financial support failed to materialize. All efforts to stir up interest in a subscription, efforts to which Mr. Winthrop, Edward Everett Hale, and Phillips Brooks lent their support, failed utterly. "That there ought to be a good statue of Eliot in the square [Eliot Square, Roxbury] I am sure and that yours is a good statue I am sure," Hale wrote, but with depression in the air, Rogers' timing was unpropitious. In 1895 he finally broke up the huge plaster model and threw the fragments of what he had hoped would be his masterpiece into the waters of the East River.

If other things had been going well Rogers might not have pinned his hopes so desperately on the Eliot Memorial proposition, but other things were not going well. Beginning in 1888, it was apparent that the "group" business was going into its inevitable decline. The public, moreover, had shown little interest in Rogers' new style of work exemplified by "Ichabod

Crane and the Headless Horseman." And against one completed commission between 1888 and 1892 (a bronze bust [191] of General Antonio Paez of Venezuela, ordered for $1,750 by a descendant in 1890), Rogers had to balance three prospective commissions that came to nothing — the "John Eliot"; a statue of John Stark [187] for the State Capitol in Concord, New Hampshire, submitted in January 1890 in competition with ten other designs and rejected because it was feared weathering would eventually blunt the General's pointing finger and the tip of his sword; and finally, in 1892, a $35,000 contract for a monument commemorating the 250th anniversary of Stamford, Connecticut, which failed to materialize for lack of public support [200].

Possibly as a result of the strain he was under, trying to make the grade as a monumental sculptor after a lifetime in a vastly different type of work, Rogers' health began to give way about 1891. In earlier years, he had occasionally complained that working steadily on one model for a long time made him nervous. In 1874 months of work and worry over his lawn figures had, indeed, brought on a sort of nervous breakdown, complicated by bronchitis, from which he recovered only after his wife brought him back from the South Carolina health resort where he was wasting away and took him up to New Canaan for a month of therapeutic horseback riding. After this experience Rogers enjoyed relatively good health again until about 1891, when a slight tremor appeared in his right hand and did not respond to treatment. "I am getting too old & *shaky* to expect to do very much more work — though I won't say too old for I don't *feel* so," Rogers wrote in August 1891 (he was approaching his sixty-second birthday), "but my shaky hand interferes a good deal now and does not grow any less certainly."

During the three years that remained before advancing paralysis forced him into retirement, John Rogers kept tenaciously at the work which had been his "great resource & enjoyment" for more than forty years. Two more groups in the style which had made him famous issued from his studio — "Football" [199] in the fall of 1891 and "The Watch on the Santa Maria" [204] in October 1892. Neither was among his most inspired works, but they were both up to his average and gave no hint of failing powers. "The Watch on the Santa Maria" was, however, the last group published by John Rogers. On February 1, 1893, he announced to the world in a printed circular that he had sold his right in his groups to William Brush, long the foreman of his plaster shop. He had done so, the sculptor stated, in order to pay closer attention to his studio work.

Despite his increasing infirmity, Rogers was determined to work just as long as he could hold modelling tools in his hands. It was fortunate that he did so, for, ironically, four of his most interesting and impressive works date from the last two years of his artistic life. Three of the four date from 1892. In January of that year he executed a roguish caricature portrait of Judge Henry E. Howland, Secretary of the Century Club, of which Rogers had been a member since the 'sixties. Described by the artist as "a statuette of an officer of the club as seen through Twelfth Night glasses" [202], it is one of the most light-hearted of all Rogers' works. From the same year dates a bust of another Centurian, the poet-editor William Cullen Bryant [205], whom Rogers in his younger days had avoided meeting for fear he would talk poetry. The "Bryant" was one of Rogers' best portrait studies, full of character and feeling.

But the ailing artist's most important work in 1892, and one of the finest of his career, was a life-size seated "Lincoln" [203]. What prompted Rogers to undertake this work at the time he did is unknown, nor is there any indication that he ever made any attempt to sell it. Completed in March 1892, it was not exhibited until a year later, when it earned John Rogers a bronze medal at the World's Columbian Exposition, one of twelve awarded to American sculptors. The praise it received at the time and later was well deserved, for the "Lincoln" is a work of real dignity, a fine likeness, well characterized and pleasingly composed. The sculptor gave the original plaster in 1895 to the Manchester, New Hampshire, Art Association. In 1910 a bronze cast was made from it and placed in front of the Manchester High School, where it still stands, an undeservedly forgotten statue of the Great Emancipator.

One more work came out of the studio on West Twelfth Street before illness finally forced Rogers into complete retirement in the summer of 1893 — "Landing of the Norsemen" [207], representing three Vikings disembarking on the shores of Vineland. With his usual attention to detail, Rogers consulted Professor William H. Carpenter of Columbia College for advice on certain elements of the design. One thing he particularly wanted was a suitable runic inscription to place on a shield. "In the poem *Havamal* (from the ninth century) in the *Edda*," Carpenter replied, "I find the following sentence, which, it seems to me, would fit well on Leif's shield: ordstirr deyr aldrigi, fair fame dies never, *Havamal* 76." The appropriate Norse runes, supplied by Carpenter, were carefully incorporated into the sculptor's design. When it was exhibited at the National Academy the same year the work was well received. "The group is a spirited one, true to

"ABRAHAM LINCOLN"

Rogers' finest monumental work, this statue won a medal at the World's Columbian Exposition, Chicago, 1893. A bronze replica can be seen in Manchester, New Hampshire.

possibilities, very well composed," wrote Charles de Kay, critic for the *New York Times*. "If it were shown in London, with the title 'Landing of the First Danes in the Eighth Century,' many praises would greet its author."

Realizing, perhaps, that this would be the last time he would appear before the public as a working artist, the National Academy gave John Rogers in 1893, as part of its Autumn Exhibition, what today would be called a "retrospective." The show included eight early plaster groups of the Civil War period and eighteen later bronzes. It provoked little comment from the critics, except for de Kay, who took the opportunity to reflect on the meaning of Rogers' career. Noting that "circumstances of early training, or of surroundings, or of his own talents, have prevented the public from according him a high rank as a sculptor," de Kay pointed out that, "for good or evil, John Rogers has instilled in the minds of certain thousands of Americans the idea that sculpture has as good a right as painting to a place in a well equipped home."

> These bronzes are documents from the history of the country during the past thirty years, and as such ought to be kept together in some public museum. The art of some of them is not great, but the public for which they were made, the public that took the successive editions in plaster painted gray, had only a rudimentary idea of art. Thank Heaven, they are genuine, not the work of Americans who have a foreign varnish. As such, they will live. As such they are most desirable exhibits for an American Museum worthy of the name.

On May 1, 1895, Rogers moved out of the house on West Twelfth Street to go into retirement in New Canaan. Few even of the New York papers noted what one called "a somewhat pathetic piece of news," so quickly had the public forgotten the artist of whom the *Times* gently said: "If his art was not of the highest, surely few will begrudge him the success, the popularity, and the financial reward that came to him." In clearing out the sculptor's house and studio many masks Rogers had used in early portrait groups, as well as over a hundred plaster casts of groups, some never published, were discovered and sent to Pierre E. Guerin, the bronze founder, to be sold. The house was taken over by the Salmagundi Club.

As his health grew steadily worse, Rogers lived quietly with his wife and two daughters, summering at New Canaan and wintering in a New York apartment. After the younger daughter's death from typhoid in 1897 at the age of eighteen, the remaining trio moved permanently to New Canaan, where they were joined by Hattie's Uncle David. Four-handed whist, not modelling, was now Rogers' "great resource and enjoyment."

Although Rogers sold twelve of his bronzes in 1897, through Pierre

Guerin, perhaps to help meet his private expenses, he still retained thirty-six in 1898 when a movement to get them into a museum got under way, led by his old friend of Manchester days, the poetic Francis LeBaron, whom Rogers had once dubbed "the reverend cream cheese." The dying sculptor found comfort in the hope that his bronzes would be kept together, but Mr. LeBaron's high-pressure salesmanship met with little success in the end. Despite favorable publicity between 1898 and 1903 in some widely read periodicals, as well as published testimonials from National Academy President Daniel Huntington, from sculptors Daniel Chester French and John Quincy Adams Ward, and from the National Sculpture Society, the best that could be done was to persuade the Metropolitan Museum to buy one bronze ("One More Shot" [105]) and to exhibit six others in 1900–1902 and the Brooklyn Museum to exhibit nine others in 1901. Not until 1937, a generation after John Rogers' death, did the collection pass intact into the museum of The New-York Historical Society.

John Rogers' slow decline came to its inevitable end in 1904. The creeping paralysis which had first made its appearance in his right hand a dozen years before had bent his erect figure nearly double and deprived him of the use of his arms and legs, finally even of the power to feed himself. At last in mid-July bronchial pneumonia set in and drained away the last of his strength. His mind remained clear, however, and he clung desperately to life, murmuring over and over in his last days, "I don't want to die, I don't want to die." Hattie and the children were at his side when the end finally came on July 26, 1904.

The death of John Rogers, though duly noted in papers all over the country, occasioned little comment. The modern generation which knew not the Rogers Group or wished to forget it, along with the Victorian parlor it had once adorned, had already consigned him to oblivion. Among artists, however, the retirement and death of Rogers were not so lightly taken, for to them he represented, if not a great artist, at least a vital historical force in the development of American sculpture.

The most thoughtful analysis of Rogers' work by another sculptor was made by William Ordway Partridge in 1898. Pointing out, quite correctly, that Rogers lacked that "monumental quality or sense" which would permit him to be compared with the great figures of Classical and Renaissance sculpture, Partridge went on to name certain other qualities which made him great "after his kind" — a gift for rendering characteristic expression; spirited composition, exhibiting in such works as "Football" [199] careful study of the laws of line; the "sweet feeling" of Donatello in such a work as "The Charity Patient" [110]; and good disposition of masses in "Rip

Van Winkle at Home" [122]. It was the social effect of his work, rather than its aesthetic claims, however, that Partridge emphasized.

> He has done for us [the younger sculptor concluded] a work for which we cannot be too grateful; he has served his people conscientiously; he has dealt honestly with himself and his time; he has fulfilled his mission with dignity, and may rest quietly, not as the old men on the walls of Troy who watched the young warriors go forth to the conflict, but as one who must remain forever young, because his life has been upright, manly and true.

Other artists were less generous in their estimate of Rogers' artistry but one thing on which all could agree was that Rogers' success in getting his works into "common homes and the country" had made a revolution in the people's attitude toward the art of sculpture. The average man or woman who, before Rogers came along, had known sculpture only as something too expensive for any but "rich men's parlors" now, thanks to the inexpensive Rogers Groups, had acquired an interest in the sculptor's art which assured its modern practitioners wide public respect and patronage. It is difficult to judge how much truth there was in this point of view, but there is no question that the sculptors of the younger generation sincerely believed, with Edwin Elwell, that John Rogers "made American sculpture possible."

Standing alone in his field, John Rogers holds a peculiar place in the history of American sculpture. Considered solely as a plastic artist, it seems almost as if he had been caught in a little backwater just out of the current of its historical development. Seen in relation to American art in its broadest sense, however, John Rogers clearly was in the main stream of the Realistic movement which touched every aspect of the American imagination during the latter half of the nineteenth century. It seems reasonably certain that the special sanctions Van Wyck Brooks says govern ballads, folk-poems, hymns, and national anthems will assure John Rogers a degree of immunity from the oblivion that has already engulfed most of the more ambitious artists of his day. A genuine "Artist of the Common People," he will surely always have, as Whitman said of Robert Burns,

> a nestling niche of his own, all fragrant, fond and quaint and homely — a lodge built near but outside the mighty temple of the gods of song and art. . . .

Catalogue of the Works of John Rogers

Catalogue of the Works of John Rogers

Introductory Note

IN THIS CATALOGUE are listed the 208 known works in sculpture of John Rogers, from his first clay model of April 2, 1849, to his bust of Henry Ward Beecher, published in 1896; his sixteen known casts from the human body; and several works which have been wrongly attributed to Rogers.

The arrangement of the catalogue is as follows:

Nos. 1–51 are the works Rogers produced as an untrained amateur between 1849 and 1858 at Roxbury, Massachusetts; Manchester, New Hampshire; and Hannibal, Missouri. Of these, only two are known to have survived: "Checker Players" [3] and "Nightmare" [20]. The others are known mainly through descriptions in Rogers' own letters or, by titles alone, from a pencilled list in Rogers' hand (The New-York Historical Society) which contains the names of forty-five subjects and sketches of four others. Although this list, probably compiled in 1857 or 1858, is not arranged in correct time sequence, it has been deemed simplest to retain in the present catalogue the numbers and titles as assigned by Rogers, adding whatever supplementary information is available. After No. 45 the numbers have been supplied by the author.

Nos. 52–55 are the models Rogers is known to have worked on as an art student in Paris and Rome in 1858–59. These were only exercises and were not preserved.

Nos. 56 and 57, Rogers' last amateur works, were modelled while he was employed as a draftsman in Chicago in 1859.

Nos. 58–208 constitute the heart of the catalogue, Rogers' work as a professional artist from 1859 to 1894 (Nos. 118 and 208 were published after his retirement). Among these titles will be found not only the so-called "Rogers Groups" which brought fame to the artist, but also the many other types of sculpture he produced during a thirty-five-year career, including portrait busts and statuettes, two monumental bronze statues and designs for others, one marble "ideal" figure, anatomical studies of the horse, medallions in low relief, and many designs for groups which never left his studio. *The arrangement is chronological,* so that the catalogue presents as clear a picture as possible of how Rogers worked. Those who may be primarily interested in knowing which of these works are collectible are referred to Appendix II, A, where the true "Rogers Groups" (those works Rogers actually sold to the public) are listed in the order of their publication.

Nos. 209–224 are the casts of human faces and limbs that Rogers is known to have made.

The concluding, unnumbered section of the catalogue (pages 277–280) deals with works which have been wrongly attributed to John Rogers in earlier publications, with works which are sometimes mistaken for Rogers Groups simply because of their general appearance, and with the mysterious parian and creamware copies of groups by John Rogers. For information on early photographs and stereopticon views of Rogers Groups, the reader is referred to Appendix II, D.

Key to Collections Cited in the Catalogue

Examples of Rogers' works can be seen in many museums. For the reader's convenience public collections where each group may be seen are listed with each entry. The numbers after the word "Collection" refer to the collections listed below.

(1) Albany Institute of History and Art, Albany, New York
(2) Brooks Free Library, Harwich, Cape Cod, Massachusetts
(3) Essex Institute, Salem, Massachusetts
(4) Robert Hull Fleming Museum, University of Vermont, Burlington, Vermont
(5) Harold Warp Pioneer Village, Minden, Nebraska
(6) Lightner Exposition, St. Augustine, Florida
(7) Manchester Historic Association, Manchester, New Hampshire
(8) John Rogers Studio, New Canaan Historical Society, New Canaan, Connecticut
(9) The New-York Historical Society, New York City
(10) Society for the Preservation of New England Antiquities, Boston, Massachusetts
(11) Toledo Museum of Art, Toledo, Ohio
(12) Lincoln National Life Foundation, Ft. Wayne, Indiana
(13) Henry Ford Museum, Dearborn, Michigan
(14) Museum of the City of New York
(15) Neville Public Museum, Green Bay, Wisconsin

1. DUTCHMAN

Although Rogers listed this first, it is not at all certain that this was the subject of his first effort in modelling with clay, thus described in his own words a half-century later:

> One day I met a friend in Boston, who was a young dentist. He invited me into his office, where he showed me a little figure which he had modelled in clay. I took a great fancy to it; immediately went to Charlestown, to an address, which he gave me, of a pottery; and there I got some clay & carried it home; whittled some modelling sticks, & set up my first figure. I was quite successful. I could work on it without straining my eyes and found it a great resource and enjoyment.

From Rogers' account book this encounter with the dentist can be dated exactly, as April 2, 1849. Nowhere does Rogers name this first group, unless his putting "Dutchman" down first on his pencilled list in 1857–58 can be interpreted literally.

2. IRISHMAN. See No. 33.

3. CHECKER PLAYERS

In 1855 Rogers referred to this as "one of my first figures" and rather discouraged its exhibition that year at a fair in Boston on the grounds that it was "so old & has been seen by so many that it has lost its novelty," and that it was "liable to get broken . . . for it is not strengthened & supported well." He had given it, apparently, to his mother. A photograph of the Rogers' parlor in Roxbury about 1880 shows the group in a glass case on a wall-bracket. The sculptor's sisters later presented "Checker Players" to the Society for the Preservation of New England Antiquities, its present owner. The group, in clay, painted, is 6 inches high, the base 8 inches by 5 inches. The composition is very clearly derived from Sir David Wilkie's painting of the same subject, with which Rogers was familiar as an engraving.

4. DOMINIE SAMSON

This dates from before March 23, 1851, when Rogers asked his sister to send him "a small piece of the stuff with which I made the impression on the Dominie's stockings."

5. HAYMAKER

This dates from March 1851, and may have been made for Mr. Benjamin Kent, a prominent schoolteacher in Roxbury and librarian of the Fellowes Athenaeum. Mr. Kent visited John in Manchester in March and was "mightily pleased" with the figure of the haymaker. "He said it carried him back to his boyhood & he thought the boy looked very much as he did at his age. He said that same evening he sat down & wrote over a hundred lines about the scenes of his boyhood of which I & my figure were prominent objects. He *attempted* to criticize it. He said the rake handle was too large, the jug was too large & the boy's hand not 'chubby' enough."

6. BOYS FIGHTING

7. APPLE WOMAN

John Rogers' pocket account book contains the following entry relating to this early group:

Cash	Dr	1850		Contra	Cr
	In acct with the Apple Woman group				
To group to Mrs. Quincy	2.00	Jan.	By having it cast		7.50
			" linseed oil &c		.57
			" plaster		1.75
			" oil &c		.33
		Mar. 7	" Mulrey for moulds &c		10.08
		or 8	" " " casts &c		13.37
			" teaming		.50

This was the only one of his early works that Rogers cast in plaster or sold.

8. OLD BACHELOR

Rogers modeled this in March 1851 at Manchester. It was 11 inches high, with a base 11¾ by 9¾ inches, and John recommended that it be placed in a four-sided glass case for protection, since it was going to be exhibited at the Roxbury May Fair. "If it should be put in a lottery," he added, "I hope it will be drawn by one of the family for I have taken more interest in it than I did in the last." He reported on April 20 that his solitary friend" had inspired some amusing remarks from his fellow mechanics. "Well, I swow," said one, "if that ain't considerable of a git up." In 1856 it was owned by a Mr. Ellis. See No. 21 for another version of "Old Bachelor."

9. GOSSIPS

10. SATURDAY NIGHT

11. ROBINSON CRUSOE

This seems to have been John's Christmas present to his uncle Henry Bromfield Rogers in December 1850. Before giving it he wrote to his father to ask what criticisms had been made of it. His mother had relayed the message that Uncle George Derby "thought his cap should be on his head, but he must recollect," the artist responded, "that Robinson is *at home* — in his house — & has manners enough to take his cap off. This is the only fault I have been told of," he added. Rogers had a beautiful note of acknowledgment from Uncle Henry after Christmas. When he heard that "the cat's legs have got broken in Robinson's family," John told his father to save the pieces and try to put them back together with "that sticking gum" in his brother's closet, rather than wait for him to come down from Manchester.

12. UNPROTECTED FEMALE

"I hope you will see that the 'Unprotected Female' is put out of sight," Rogers wrote to his mother on June 17, 1851, leaving us to guess why.

13. VICTORY

14. SANTA CLAUS

This was one of the groups in the house at Roxbury. John mentioned it in a letter from Chicago in 1859, saying only "I am sorry to hear the Santa Claus is so badly broken."

15. FRIAR TUCK

On August 26, 1855, Rogers wrote from Manchester: "I have commenced a group of the Black Knight & Friar Tuck in the hermitage," a scene from Sir Walter Scott's *Ivanhoe.* "It will make a spirited group," he added on the 29th, "if I finish it as I have formed it in my mind." This may be the group in clay Rogers exhibited at the New Hampshire Agricultural Society Fair in Manchester in September 1855, for which he won a prize. "It was quite amusing to stand by & hear the remarks that were made," Rogers wrote, "though I was a little bashful in standing by myself, but heard them through others. It was finished up in such a hurry that I felt rather ashamed of it but consoled myself with thinking that the countrymen would hardly know the difference." The group wound up in the Rogers' parlor at Roxbury. John wrote home in January 1856 that a bracket 18 inches by two feet would be large enough for "the Friar Tuck piece."

16. CURIOSITY SHOP

Rogers made this in Manchester, probably in 1856. It was the first for which he had a live model. "You have heard me speak of a little girl who is so beautiful in Manchester," he wrote to his sister Clara in February 1857. "She is a daughter of Mrs. Dodge's. . . . I hope you will see Kitty Dodge sometime. I quite fell in love with her. I got her to sit for me when I made Little Nell in the Curiosity Shop but was about as successful in getting a likeness as I was with Mother. If she was only a little older she would be a very dangerous acquaintance."

17. DESERTED VILLAGE. See Nos. 35 and 63.

18. OLD OAKEN BUCKET

"I have begun to work out my *'idee'* & am quite pleased with it," Rogers wrote to his mother on July 16, 1855. "It is the poem 'the old oaken bucket, the moss covered bucket, the iron bound bucket that hangs in the well.' " After it was finished, Rogers placed it on exhibition with a Mr. Nichols in Boston, removing it about the end of August. Rogers promised the group to a family friend, Mrs. Wendell, but another friend, Mrs. Charles Stetson, fell in love with it and offered to buy it. "It is very gratifying to have Mrs. Stetson like it so much," he wrote, "but it disturbs my arrangements dreadfully. . . . I have already delayed Mrs. W's so long that I don't like to postpone *that,* but if Mrs. Stetson is *set* upon having the Old Oaken Bucket, why, I can make another for Mrs. W. I have never sold any clay group yet & I certainly shouldn't begin with Mrs. Stetson. So, if she takes it, it must be as a present. I shall wait before writing anything to Mrs. Wendell, to hear from you, whether it was one of Mrs. Stetson's sudden fancies or if she is determined to covet it." The outcome of this is not known.

19. NIGHTMARE

Rogers modeled this in December 1853 as a gift for Mr. Oliver W. Bayley, superintendent of the Amoskeag Machine Shop in Manchester. He described the subject as "a man in a nightmare. The 'adversary' is quietly sitting on his chest looking him in the face. One little imp is pulling his hair out, whilst two others are engaged in sawing his legs off. A few snakes complete the picture. I might have made it a little more *horrible* but concluded it would answer as it was for all *practical purposes*."

20. NIGHTMARE

From Hannibal, Missouri, on April 5, 1857, Rogers wrote: "I am making a nightmare scene to ornament my room which is expected to be surpassingly horrible. You may wonder at my selection of such scenes but it will be appreciated in Hannibal better than anything else." A fuller description followed on April 27:

> I have finished my nightmare scene. It is strange how the subject seems to attract people more than any other. It was so with the one I gave to Mr. Bayley at Manchester [19]. Nearly every evening I am at home I have a crowd come in to see it. The design is partly similar to Mr. Bayley's only the Agony is piled up a little more. The victim is in bed & is being hugged by a skeleton from which he is *squirming* to get away. The old devil himself is leaning over the head board, quietly grinning & admiring the scene. Two little imps are sawing the man's leg off and a few small imps are scattered round engaged in various kinds of mischief. I have it understood as I think I told you that the poor fellow has been boarding lately at the same house where I board & the hard fare don't agree with him. My landlord was up here to see it a little while since but I concluded it was most too pointed a joke to tell him.

This spirited figure in painted clay has remained in Hannibal ever since. It is now in the Gladys A. Hawkins Memorial Museum.

21. OLD BACHELOR

"I believe I did not speak last week of a group I have made," Rogers wrote from Hannibal on November 30, 1856. "I came across some excellent clay & could not resist working in it. The scene was like the one Mr. Ellis has of an old bachelor [8] but varied in the composition. I was quite successful & my stock of popularity has risen about fifty per cent on account of it." Rogers apparently presented this model to his Hannibal friend, Miss Kate Hayward (sometimes given as Haywood), who in the spring of 1859 lent it to Chicago's first Art Exhibition. It was listed in the third edition of the catalogue as "Model in Clay Rogers Miss Haywood." When Rogers came to Chicago later the same year he found that the "Old Bachelor" was "a capital introduction." "It seems to have been about as attractive as anything on exhibition," he told his mother on August 28, 1859; "everybody is curious to know how it is done & I have frequent opportunities to talk very wisely about it." In Smith, *Rogers Groups*, p. 109, this is listed as "Irish Bachelor Mending a Pair of Breeches."

22. PLAYING MARBLES

In the *Amoskeag Bulletin* of the Amoskeag Textile Club of Manchester, New Hampshire, April 15, 1916, it was stated that John Rogers exhibited two groups at the annual fair of the New Hampshire Agricultural Society when it met in "the old rye field" at Manchester in 1851 (actually 1855). One of the two was "an old friar" [15]; the other, in gray clay from Hooksett, near Manchester, was a figure of a boy playing marbles. This was also mentioned in the Manchester *Mirror* in May 1895.

23. DOG AND CAT

This might be the "little boy with cat on shoulder and dog at his feet," mentioned in a letter of Sophia L. Pitman, Providence, Rhode Island, to Katherine R. Rogers, June 28, 1935 (New Canaan Historical Society). It was given by Miss Rogers to her former governess, Miss Mamie Pitman, along with some other clay sketches by John Rogers.

24. GIRL AND KITTEN

According to an article in the Manchester *Union*, May 14, 1895, Mr. Charles L. Richardson of Manchester, an old friend of John Rogers, was the possessor of one of Rogers' early clay models, "wherein the modeler represented with considerable skill a little girl and a kitten."

25. GIRL AND KITTEN

26. CHRISTMAS

27. GIRL AND BOY AND UMBRELLA

28. MAN'S HEAD

29. WOMAN'S HEAD

30. BURGLARS

On August 20, 1859, Rogers wrote from Chicago about a group at home in Roxbury: "I would advise that the Burglars should not be put in a very conspicuous position." It was probably the same group he was referring to when he told his father, August 27, 1861, that the "Picket Guard" [83] he was sending up was "intended to take the place of the Little Thieves at home," which he wanted broken up. Cf. also 39.

31. COUNTRY COURTSHIP

This was a design similar to, but more complex than, the later group known as "The Town Pump" [57]. The only reference to "Country Courtship" is in a letter of September 10, 1859, in which it is contrasted to the later version.

32. BLIND MAN'S BUFF

This may have been based on an engraving of Sir David Wilkie's painting of this subject. In a letter of April 9, 1854, Rogers wrote to his mother: "I send down two more Wilkies for you to see. I think that 'blind man's buff' is a fine study. You seem to find something new the longer you look at it. The grouping is capital but I will leave it to you to find out the beauties of it." Rogers used the same subject in two later works, his outdoor vase [148] and "A Frolic at the Old Homestead" [174].

33. IRISHMAN AND PIG

In October 1853 Rogers turned out in only four days a figure which he presented to his new friend, the Rev. Francis LeBaron, minister of the Manchester Unitarian Church. The subject was "an irishman with a pig on his back and a pipe in his mouth." Two months later the artist had a story to tell about it:

> I believe I told you [he wrote to his sister Ellen on Christmas Day, 1853] that an old lady came into Mr. LeBaron's room one day and took up the irishman I made him & let it fall, breaking it all to pieces. I took it home to mend it and after wetting it commenced to build it up again last Thursday evening. I had got it pretty well along when over it tipped onto the floor and broke & bent all to pieces again. I had one or two more mishaps with it again that evening but got it pretty nearly done before going to bed. On Friday night I had been out passing the evening and got home about eleven o'clock and went to work on it to finish it up as there was but little to do. About one o'clock I was just putting the finishing touches on it and would have been done in five minutes when its legs proved too weak for it and over he pitched again — this time falling on his face and spoiling that & breaking him to pieces as much as he was in the first place. I *did* feel like stamping him completely out of shape, but I picked up the pieces and after looking at it a while to get reconciled to it began to work on it again, determined I would not give it up so, and by three o'clock got it all done but a few finishing touches to be put on this week. I made more sure of my foundations this time. I tell them here that I experienced religion when I concluded to go to work after the last catastrophe.

This anecdote had the honor of being used as a Sunday School lecture by the Rev. Edward Everett Hale, a friend of LeBaron's but best known for his own story, *The Man Without a Country*. The last word on the group, appropriately, was written by Francis LeBaron, as editor of the *Furniture Trade Journal,* Chicago, October 1879: "We recall a work of this period, an Irishman carrying home a pig on his shoulder. The pig fairly squealed, and the Irishman laughed and swore by turns. The fun of it was delicious and irresistible, everybody who looked, laughed."

34. YOUNG AMERICA

35. DESERTED VILLAGE. See Nos. 17 and 63.

36. POCAHONTAS

37. ALARM OF FIRE

38. BOYS FISHING.

39. BOYS STEALING. See No. 30.

40. DOCTOR

41. INDIAN IN AMBUSH

42. LEISURE MOMENTS
This title is almost indecipherable. "Leisure Moments" seems a reasonable interpretation, since Rogers used this title again [60] early in his professional career, when he did occasionally re-use ideas from his amateur days.

43. PEDLAR

44. RETURN FR[OM THE] FIELDS

45. TANGLED SKEIN

[Rogers' numbered list in pencil ends at this point. On the back of the same sheet of paper are four crude sketches, also in pencil, which bear titles. These are probably ideas Rogers thought of using but never worked out in the clay. They are listed in this catalogue for the sake of the record.]

46. WAKING UP THE DOCTOR

47 THE LITTLE BEGGAR

48. READING THE NEWS

49. ADDRESS TO THE JURY

[The following two titles do not appear in Rogers' list, although they certainly date from the same period:]

50. AT THE CONFESSIONAL
In a clipping from a Manchester newspaper, May 1895, it is stated that one of Rogers' early clay groups bore this title.

51. SARAH ELLEN DERBY ROGERS (1805–1877)
Rogers undertook to model a portrait bust of his mother very early in his amateur career, possibly in 1849 or 1850. On April 16, 1854, he wrote of this attempt: "I would

give anything in the world, Ellen, if I could complete Mother's bust . . . & if I felt that I could do it I would willingly try again on it. But you know how hard I tried when I was at home. It has mortified me exceedingly. I believe it is the only thing that I ever undertook that I could not complete. I could not tell why, but my powers of imitation seemed to be taken away on that particular subject. It does not seem as if it would be so difficult as to make a figure from my fancy, for it was nothing but an imitation of nature, a low branch of the art. But it nevertheless was true. I will give it a look again when I come down." Rogers made another attempt in 1861 [85], still without success. It was not until 1862 that he finally produced what he considered a good likeness of his mother [96].

[The next group of works are those executed by Rogers as a student in Paris and Rome in 1858–59. These were only exercises and were not preserved.]

52. ANATOMICAL FIGURES

On October 6, 1858, Rogers wrote from Paris that he had joined the class conducted by Antoine L. Dantan, a respected sculptor who won the Prix de Rome in 1828. The young American's first assignment was to model an "anatomical figure, to learn the muscles." Dantan gave it a *"très bien."* By October 6, Rogers had finished the first and begun his second anatomical figure.

53. INDIAN SHOOTING A BOW AND ARROW

On October 18, 1858, Rogers reported that M. Dantan had asked him to make a composition of his own, so he made "a figure of an indian shooting a bow & arrow." Dantan was "mightily pleased with it," John wrote, "& wants to have me cast it in plaster. I suspect they think I have lived amongst the indians, I dressed mine up so readily & spoke so knowingly of what was right & wrong. It is just as well to appear wise when we can."

54. COPY FROM THE ANTIQUE

After his removal to Rome in December 1858, Rogers found a place in the studio of the English sculptor Benjamin Spence. His first assignment was to copy an antique statue. "I have now been at work three days," he wrote on January 9, 1859. "He [Spence] has seen a specimen of my modelling for I have been copying an antique statue and now he wants me to start a figure of my own and carry it on at the same time that I am copying from the antique."

55. ROUGH DESIGNS IN CLAY

On January 26, 1859, Rogers reported from Rome:

> I am progressing very satisfactorily at the studio. I have not commenced any figure yet. I made several little rough designs in clay but they did not exactly suit Mr. Spence and I have been trying to think of others. You have no idea how difficult it is. I used to think it was hard enough when I made designs for a group but this seems worse because according to the classical ideas prevailing here, and no doubt they are the true principles, statuary should be as simple as possible, with very little drapery and no *accessories* as they call all the little odds and ends that I used to put

round my groups to help tell the story. You see when you leave all *those* out it is very difficult to make any particular action or position tell the story. It may be true in *theory* to leave all the accessories out but I don't believe in it altogether. . . . When I get any subject that is satisfactory I will let you know. Those that I had already thought of were not simple enough. He wanted something quite simple to begin with. There are plenty of characters in books but they will not suit the scanty drapery that is necessary — so you can imagine how difficult it is — but I shall get hold of something before long.

[Rogers' last works as an amateur were produced in Chicago during his brief residence there in 1859:]

56. CHECKER PLAYERS

In August 1859, while working in Chicago as a draftsman in the City Surveyor's office, Rogers modelled a group of checker players to be disposed of by lottery at a charity bazaar. "My group is all ready but the glass case," he wrote on August 20, "and is quite successful. I don't know but quite as good as your checker players [3]." He brought it to the office the following week, with dramatic results. "The editor of one of the papers saw it," the artist related, "& was mightily taken with it. There is a police court room directly across the entry from our office & this man went in there & brought out the judges & clerks & all hands to see it." The next day there appeared in the newspaper the following flattering notice:

> We were shown yesterday a very meritorious piece of miniature statuary modeled in clay by our young townsman Mr. John Rogers. The model represents two old-fashioned yeomen, in rustic garb, seated on an old-fashioned settee, and engaged in the old-fashioned game of chequers. The game has progressed to the close, each having but two kings left on the board, and by the moves one player has *penned* the other so that he has no move left without losing all his remaining forces. The winner leans back and enjoys his victory in a hearty haw-haw; while the loser, pinching his nether lip, appears to be both pleased at the adroitness of his adversary, yet puzzled to understand how it happened. The expression in the features of both is conveyed with wondrous faithfulness, and there is an ease and freedom in every line of this little clay model which indicate the maker as the possessor of no ordinary artistic skill.

The publicity brought still more visitors. "I have to give so many explanations as to what it is made of & how it is done that I am getting to be a perfect machine & just want to be touched off with a question to wind off the same yarn every time. . . . I have been interrupted three or four times while I have been writing this letter [September 10, 1859] by ladies & gentlemen, strangers to me, who have climbed up eighty-two steps to see my checker players. I am in a fair way of being spoiled at last by flattering remarks." The group was raffled off for $75.00, by selling three hundred tickets at twenty-five cents each, and was won by a young lady. "A great many had invested in a large number of tickets and were disappointed in not getting it," Rogers gleefully wrote home on September 24. "Two or three people have spoken about buying some of me and I have no doubt I could do pretty well by getting some up for sale."

The popularity of his first two versions of "Checker Players" led Rogers to use the same theme, with variations, three more times. See "Checker Players" [3], "Checkers Up at the Farm" [145], and "Chess" [184].

57. THE TOWN PUMP

Inspired by the success of "Checker Players" [56], Rogers got a fresh supply of clay from the Chicago sculptor Leonard W. Volk ("the best I think I ever used") and set to work on another model, "the same idea as Country Courtship [31] though simpler." By October 8 he was finishing it. "I had it all put together but found it did not balance well & I was quite disgusted with it but this morning I cut it to pieces & twisted it round & with a few additions it is quite satisfactory now. A few hours work will finish it. I am anxious to get it done & at work on my next, The Slave Auction [58]." Although he originally intended "The Town Pump" as a gift for Mrs. Samuel Greeley, his employer's wife, need for cash led him to offer it publicly for sale, in the bookstore of D. B. Cooke & Co. on Lake Street. It was described and praised in one of the newspapers on October 28, 1859:

> "The Town Pump" is a composition of four figures. At the pump a plowboy is watering his horse, while a rustic fair one, with basket on arm stands waiting for her chance to use the pump, beguiling the time with conversation, while her dog lies down at her feet. The position of the figures is extremely natural and easy, and the expression of the countenances of the man and girl is life-like beyond description. What will also strike the critical observer is the faithfulness in the anatomy of the horse, viewed in connection with the pasture. The accuracy in this respect is really wonderful. The drapery of the human figures is well arranged, and the entire group has an air of ease and naturalness that speaks well for the genius of the artist.

It is interesting to compare this description with the group published by Rogers in 1862 under the same name [89].

Despite the above "puff," Rogers had trouble disposing of his group. "I have had several offers to buy 'The Town Pump' by parties living out of the State," he reported on November 13, "but I could not warrant the safe transportation — but I have had no offers in town. . . . I want the money or I would give it away to a friend of mine." Just before he left for New York, however, he gave "The Town Pump" to the Chicago Historical Society. It was later lost in the great fire of 1871. This group was also referred to as "Watering the Horse" (Smith, *Rogers Groups,* p. 112).

[Rogers' professional career begins at this point.]

58. THE SLAVE AUCTION

Plaster painted or dipped in spermaceti or steerine; height 13¼ inches
Signed JOHN ROGERS/NEW YORK
Price: $3.00 (1859–60); $5.00 (1861)
Collections: 1, 2, 3, 9

John Rogers' first offering as a professional sculptor was, in the words of Theodore Tilton (*The Independent and Anti-Slavery Standard,* September 20, 1860), "a testimony to that love of freedom which was born in him under the shadow of his New England hills." The idea of the group came to the artist in Chicago in September 1859, was put into clay by November, and was cast in New York in December. In spite of its timeliness — Rogers first offered it for sale a fortnight after John Brown's execution — "The Slave Auction" was not the success Rogers had expected. "I find the times have quite headed me off," he wrote on Christmas Eve, "for the Slave Auction tells such a strong story that none of the stores will receive it to sell for fear of offending their Southern customers."

Although Rogers achieved some notoriety and a few sales to abolitionists early in 1860 by employing a Negro to hawk it about the streets of New York, "The Slave Auction" never paid its way, even after the sculptor brought out improved casts from a new model in April 1860 and again in November 1861. "The Slave Auction," he wrote in 1863, "gave me probably more satisfaction to make than any other of my small groups, but I sell less of it than of almost any other group. By taking a subject on which there is a divided opinion, of course, I lose half my customers." The group was withdrawn from sale before 1866 and is consequently now quite rare.

59. THE FARMER'S HOME

Plaster; height probably about 13 inches
Price: $3.00
No copies located

Begun early in December 1859 and put on sale in January 1860, "The Farmer's Home" offered a marked contrast in spirit to its predecessor. Dr. George B. Cheever gave the following description in *The Independent and Anti-Slavery Standard,* February 16, 1860:

> [It] represents a farmer's family in New England. . . . The hearty, happy father, after his day's work, or on his return from the field, is seated beside his wife, with a laughing baby astride his foot and held by both hands to be tossed up and down to a tune which the father is whistling. Another frolicking fat urchin is climbing on his shoulder, and grasping him by the hair to hold on. A dog on one side, in the most natural attitude possible, is looking up at his master's face, at the noise of his whistling, as if to say, That's good, I like that! A kitten on the other side, at the foot of the wife, is playing with her ball of worsted, and the plain but pleasant intelligent face of the mother bespeaks the very perfection of household contentment and happiness.

Although Rogers was sure "The Farmer's Home" would sell better than "The Slave Auction" ("home scenes," he said, "interest *everybody*"), this proved not to be the case. After making a few dozen casts he decided to withdraw it because of unnamed defects which made it too complicated to cast profitably. He did sell (at $3.00) or give away at least four casts. One went to Dr. Cheever, a prominent abolitionist who found it useful for propaganda contrasting life at the North and South. Another abolitionist, Lewis Tappan, had the two groups photographed in April 1860 and sent copies of the photographs to England. Rogers was supposed to receive copies too, but they are not among his papers.

60. LEISURE MOMENTS

Plaster; destroyed

On February 27, 1860, Rogers wrote to his cousin Anna H. Peabody that "Leisure Moments" was "defunct," spoiled in a casting experiment. This was in all probability the "little group" he began after completing "The Farmer's Home" [59] in January. On January 15 he reported that the "little group" he was then modelling was "very simple [and] could be cast very easily in this cheap bronze which is simply zinc bronzed over." On January 20 he described the "little group" as cast but not yet finished up. There is no further mention of this abortive work until the announcement of February 27 that "Leisure Moments" was defunct. See also No. 42.

61. CHECKER PLAYERS

Plaster, painted; height 8½ inches
Signed JOHN ROGERS/NEW YORK 1860
Price: $5.00 (April 1860); $3.00 (November 1860); $6.00 (1866)
Collections: 3, 6, 9, 10

Disheartened by the successive failure of "The Slave Auction" [58] and "The Farmer's Home" [59], Rogers turned reluctantly in February 1860 to a subject he had used twice before as an amateur, a game of checkers. "I only wish it was more original," he lamented, "for I don't like to make anything that can be traced to a picture," in this case an engraving after a painting by Sir David Wilkie. "But still this is only the *idea* that is copied," he added. "The arrangement is different." The design was the same, however, according to the artist, as the "Checker Players" [56] he had made for the Chicago Charity Fair the previous year. His first "Checker Players" [3] was much closer to Wilkie.

The 1860 model, begun about February 10 and finished in the clay by February 25, proved difficult to cast. The first casts were ready just in time for the artist to put one in the Spring Exhibition of the National Academy of Design along with "The Slave Auction" and "The Village Schoolmaster" [63]. It was on sale at Williams & Stevens art store on Broadway the week of April 22 and at first sold "readily" at $5.00. It was also on sale at Rogers' studio, where a copy was bought by Mrs. William B. Astor. Within a few months Rogers lost faith in this, his first modestly successful work. "I am not very anxious to have any of them go into 5th Ave. houses," he wrote on October 7, "for I don't feel so proud of them as I did once as my taste has somewhat changed." The price was lowered to $3.00 in November 1860 and by August 1861 his stock was exhausted. In October 1861, inspired by the unexpected popularity of "The Picket Guard" [83], Rogers remodelled "The Checker Players" and the following March was able to report that it seemed "to take pretty well." The group was belatedly patented on May 27, 1862. It appeared in the first Rogers catalogue (1866) but was finally withdrawn in 1868.

This group was copied in parian. The only example known is in the collection of the Harold Warp Pioneer Village, Minden, Nebraska. See Appendix II, Section C.

62. THE FIREMAN

Plaster, probably painted; height probably about 13 inches

No copies located

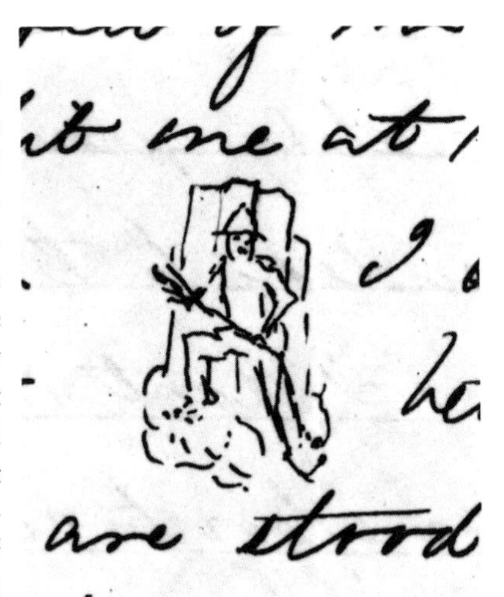

On March 3, 1860, John Rogers reported home that he had begun modelling a fireman which he thought would "sell well to an immense body of men here in N. York & in every city of the Union." The piece represented a single fireman standing behind "some boards . . . stood up against some burnt rubbish to shield him from the fire while he is holding the hosepipe & calling out to play away." Rogers employed a model for a while but found that it was "so difficult to make a model take the *action*" that he got along better without him "except for some of the smaller details." Rogers made the first cast of "The Fireman" himself on April 22. On May 5 he announced that he had

had "a few" casts made and planned to exhibit one at Williams & Stevens the following week. Whether he carried out this plan or not is not known. A week later Rogers wrote that he was not going to hurry "The Fireman" until he had put "Night" and "Morning" [65, 66] on sale first. Before the propitious moment arrived, however, the artist had decided plaster was beneath his dignity and "The Fireman" apparently never did go on sale officially. How Rogers disposed of the casts on hand is not known, but it seems unlikely that he would have wantonly destroyed them. However he disposed of them, no copies are known to survive. Some idea of the group's appearance can be gained from the rough sketch reproduced here from Rogers' letter to his mother, May 5, 1860, owned by The New-York Historical Society.

63. THE VILLAGE SCHOOLMASTER

Plaster, painted; height 9¾ inches
Signed JOHN ROGERS/NEW YORK
Price: $5.00 (1861–62); $6.00 (1866)
Collections: 1, 3, 6, 9

The clay model of this little group was already "well along" when Rogers first mentioned it in mid-March 1860. It illustrated the line in Goldsmith's *The Deserted Village,* where the Schoolmaster argues with the Parson, "For e'en though vanquished, he could argue still." The artist intended, as an experiment, to leave it in the clay and see if it would sell that way, saving him the trouble and expense of casting. He finished it in time to enter it in the Spring Exhibition of the National Academy of Design. "It seems to be liked very much & is thought the best I have done," Rogers noted, "but that is partly owing to its being in the clay which has a better effect than the plaster." Priced at $50.00, the clay model was still unsold in September 1861, when Rogers finally made a cast of it, after "The Picket Guard" [83] had demonstrated the saleability of plaster groups. "I think you will like it better than anything," he told his mother. "I have always considered it my best group in some respects but thought it too difficult to cast till lately." Six months later he reported that as far as sales were concerned this group was "about the most unprofitable," though he thought it still one of his best designs. Rogers patented "The Village Schoolmaster" on May 27, 1862, and kept it in stock until 1868.

64. EVANGELINE

Clay sketch; destroyed before completion

At the end of March 1860 Rogers commenced "a figure of Evangeline" based on a popular engraving, possibly one after Faed's painting advertised by Goupil in *The Crayon* in October 1856. He did so at the urging of a Mr. Doll, an employee of Williams & Stevens, the New York art dealers, who felt that a cheap plaster copy of a high-priced engraving, the original plate of which had been destroyed, would be a profitable venture. Doll's advice was hardly disinterested, since he was at the time trying to persuade Rogers to make him his business agent. Feeling as he did about copying the work of other artists, Rogers could generate little enthusiasm for the project and dropped it within less than two weeks. "I have commenced but it comes hard," he wrote on March 31. "I think I shall get it after a while though." On April 15, however, he wrote "Evangeline didn't come out satisfactorily & I changed her into a *fireman* [62]." Speaking of it later (July 15, 1860), he told his mother: "Evangeline, whom you inquire after, passed a very precarious life of a few days & was buried in the clay pail."

65, 66. NIGHT and MORNING

Medallions in low relief, plaster, white on blue ground; diameter 18 inches
Price: $15.00 (pair)
No copies located

Among the favorite art works of the mid-nineteenth century were the bas-relief medallions entitled *Night* and *Morning* created in 1815 by the great Danish Neoclassicist Berthel Thorwaldsen (1770–1844). Reproductions in plaster, beadwork, and other media were common in Victorian homes. New York's Cosmopolitan Art Association distributed engravings of these subjects in March 1860. A month later, Williams & Stevens suggested to John Rogers that he turn his hands to making copies in plaster. Since none of the original casts was available, they explained, plaster copies would "sell like hot cakes" at $25.00 a pair.

Rogers modelled and cast both medallions between April 29 and May 26, 1860. Although he expressed satisfaction with the result and admitted that making these careful copies was "a very good experience," Rogers apparently did not experience any sort of conversion to the Neoclassical mode. "I never expect to do anything of *that* style," he told his mother, "for my forte lies more in spirit & action."

When he started work on "Night" and "Morning," Rogers had predicted they would yield a good profit because they would be easy to cast in spite of their size. Casting proved more tricky than he had anticipated, however, because he tried to cast in color. "The trouble," he wrote home on June 17, "is in the blue background. I had cast them too light a blue & as I had got so many cast I could not afford to throw them away, so

I have been trying to tint them by hand in numberless ways. . . . I have got very nearly the thing now & will soon have it all right."

At first Rogers intended casting the frames in plaster too, but this proved too difficult, so he reduced the price to $15.00 and suggested they be framed in maroon velvet "like the common way of binding engravings." When Williams & Stevens told him he was foolish to price them so low, his characteristic reply was "I prefer to put them at a price that no one who likes them need hesitate to buy."

There is no way of knowing how many pairs of "Night" and "Morning" were sold. On July 15, 1860, Rogers reported that he had sold several pairs but did not expect to sell many till fall. Several copies went to his family and one was sold in October to a friend, Mr. Duff. Williams & Stevens probably sold some also. Apparently the whole venture proved to be more trouble than it was worth, for on December 9, 1860, Rogers reported to his family that he had got rid of his remaining stock of "Night" and "Morning" to an unnamed buyer for $100.00 and was glad to have them off his hands. It is quite possible that copies may have survived unrecognized as the work of John Rogers.

67. BAS RELIEF (untitled)

On May 26, 1860, in a letter to his mother, Rogers stated: "I have taken quite a fancy to bas reliefs since I modelled Night and Morning [65, 66] & think it is the most desirable form to put my groups in. . . . I have commenced a group to try it." It is not known what the subject was nor whether it was completed.

68. THE FISHER GIRL

Parian statuette; height 15 inches

Inscriptions on base: (left) A PREMIUM AWARDED BY THE COSMOPOLITAN ART ASSOCIATION 1861; (front) THE FISHER GIRL; (rear) AFTER BARBEE'S STATUE BY JOHN ROGERS/COPELAND

Collection: The New-York Historical Society

Probably because of his competent handling of the "Night" and "Morning" plaques [65, 66], Rogers was commissioned in June 1860 by the Cosmopolitan Art Association to make a reduced copy of William Randolph Barbee's statue "The Fisher Girl," an ideal nude "sitting by the lonely sea alone, gazing in puzzled wonderment upon the broken meshes of her net." The Association had recently bought the much publicized original marble at auction for almost three thousand dollars and wished to distribute reproductions by lottery to members of the Association. Rogers began his clay model on June 23, 1860, working under the public's eyes in the Dusseldorf Gallery on Broadway, and had it finished and cast in plaster by July 15. It was then shipped to the famous Copeland pottery in England, where it was reproduced in "parian," a soft-paste unglazed porcelain with a marble-like finish. Eleven of these copies in parian were distributed in 1861 by the Cosmopolitan Art Association. There is no record of what Rogers was paid for this job, but he certainly got good publicity out of it. The *Cosmopolitan Art Journal* told its readers in December 1860 that he had executed the commission "in such a manner as to excite the utmost praise and satisfaction from all who beheld the artist's work." Rogers himself was so pleased with the result that he decided to abandon plaster genre and aim thereafter rather higher. "The Fisher Girl" was, however, his last copy.

69. GENTLEMAN SITTING IN A CHAIR WITH A NEWSPAPER

Portrait statuette in clay
Unlocated

On June 29, 1860, while still working on his copy of "The Fisher Girl" [68], Rogers told his mother "the plaster business" was so bad he had decided to turn his attention to portraiture. "It will take some little practice to acquire a facility at catching likenesses," he wrote, "but I shall do it eventually & it will be sure to pay & not keep me in such constant uneasiness as my groups do. The style that I have started on," he continued, "is a statuette of a gentleman sitting in a chair with a newspaper. Those who have seen it like the idea of the full length statuettes. Mrs. Oakey was in a few days since & was particularly pleased with it." The identity of the gentleman who sat for this portrait was not revealed nor was the portrait mentioned in any newspaper notices.

70. CLAY GROUPS

On July 1, 1860, just two days after speaking about his portrait statuette project [69], Rogers announced in another letter to his mother a complete revulsion from plaster, the very name of which, he said, "condemns any work of art." "So lately," he added, "I have given up all thoughts of plaster & have turned my attention to making clay groups which seem to meet with a ready sale at a fair price, but though I intend to devote more care to these & make them studies to improve myself, I feel ambitious to put something in marble now." A fortnight later (July 15, 1860) he was still in the same mood: "Lately I have been in a sort of intermediate stage of clay groups which is more profitable as it brings a more ready return — but now I aspire to *marble* & next winter I expect to come out a full fledged sculptor." The artist failed to identify the subjects of these groups, none of which is known to have survived.

71. THE FAIRY'S WHISPER

Plaster, soaped or painted; height 21 inches length 28 inches
Signed JOHN ROGERS/NEW YORK/1860
Price: $25.00; withdrawn about 1882
Collections: 1, 2, 3, 5, 8, 9

With his heart at least momentarily set on becoming a sculptor in marble, Rogers turned his hand in the summer of 1860 to his "first attempt at anything ideal." Begun early in July, the clay model of "The Fairy's Whisper" (or "fairy in the bullrushes" or "my boy" as he variously referred to it) took shape slowly and was not completed until late in September. It was mid-October before the first plaster casts were ready and his first recorded sale was made on October 31. Early the next month he made a new model, incorporating some changes not described, and it was from this model that all subsequent casts were derived.

Rogers' first essay in the "ideal" was a lifesize figure of a boy described by a contemporary as "sitting with all the unconscious grace of childhood upon a bank of flowers, while a fairy which has just sprung from a clump of delicate fern leaves (its evident hiding place) is whispering in his ear. . . . Entranced by the mysterious visitant," the same writer went on, "the flowers have fallen unconsciously from the dimpled fingers. A dreamy smile hovers around the parted lips, while the eyes half closed as in a delicious dream, have still an eager, earnest expression, as though he feared his low, tremulous breathing even, might break the witching spell" (*Boston Transcript,* November 12, 1860). "The Fairy's Whisper" was indeed, as Rogers told his mother on July 1 when the design was still only in his head, "something which the ladies would call a 'sweet thing' (emphasis on the *sweet*)."

As he was anxious for his first "ideal" figure to be as correct as possible, Rogers went to "a heap of trouble" to find a model for the boy, finally settling on a little German boy he had spotted running into a tenement. The negotiations were carried on through an interpreter. For certain detail the artist used casts taken from other young models when he "could persuade them by large bribes of sugar plums & cents, though to the mortal terror of some of them."

Although it was hailed almost universally as a work "of exquisite beauty and tenderness of feeling" (*New York Tribune,* September 8, 1860), "The Fairy's Whisper" did not make its creator's fortune. It did, however, advance his reputation, especially with connoisseurs and dealers who were a bit leary of everyday scenes in plaster. With this work Rogers won the hearts and influential voices of men like Dr. Magoon of Albany, collector and critic of art, who was so "haunted" by his first view of Rogers' "little boy" that he went back to see it again before leaving New York City (September 1860). Magoon later returned to buy one copy for himself and another for the president of the University of Rochester, albeit at a reduced price, since the artist expected these gentlemen would be "the means of bringing in other orders."

Slow seller though it was, "The Fairy's Whisper" remained in Rogers' stock as late as 1882, consistently priced at $25.00. Rogers tried to spur its sales appeal by pointing out that it could be used out of doors in summer if painted and raised off the ground.

72. THE CHILD'S DREAM

Design for a marble statue, destroyed before completion

On December 9, 1860, Rogers reported cryptically that he had got hold of a new design which took after "The Fairy's Whisper" [71], but he declined to describe it, wishing as he put it, to give no more false alarms. The very next week the aspiring sculptor received his first commission for an original work in marble. His second-cousin Hattie Appleton (half-sister of Frances Appleton, Longfellow's second wife), having come into a little money, offered him $350 to $400 for a small marble statue. "Of course I shall lay myself out on the occasion," Rogers wrote his mother, "as it is a chance that I have been wanting. The design I am at work on now is a fairy scene like the last, but is meant to represent a child's dream. A child has fallen asleep on a bank & two or three fairies are dressing its hair with flowers &c." He offered more details a month later (January 12, 1861):

> The child is lying on her side with her left arm under her head & her body rather *cuddled* up. A sprig of grape vine intermixed with fern leaves makes some foliage about her head, which partly conceals one fairy who is dressing her hair with flowers while another is floating up through the leaves & bringing flowers in her scarf.

In spite of encouragement from several visitors to his studio, including the proprietor of the Dusseldorf Gallery, Rogers made only slow progress on "The Child's Dream" through January and February 1861. The longer he worked on it the less he liked it.

> I can't get interested in the fairy business [he wrote on February 24]. I intend to make some alterations in Hattie's piece but if it doesn't come to suit me at once I shall pull it down. I shall aim at bronze & parian after this and not be bothered with marble. I am not sure but it will be economy for me to give up the attempt on the fairy piece at once without wasting any more time on it for at the price I told Hattie I should do it for I will not make a cent. The design is too much like the Whisper to give me much credit for originality in it.

Soon after, on March 3, Rogers reported that his "little girl" had come "to an untimely end." "I knocked it all to pieces," he explained, "& have set up another in a different shape though carrying out the same idea on a smaller scale, but I can't get up the least enthusiasm about it. There must be some spirit about a piece to interest me." This too came to an untimely end, though Hattie Appleton eventually got her marble statue in the guise of "Air Castles" [80].

73. THE ARTIST AND HIS PATRON

Design for a group; not completed

This "very fine group" was mentioned in the *New York Times* on December 29, 1860, as one Rogers was working on at that time. It was not mentioned by name in any of Rogers' surviving letters, but it may have been the design referred to in a letter of December 29 as looking "foggy": "It is all right in principle but there's a screw loose in the practice I find. I may twist it into something yet." Since there is no further mention of this group it probably was never completed.

74. A BRIBE

Design for a group; not completed

The *New York Times* reported on December 29, 1860, that Rogers was working on several statuette groups. "There is one," it said, "which he calls 'A Bribe,' but which looks like the Devil and an Alderman, which will be peculiarly appropriate at the present time." This group is not mentioned in Rogers' correspondence and presumably was never completed.

75. THE VIGILANCE COMMITTEE

Clay; probably destroyed

The violent actions of Southern Vigilance Committees toward Negroes and toward whites suspected of abolitionist views were much in the news during the months immediately preceding the outbreak of the Civil War. John Rogers showed where his feelings lay in this group, executed in clay during the first week of 1861. He hoped to put it on display in the window of some shop on Broadway, if he could find one willing to show it. "I am afraid they will think it hits rather too hard," he wrote on January 6. The group was described in the *New York Post* in March:

> [It] is composed of three figures, one with a rope round his neck, one end of which is in the hands of an ugly looking fellow, whose attention is equally divided between a paper which seems to have been found on the prisoner's person and a tar-pot significantly placed in the background. The subject is the 'Vigilance Committee.'

Rogers himself wrote of this group on January 19, 1861: "The Vigilance Committee did not amount to much," indicating that it was never completed for sale, although the original model may have stayed in his studio for a time.

76. SIR JOHN FALSTAFF

Clay; unlocated

Rogers reported in a letter of January 26, 1861, that he had received from a "5th Ave. man" a commission for a clay group but that he had not yet settled on a subject. The following week he said that he was doing a small figure of Sir John Falstaff on commission. Although Rogers did not mention this group again, it is quite possible that he did complete it and deliver it, in the clay, to his unnamed patron.

77. THE MERCHANT OF VENICE

Clay; unlocated

Rogers' first group depicting the trial scene in Shakespeare's play, *The Merchant of Venice,* was begun in February 1861 and completed, in the clay, in time to send it to the National Academy between March 3 and 10. "The group does me but little credit," he wrote of it, "but it was too late to remedy it." The catalogue listed the work as "Portia, Shylock and Antonio — in clay, for sale." Rogers reported home that the group had been put "in a miserable place," about which he would have felt badly "if it had been a better work." None of the critics mentioned it in their reviews of the Academy exhibition, but one who saw it in the artist's studio before hand praised the "vigorous modeling of Shylock." Still in clay, the group was in Rogers' studio in October 1861, when he reported taking molds from it. Nothing more is heard of it, except for brief notes in the *Springfield Republican,* November 30, and the New York *Home Journal,* December 1861. The absence of any further reference to "The Merchant of Venice" in Rogers' correspondence suggests that he made and sold no casts. The fate of the original clay is not known. Rogers used the same scene again in 1880 in the group entitled " 'Is It So Nominated in the Bond?' " [160].

78. RICHARD III

Clay and plaster; both unlocated

In the first flush of enthusiasm over his "Merchant of Venice" [77], Rogers conceived the idea of devoting himself to illustrating scenes from Shakespeare. "As my plan is now," he wrote on February 24, 1861, "I should make them about 15 inches high and after it is nicely modeled up to invite people to see it & get subscribers to a limited number in bronze. I wonder I have never undertaken Shakespeare before," he continued. "I could find illustrations for anything in it and taking it from such a source would make it familar to everyone — then again the costumes are so much more picturesque." "Taking my designs from Shakespeare," he added a week later, "will give them a dignity that everyday subjects don't have."

For the first of his planned Shakespearean series, Rogers selected the third act scene in *Richard III* in which Queen Margaret curses Richard. "If you read over the scene," the artist told his mother, "you will see that the curse is tremendous." Work on the model, begun about March 1, 1861, was slowed after two weeks by uncertainty over costumes. On this point he consulted with the famous actor Edwin Forrest. "The Lion received me very cordially into his den," Rogers reported on March 17, "& kept me there nearly an hour showing me books of costumes, pictures &c." A week later Forrest came to see Rogers' studio and then took the young artist to Mathew Brady's to show him photographs of himself in various characters. In spite of Forrest's help and encouragement, the group would not come out to suit. "After all, Shakespeare stock is down," Rogers wrote on March 23. "I had worked a fortnight on Queen Margaret & yesterday I took the greatest satisfaction in pounding her into a jelly. I could not get her to suit me. You can imagine that it takes some philosophy to keep one's spirit up to sell nothing, to have no one come to see you & to work a fortnight on a queen & not make even a decent looking old hag out of her. I will finish up Richard," he concluded, "& let him stand alone in his glory."

By March 30 Richard was finished in the clay to the artist's satisfaction. "It will be a good advertisement for me amongst a certain class," he decided, "for it is better & more carefully modelled than anything I have done, but it will never pay for it is not a taking subject." On April 6 he made a mold on "Dick" and got a good cast which, he said, took a weight off his mind. What happened after that is a complete mystery, for Rogers never mentioned "Richard III" again.

79. ST. CATHERINE

Bas-relief medallion, plaster, white on blue ground; diameter probably about 18 inches

No copies located

During the first week of April 1861 Rogers received a commission from an unnamed patron to make a bas-relief of St. Catherine borne aloft by four angels, derived from a popular engraving. "I have worked about a day on it," he reported on April 6, "& am satisfied that I can make a good thing of it." "My bas relief of St. Catherine is a complete success," he wrote on the day Fort Sumter was fired on, "& will be very beautiful on a blue ground. . . . I shall probably finish modeling it this next week."

The outbreak of war caused Rogers' patron to withdraw the "St. Catherine" order, much to the artist's annoyance. "I expected to get a hundred dollars for it," he complained, "but instead of that I must go to the expense of getting up casts & dispose of them myself. I have no doubt that I shall realize more in the end by doing so . . . but still it is not ready cash which is desirable these hard times." He had some casts ready by May 25. "The outlay is not much," he wrote on the 28th. "I had a man only a few days casting & I shall do the finishing myself. With the frames & glass they only cost about $3 & I think they will sell readily at $10. in ordinary times." Copies soon after went to his cousin Susan Welles of Boston, to Mr. Supply C. Thwing of Roxbury, and to a Mrs. Ropes of Salem, the last priced at $12 because it was in a rosewood frame. The artist later gave a copy to the Charles Stetsons, old Cincinnati friends lately moved to New York, and sold a second copy to Mrs. Ropes "delivered according to her direction."

There is no evidence that "St. Catherine" was sold by any of the New York stores, but it was on sale at Williams & Everett's in Boston. In fact, Rogers complained in December 1861 that the Boston firm was indulging in unfair price-cutting. "They have no business to offer them at that price [not mentioned] & I have written them so — that is, with the frames — $6 for the casts is what I have offered them at but my frames cost me nearly $4 & I don't see how they can offer theirs at $3. Those frames belong to them. The casts with the frames should be $12, but I shall hear from them soon I suppose."

Although Rogers had tried to "sell out" his stock of "St. Catherine" as early as September 15, 1861, he still had some on hand the following June, when he sold two copies — one to Mrs. Ropes again, and one to a Mr. and Mrs. C. S. Thayer. "St. Catherine" was not mentioned in newspaper accounts of Rogers' work. Unrecognized copies may exist, but none has been reported.

80. AIR CASTLES

Marble

Collection: Society for the Preservation of New England Antiquities, Boston

After abandoning his "Child's Dream" [72] in March 1861, Rogers did nothing for a month toward fulfilling Hattie Appleton's commission for a small marble statue. On April 13, however, he reported that he had a new design in mind, "a female figure — very simple & telling," about which he felt "in high feather." He did not begin the actual modelling until after his move into his new studio on April 29. He thus described what he had in mind, on May 5:

> "Air Castles" is the title I proposed for it & the design is a country girl who has gone to a spring for water & becomes absorbed in thought, building air castles. She is leaning against a rock from the cleft in which is the spring. Her pail is standing under it & the water has filled the pail & is running over which shows she has forgotten herself. She is playing thoughtlessly with her curls with one hand & with the other holds the end of her shawl which has dropped from her shoulders. . . . She will have a pleased expression & as it is a single figure, simple & tells the story I flatter myself it is a good design.

In spite of his initial enthusiasm, Rogers found it difficult to keep up his interest in "Jemima" as he sometimes called her. "It's not my style," he wrote on May 18, "and don't interest me much." By June 29, however, he had "finished up Jemima roughly & covered her up for the present. I found I was getting tired of her," he explained, "& was afraid I might spoil her by finishing her in a hurry."

In late July, after a visit home, Rogers returned to "Air Castles" with revived interest and made a number of changes, including altering the "whole arrangement of her drapery." During his visit in Roxbury he had made casts [214, 215] of his twin sisters, Fannie and Bessie, then sixteen years old, which casts, he said, were of great assistance "to me & Jemima who shows her gratitude in her improved looks." "She has got real country girl's feet, if they *are* Bessie's," he wrote in another letter. Rogers completed the clay model in mid-August and cast it in plaster by the 25th. He was cautious in his estimate of the result: "I think the design & general effect will be liked, but the detail will be criticized by the knowing ones." Before having the figure put into marble, Rogers sought advice from artist friends and relatives in New York and Boston. For this purpose he had a photograph taken.

From late September to late November 1861 "Air Castles" was in the hands of a stone cutter. Rogers then undertook to finish the marble himself but gave up in despair after two weeks, handing the job over to a man with experience. "It would ruin me," he complained on December 8, "to go into such a state of mind over another large statue as I have got into over Air Castles. . . . I hope it is the last piece of marble I shall ever see in my studio." "I am very glad it is out of my hands," he added a month later. "I should certainly have spoilt it with my impatient way of going to work on it." The man who did the work for Rogers was a former student of the American sculptor Henry Kirke Brown, but Rogers never mentioned his name.

On March 1 Rogers reported that, at long last, the marble, almost finished, was back in his studio.

> I have been kept in a world of worry ever since the marble was commenced on to make the man keep at work. He does the work by contract & seems every once in a while to get tired of it & lets it drag. He worked steadily on it for several days when he first brought it to my

> studio & then was off several days till at last I got out of all patience & sent him a note which had a good effect & for several days past he has done well. He is a good workman but under the circumstances I am quite at his mercy. . . . I begin to feel a little better satisfied than I did with it now that it is being finished up. It will make quite a decent thing after all.

In the end the temperamental marble cutter let the sculptor down and Rogers worked night and day putting the final touches to the work in order to have it ready for the last Artists Reception in the Dodworth Building, March 13, 1862. "The reception was a success," he announced on the 15th. "I had Jemima put in position with drapery behind her & I think she did me credit. She certainly looked well & seemed to be admired." "It is a different style from my other works," he added in a later letter, "& visitors seem to be more attracted by the originality of my smaller works than the simplicity requisite for marble." Hattie Appleton, his cousin-patroness, saw the figure soon after and gave the artist her permission to enter it in the National Academy's spring exhibition. Rogers was a bit nettled to find, after all his trouble with the marble, that "Air Castles" was less noticed than "The Town Pump" [89].

"Air Castles" was finally sent off to Miss Appleton on July 3, 1862, almost eighteen months after it had been commissioned. Hattie expressed "entire satisfaction," however, and proudly displayed it in her home for the next sixty years. During most of that time it stood on a marble-top table between the dining room windows of No. 28 Mt. Vernon Street, Boston, Hattie's home after she married Greeley Stevenson Curtis. After her death in 1923, the statue was presented to the Society for the Preservation of New England Antiquities as an unsigned work of William Wetmore Story. It was only after the publication of an 1861 photograph in Mr. and Mrs. Chetwood Smith's *Rogers Groups: Thought and Wrought by John Rogers* (1934) that the Society realized it owned a "lost" work of John Rogers, his only work in marble. The original clay or plaster model of "Air Castles" was still in Rogers' studio in February 1867 but has apparently not survived.

81. PORTRAIT BUST OF AN UNIDENTIFIED WOMAN

Clay
Unlocated

Early in May 1861 Rogers' interest in doing likenesses revived. "As there is scarcely anyone in the city who does it," he wrote on May 5, "I will stand a first rate chance if I once get started. I think I should succeed without any trouble now." He apparently went right to work, for on May 18 he reported to his mother: "I have worked on the bust I told you of [probably in a letter of May 12, now lost] & improved it some but I could not afford to hire a sitter any longer so I let her go. I shall continue to practice when I have a chance." Since this was a practice piece, it may well have been destroyed at the time.

82. WINFIELD SCOTT (1786–1866)

Uncompleted design for a statuette

On May 25, 1861, Rogers told his mother that he wanted to make a statuette of General Winfield Scott, then in command of the Union Army. "It would certainly take now & for some time to come," he wrote, "for he is to be the hero of the war. I hardly know how to place him or what material to get to work from — but I shall look round next week & see." In a postscript the following day, he asked Mrs. Rogers not to mention this to anyone, "for it is very probable I shall not go on with it, as these private adventures are expensive & risky." He did, however, set up "a rough design" of General Scott early in June, only to abandon it in a few days, explaining on June 8 that it was too difficult to get a perfect likeness with the material he could find to work from, presumably photographs and newspaper cuts.

83. THE PICKET GUARD

Plaster, painted, dipped in steerine, or unfinished; height 14½ inches
Signed JOHN ROGERS/NEW YORK
Patented April 1, 1862
Price: $5.00 (1861); $6.00 (1866); $10.00 (1871–82)
Collections:
Type A: 3, 5, 6, 8, 9
Type B: 1, 2, 5, 9

"The Picket Guard" was begun in the latter part of June and cast by July 14, 1861, while Rogers was temporarily out of sorts with his ambitious "Air Castles" [80]. Although he thought the group looked "bully," Rogers was in no hurry to have additional casts made, past experience having convinced him that the cost would outrun

sales. Very soon after they did go on sale in New York and Boston in August they were attracting notice by their "timely appearance and great cleverness in execution and design" (C. K. Tuckerman in the *Commercial Advertiser*, October 1861). Almost by accident Rogers had found just the right vein for the times, a topical subject inspired by the war, blending drama with homely humor. Sales rose steadily until winter, when Rogers found himself making a profit for the first time. Despite serious later setbacks, largely owing to his reluctance to devote himself exclusively to "small work," Rogers' popular success stemmed from the unforeseen appeal of this group.

Two versions of this group are known, both bearing the same signature and patent date. The differences are as follows:

Type A: The earlier version is distinguished by the following features: a veil hangs from the back of the Zouave officer's cap, the officer's mustache is parted and the tips curled, the private on the viewer's left is clean-shaven.

Type B: The officer's cap has no veil, his mustache is not parted and the tips not curled, and the private on the left has a goatee.

A drawing of Type A accompanied Rogers' patent application. Photographs of Type A were published in 1863, 1865, and 1868, and photographs of Type B in 1867–68. Rogers' 1866 catalogue illustrated Type B. Although the evidence is inconclusive, it seems likely that Type B replaced Type A about 1865–66.

84. JOHN ROGERS (1800–1884), father of the sculptor

Portrait bust, plaster; half life-size
Presumed destroyed

Using as his model the life mask he had made at Roxbury in July 1861 [211], young John modelled a bust of his father during September of the same year. Family friends in New York thought the likeness excellent. The costume worried the sculptor somewhat. Although his own inclination was to use modern rather than classical dress, he felt it advisable to secure family consent to this innovation. "I want some advice as to the proper drapery or dress," he wrote his mother. "I never agreed wholly in the way of making busts, with bare necks and drapery over the shoulders. Father has always worn the same kind of collar and it seems as much a part of him as his whiskers. Then why should his bust not be made so. That is the way I have it now with a little drapery over the shoulders to relieve them. Nobody would know him with a bare neck like a Roman gladiator for nobody ever sees him so. It seems to me this is common sense — how does it strike you. . . . Please drop me a line and let me know the united wisdom in family council assembled." The family's judgment is not recorded, but Rogers finished the bust, made one plaster cast, and sent it home for criticism early in October. "If there is anything that you can point out to me distinctly so that I can improve it," he told his mother, "please do so & when you are satisfied let me know how many copies to cast. I want to give one to Uncle Henry [Henry Bromfield Rogers, the subject's brother], Aunt Hannah [Mrs. William Powell Mason, his sister] & Daniel [Daniel Denison Slade, his nephew] & whoever else you may say. . . ." Nothing more came of it, however, for the subject himself "put an injunction on his bust," much to the artist's discomfiture. It is presumed that no casts were made and that the original was destroyed.

85. SARAH ELLEN DERBY ROGERS (1805–1877)

Portrait bust, clay
Not completed

Having failed in his first attempt to model a portrait of his mother in the 1850s [51], Rogers approached the second with trepidation. He spoke of it in May 1861 but did not begin the modelling until September, after securing a cast of Mrs. Rogers' face [212]. The cast was not entirely satisfactory, however, and the sculptor decided to postpone further work on the bust until he could get his mother to sit for him. A year passed before he tried again [96].

86. THE FLIGHT OF THE OCTOROON

Uncompleted design in clay for a life-size marble statue; destroyed

As soon as "Air Castles" [80] was ready to turn over to the marble cutter, Rogers forgot the agony it had caused him and enthusiastically launched into an even more ambitious project, which he wanted to be for him, he said, "what the Greek Slave was to [Hiram] Powers." "I want to make a careful study of it first on a small scale & eventually to make it life size. It is full of spirit, character & sentiment & suits me exactly so far," he wrote on September 21, 1861. "I want to be a year about it & shall stake my reputation on the result." By mid-October Rogers had the clay model well along and felt confident enough to reveal its name — "The Flight of the Octoroon" — and describe it to his mother:

> It represents a mother with her child in her arms who is just checking her flight to listen for pursuit. It will be very lightly draped which will give me a good opportunity for modeling form & with the great interest which slavery is exciting & the amount of expression & spirit I can put into the figure I feel every confidence in its success. You know an octoroon can have perfectly classical features & the only distinguishing mark will be a very pretty waviness to the hair.

Although Rogers could claim his design to be original, it obviously owed something to *Uncle Tom's Cabin* and its title, at least, to Dion Boucicault's popular play, *The Octoroon,* then showing in New York.

Time-consuming troubles with the marble of "Air Castles" and the unexpected spurt in plaster sales after the appearance of "The Picket Guard" [83] left Rogers little time for work on "The Octoroon." By mid-November he was wondering whether he "was wise in commencing so large & difficult a work" and thought that other commissions might induce him to put it aside altogether. A few weeks later he decided to destroy the uncompleted model. "I have got into such a nervous impatient state over my Air Castles," he explained, "that I fear I should get in the same state with any large figure which takes a long time to finish, so that I feel convinced that my temperament is not suited for such works." The Octoroon's obituary appeared in the artist's letter of December 10, 1861, to his sister Ellen: ". . . the poor thing died the other day."

87. CAMP LIFE: THE CARD PLAYERS

Plaster, painted; height probably about 12 inches
Signed JOHN ROGERS/NEW YORK
Patented April 15, 1862
Price: not known
Collections: 15; three in parian are also reported

"I have commenced a little group of soldiers playing cards," Rogers wrote on December 14, 1861, "which will be the best comic thing I have ever done." The clay model was finished by December 28 and cast the following week. He sold the original clay model, a profitable change from his usual practice of using the original for casting until it wore out. Unfortunately, "Camp Life" proved difficult to cast. In February he reported that he had made four lots, "each time thinking they would come out well & all have proved bad." Although he hoped for better luck with a fifth lot, then in the works, Rogers did not mention this group again in his letters. He must have got some successful casts, however, since he patented it in April 1862 and had examples on sale at Schaus & Goupil's in New York in June 1862 and in Boston and Chicago stores as late as 1865–66. It was also included in the sets of photographs and stereographs of Rogers' groups published between 1863 and 1868. It was not listed in the first Rogers catalogue in 1866. One copy in plaster has been located. Three copies in parian have been reported (one in a private collection, the others at the Albany Institute, Albany, N.Y., and the Harold Warp Pioneer Village, Minden, Nebraska). Since there is no contemporary evidence that Rogers issued any of his groups in parian, this writer believes that the parian Rogers Groups were unauthorized productions by English or French manufacturers who made their molds on Rogers' plaster groups. See Appendix II, Section C for a discussion of the parian problem.

88. THE CAMP FIRE: MAKING FRIENDS WITH THE COOK

Plaster, painted; height 12 inches
Signed JOHN ROGERS/NEW YORK
Patented May 27, 1862
Price: $5.00 (1862); $6.00 (1866)
Collections:
Plaster: 1, 3, 5, 9
Clay: Mr. Mills, Brooklyn, 1862; not located

Even before "Camp Life: The Card Players" [87] was out of the molds, Rogers set to work on a new military design, a scene around a camp fire, which he modelled with more care and made "more picturesque" than any of its predecessors. Begun about the middle of January 1862, "The Camp Fire" was finished in time to be displayed in Rogers' studio during the February 13 Artists Reception at the Dodworth Building. The clay original was sold to a Mr. Mills of Brooklyn. Plaster casts were in the stores by March 9 and "took pretty well." The group was among those withdrawn about 1868.

89. THE TOWN PUMP

Plaster, painted; height 13 inches
Signed JOHN ROGERS/NEW YORK
Patented May 27, 1862
Price: $5.00 (1862); $6.00 (1866); $10.00 (1871–78)
Collections:
Type A: 3, 5, 6
Type B: 1, 4, 5, 9
Clay: Rev. Octavius B. Frothingham, New York, 1862; unlocated

In March 1862 Rogers produced an up-dated version of a group which had won him praise in Chicago in 1859. The first "Town Pump" [57] had represented a pair of rustic sweethearts with a horse and dog. The 1862 version has no animals and the farmer boy has turned into a soldier on his way to camp. Rogers turned this out rather hastily for entry, along with "Air Castles" [80], in the spring exhibition of the National Academy of Design, opening early in April. The *New York Times* reported that "The Town Pump" was "one of the most admired works of art in the exhibition" and Rogers ruefully observed that it received much more notice than his more ambitious marble statue. Casts of "The Town Pump" went on sale in New York, Boston, Albany and Providence in May 1862. The clay original was bought in December 1862 by the Sunday School of the Third Unitarian Church, New York, for presentation to the pastor, Octavius Brooks Frothingham (1822–95). Rogers later visited Frothingham and found the group "placed quite conspicuously in his parlor."

"The Town Pump" is known to have been issued in two slightly different versions:

Type A: The soldier's canteen hangs directly below his hand and cup. This type appears in Rogers' patent application and in an album photograph by Stadtfeld, 1863.

Type B: The canteen hangs at the soldier's right hip. There are also small differences in the soldier's left hand and the wrinkles in his uniform. This type appears in the 1866 catalogue and in Smith, *Rogers Groups: Thought and Wrought by John Rogers* (Boston, 1934), p. 64.

This group was referred to in the *Springfield Republican* in January 1863 as "En Route for the War" (separately listed in Smith, *Rogers Groups,* p. 115).

90. SHARP SHOOTERS

Plaster, painted; height 12 inches
Signed JOHN ROGERS/NEW YORK
Not patented
Price: not recorded
Collections: 3, 5, 9

"Two of the 'dead-shots' are skulking behind a stone wall; one hoisting a figure, made up of a stuffed coat and cap, just above the wall, while his companion, with rifle in rest, 'draws a sure bead' upon the unlucky wight away yonder who may happen to show his head while aiming at the dummy target" (*Boston Post,* May 24, 1862). The exploits of Berdan's famous regiment of "sharp shooters" furnished the theme for Rogers' fifth military group, produced in May 1862. Mentioned only once in the artist's letters and only a few times in contemporary newspapers, this offbeat work probably sold poorly because of the rather gruesome scene it depicted. Although it was included in most of the album photograph and stereograph series published between 1863 and 1870, "Sharp Shooters" was not patented by Rogers and it was withdrawn from sale even before the first catalogue of Rogers' Groups appeared in 1866. Only three copies are located.

91. PORTRAIT BUSTS AND STATUETTES

Plaster; six inches to a foot high
Unidentified and unlocated

During the summer of 1862 the plaster business was so poor that Rogers turned to portraiture in the hope of a more immediate source of income. In July he began to take likenesses for practice, but failed to mention the names of his subjects.

In September and October he resumed portrait work, reporting that he was "at work on heads mostly of friends" and that he had made "several quite successful little busts." Among the portraits he is known to have done at this time are those of Barry Gray [92], Henry T. Tuckerman [93], Mrs. Holyoke [95], George Welles [94], and Sarah Ellen Derby Rogers [96]. Other sitters are not identified.

That Rogers intended to specialize in portraiture at this time is evident from the notices he planted in the New York *Evening Post* and *Commercial Advertiser* in October 1862. According to these notices he was prepared to produce at a "trifling" cost, in as many plaster copies as desired, full length, standing or seated statuettes about a foot high or busts about half that size. This venture did not prove particularly lucrative, however, and Rogers was soon at work on his "groups" once again. He did occasionally do busts and statuettes thereafter [see 100, 104, 115, etc.].

92. BARRY GRAY

Portrait bust in plaster; about six inches high
Unlocated

On September 6, 1862, Rogers wrote home that he had been "quite successful in making a little bust" of his friend Barry Gray of the *Home Journal.* "Barry Gray" was the pen-name of Robert Barry Coffin (1826–?), an associate editor of the *Home Journal* and author of several popular volumes of light essays, including *Castles in the Air.* He had first visited Rogers' studio in December 1861 and had since published a number of very laudatory notices of Rogers' works in the *Home Journal.* His support at this critical stage of the artist's career was an important factor in determining the direction Rogers was to take.

93. HENRY T. TUCKERMAN

Portrait statuette in plaster, full-length standing or sitting; about 12 inches high
Unlocated

Among the writers who publicized John Rogers in the early days of his career one of the most complimentary was Henry T. Tuckerman (1813–1871), prominent critic, poet, essayist, biographer, and travel writer. Rogers returned the compliment in September 1862 by doing a portrait statuette of Tuckerman which was praised in the *New York Leader* for its "naturalness and ease of pose." Tuckerman later singled Rogers out for high praise in his *Book of the Artists,* a comprehensive survey of American art published in 1867.

94. GEORGE D. WELLES (1843–1923)

Portrait statuette, standing or seated, in plaster; about 12 inches high
Unlocated

In October 1862 John Rogers' uncle, the Hon. Robert C. Winthrop, ordered "two groups of George Wells [sic]." The subject was Mrs. Winthrop's son by her first husband, Arnold F. Welles of Boston. Mrs. Winthrop, born Laura Derby, was a younger sister of Sarah Ellen Derby Rogers, the sculptor's mother. George D. Welles was graduated from Harvard College in 1866.

95. MRS. GEORGE O. HOLYOKE

Portrait bust, clay or plaster
Unlocated

On October 5, 1862, Rogers wrote: "This week Mrs. Holyoke is going to sit. I hope to be successful as it is my first attempt at a female head." A surviving life mask [216] made by Rogers identifies the subject of this bust as Mrs. George Osgood Holyoke. Her husband, a tobacco merchant in New York City, was the partner of Henry B. Rogers, the sculptor's younger brother.

96. SARAH ELLEN DERBY ROGERS (1805–1877)

Portrait bust in plaster, painted; height 11¼ inches

Unsigned

Collection of The New-York Historical Society, presented in 1955 by Miss Katherine R. Rogers

After two unsuccessful attempts to model a likeness of his mother [51 and 85], Rogers finally completed a portrait bust in the fall of 1862. On September 27 he urged her to come to New York so that he could try once more, now that he had had some experience. "It is my only chance to take it when you are here," he wrote, "for it is useless to attempt it when I go to Roxbury." Mr. and Mrs. Rogers did come to New York in October 1862 and it is assumed that the artist carried out his plan at that time, although subsequent letters contain no reference to the bust. The bust itself remained in the possession of the Rogers family until given to The New-York Historical Society.

97. HAMLET

Plaster, painted; height and signature not known

Price: $10.00

No copies located

Early in November 1862 Rogers began a statuette of the famous actor Edwin Booth (1833–93) as Hamlet, one of his most successful roles. The scene chosen was the dramatic moment in Act One when Hamlet cries out to the ghost of his murdered father: "On, on, I'll follow thee." Booth took a very active interest in the work, selecting the scene to be illustrated, lending Rogers his costume, permitting a cast to be made of his face [217], and giving at least one sitting. On November 30 Rogers reported to his mother that he hoped to finish the clay model that week. "There has been an immense amount of work on it owing to the amount of drapery," he explained. "It is not going to be much of a success," he added; "in trying for the expression I have not secured a very strong likeness." Two weeks later the model was completed and casts were ready just before Christmas. "They are a good deal of trouble to cast & a work of rather more pretension than my groups," Rogers wrote, explaining why he had decided to price them at $10.00 instead of his usual $5.00. "I don't expect to sell many of them," he admitted, "but, under the circumstances, I prefer to sell fewer & make more." Three days after Christmas Rogers reported that he had sold two copies but had not yet placed any in the stores because of casting difficulties which had necessitated the making of new molds. He did send some to Boston in January, only to have them broken in transit. "It is a bad figure to pack safely," he complained. All in all, "Hamlet" had proved more trouble than it was worth and Rogers made no further efforts to push it. How many copies were sold, beyond the first two, is not known. The only later reference to this work was in the *Christian Register,* Boston, 1869, where it was noted that Rogers had shown in his "Council of War" [112], "as well as in the statuette of Booth," that he could catch the expression of the living face.

98. UNION REFUGEES

Spelter (zinc bronze) or painted plaster; height 22½ inches
Signed JOHN ROGERS/NEW YORK
Patented April 19, 1864
Price: spelter, $60.00; plaster, $15.00 (1863–78), $10.00 (1882), $8.00 (1888–95)
Collections:
Spelter (Type A) : 9, 13
Plaster (Type B) : 1, 9
(Type C) : 2, 3, 5, 9
Bronze master model (Type A) : Museum of the City of New York, gift of Mr. and Mrs. Francis Rogers

An unexpected New Year's gift of five hundred dollars from his uncle Henry Bromfield Rogers enabled John Rogers to carry out in 1863 an experiment in casting his works in bronze, a more fashionable and durable material than plaster. "Union Refugees" was designed with this in mind. The artist made the model half again as large as his previous groups and modelled it with considerably more care. Although unfinished, the clay was shown at an Artists Reception in mid-January and made "a decided hit." The master cast was ready by March 1, but the first metal casts were not completed until late July, when two were put on exhibition to attract subscriptions. In order to keep the cost down, Rogers decided to have the casts made of spelter (zinc bronze) rather than real bronze. The master model, however, was cast in real bronze. On August 15 he was able to report that he had received sixty dol-

lars for the first "bronze" delivered, his profit being twenty dollars. Although he sold others, there is no record of how many.

By the end of August 1863 Rogers had decided to go back to plaster after all and save the trouble and expense of metal casting. "I assure you," he told his mother, "it is a weight off my mind & in spite of all the trouble I have had with plaster, I feel as I should on coming home from a long tiresome journey." Using the bronze master model already on hand, he turned out plaster copies of "Union Refugees" for sale at fifteen dollars. These proved very popular. The group was listed in Rogers' catalogues until 1888 and it reappeared in the 1894 and 1895 catalogues of the successor Rogers Statuette Company. The parian version, of which one copy is known, is probably of trans-Atlantic origin. See the section on parians in Appendix II. "Union Refugees" is known in at least three slightly varying states, to be distinguished as follows:

Type A:
The wife's sleeve is half-length; her shoes are cut low, exposing the ankle; her shawl is not fringed; the husband's hand grips the gun stock at its narrowest point; the exposed end of the sash across his chest barely shows; the wrinkles in his trousers at the boot tops rise diagonally toward the knee.

Type B:
Same as Type A, except that the wrinkles in the man's right trousers leg are horizontal.

Type C:
The wife's sleeve is full length, her shawl fringed, and her shoes cover her ankles; the man grips his gun stock near the butt; the sash has a prominent overlapping end; and his trousers wrinkles are horizontal, though not identical to those in Type B.

Type A is certainly the original version, since the spelter copies and the photographs published in 1863–65 are all of this type. Type B appears in a photograph published in 1868. Type C appears in all Rogers' catalogues, 1866–95 and in the *American Historical Record*, 1872.

99. COUNTRY POSTOFFICE / NEWS FROM THE ARMY

Plaster, painted; height 20 inches
Signed JOHN ROGERS/NEW YORK
Patented April 19, 1864
Price: $15.00 (1863–76); $12.00 (1882); $10.00 (1888)
Collections:
Type A: 1, 2, 3, 4, 5, 9
Type B: 10
Bronze master model (type A): The New-York Historical Society, purchased in 1936 from Katherine R. Rogers

Rogers began this group about April 1, 1863, intending to cast it, like "Union Refugees" [98], in spelter (zinc bronze). The first cast was ready toward the end of May, but Rogers delayed casting more until he had seen how "Union Refugees" went. In August, having decided against further casting in metal, he made an improved model of "Country Postoffice" and cast it in plaster. The plaster casts went on sale at the end of September 1863 and were immediately successful. Rogers presented one to William Cullen Bryant on Christmas Eve.

Two varieties have been identified, varying in several small particulars. The most readily distinguishable difference is in the girl's costume.

Type A: The girl's forearm is sleeved to the wrist.

Type B: The girl's forearm is bare.

Type A seems to be the original version, since it appears on Rogers' patent application, as well as in his 1866 catalogue, in a stereograph of about 1875, and in Smith, *Rogers Groups,* p. 68. Type B is known from a photograph by Stadtfeld, 1864, and one surviving copy.

100. PORTRAIT BUST

On June 11, 1863, Rogers wrote to his sister that he had been working all day on a little bust, trying to take it from a photograph, and that he found the effort tiring. The subject is unidentified and the bust unlocated.

101. MAIL DAY

Plaster, painted; height 16 inches
Signed JOHN ROGERS/NEW YORK
Patented April 19, 1864
Price: $10.00
Collections: 1, 2, 3, 5, 6, 9

After "Union Refugees" [98] and "Country Post-office" [99] Rogers was briefly stumped for ideas. "Mail Day" was a logical companion piece to "Country Postoffice" but the artist was almost apologetic about it. "I am now at work on a single figure, which does not amount to much," he wrote on September 5, 1863, "till I can think of something more satisfactory." Although he did not mention it again, "Mail Day" went on sale before Christmas 1863 and retained a place in Rogers' stock until 1882. As late as 1893 it was described by an art critic (Charles de Kay of the *New York Times*) as the best of Rogers' Civil War pieces, praiseworthy for its humor, good composition, and good modelling. "Mail Day" also was used as a "prop" in J. G. Brown's 1867 painting, "The Young Artist," illustrated in *Antiques,* May 1955, p. 387. There is no record of a bronze master model for this figure.

102. RETURNED VOLUNTEER: HOW THE FORT WAS TAKEN

Plaster, painted; height 20 inches.
Signed JOHN ROGERS/NEW YORK
Patented May 17, 1864
Price: $15.00; $12.00 (1882); withdrawn after 1888 but again listed in 1895 by the Rogers Statuette Company.
Collections:
Type A: 2, 3, 7, 8, 9
Type B: 1, 5, 6
Bronze master model (Type A): The New-York Historical Society, purchased in 1936 from Katherine R. Rogers

On September 27, 1863, Rogers reported that he had set up a new group which he thought would prove the most popular he had yet done. He worked on it with deliberate care in order to make it as perfect as possible. Although still unfinished, it was exhibited at the Artists Reception in mid-January 1864. The first casts went on sale the last week of February.

The two slightly variant versions are distinguished as follows:

Type A:

The head of the blacksmith's hammer is turned half to the viewer's right and the blacksmith's shoe half to the viewer's left;

Type B:

The hammer head and shoe are seen head-on.

Type A appears in Rogers' patent application, in the 1864 Stadtfeld photograph, the bronze master model, and a stereograph of about 1875. Type B is illustrated in Smith, *Rogers Groups,* p. 68.

103. THE WOUNDED SCOUT / A FRIEND IN THE SWAMP

Plaster, painted; height 23 inches
Signed JOHN ROGERS/NEW YORK
Patented June 28, 1864
Price: $15.00; $10.00 (1882); withdrawn after 1888
Collections: 1, 2, 3, 5, 6, 7, 8, 9
Bronze master model: The New-York Historical Society, purchased in 1936 from Katherine R. Rogers

"My new group, which I showed in its rough state," Rogers wrote on February 28, 1864, "brought out great praise from all the strong thinkers who pronounced it far ahead in its meaning of anything I had attempted. It represents an escaped slave leading off & protecting a wounded soldier." One of those who admired this group at its first showing was Jessie Benton Frémont, wife of General John C. Frémont, soldier-explorer and first Republican candidate for the presidency (1856). Rogers himself sent a copy of this group as a gift to President Abraham Lincoln. The President's letter of acknowledgment, June 13, 1864, has survived among the artist's papers. "I can not pretend to be a judge in such matters," the President wrote; "but the Statuette group 'Wounded Scout'— 'Friend in the Swamp' which you did me the honor to present, is very pretty

and suggestive, and, I should think, excellent as a piece of art. Thank you for it." Rogers' gift of another copy of the same work to the Rev. Henry Ward Beecher in January 1865 prompted a letter (also among the artist's papers) praising him in the highest terms, particularly for "the moral element" in his work. Still another prominent figure of the day, the abolitionist poetess Lydia Maria Childs, was tremendously moved by "The Wounded Scout." "There is more in that expressive group," she wrote in *The Independent* in December 1865, "than the kind negro and the helpless white, put on an equality by danger and suffering; it is a significant lesson of human brotherhood for all the coming ages."

This group was also produced in parian, probably in England or France without Rogers' permission. See the section on parians, Appendix II, Section C.

104. TILESTON STATUETTE
Unlocated

On May 29, 1864, Rogers wrote to his mother that he had about completed "the Tileston statuette" and expected to cast it that week. The following week he expected the Tilestons in to see it before sailing for Europe. A month later he informed his mother that he had received a note from Mrs. Hemenway expressing entire satisfaction with "the statuette." The subject of the statuette was probably the noted New York banker and merchant Thomas Tileston (1793–1864), president of the Phoenix Bank, who had died in February 1864. Mrs. Hemenway was certainly Mrs. Augustus Hemenway of Boston, Thomas Tileston's eldest daughter.

105. WOUNDED TO THE REAR / ONE MORE SHOT

Plaster, painted; height 23½ inches
Signed JOHN ROGERS/NEW YORK
Patented January 17, 1865
Price $15.00; $12.00 (1882); $10.00 (1888)
Collections:
Plaster: 1, 2, 3, 5, 6, 7, 8, 9
Bronze: one copy recorded, given to ex-Governor Buckingham of Connecticut in 1866, not now located
Bronze master model: Metropolitan Museum of Art, New York, purchased in 1917 from the Rogers family

Begun in September 1864, "One More Shot" (as it usually is called) went on sale in November and immediately established itself as one of Rogers' most popular works. Unlike most of the war groups, it remained in stock to the very end of the artist's career. It was particularly favored as a gift for veterans. A copy in bronze, costing $150.00, was presented to the wartime Governor of Connecticut by his friends in 1866. Messrs. Hovey & Nicholas of Chicago in 1868 gave a plaster copy to General Joseph R. Hawley, president of the Republican National Convention which nominated Grant for the Presidency. Rogers himself gave a copy in 1879 to the Veteran Zouaves of Elizabeth, New Jersey, and in October of the same year, fourteen years after the end of the Civil War, "One More Shot" was given Sergeant G. B. True and his bride by the Manchester (N.H.) Cadets. "Nothing relating to the war in painting or sculpture surpasses 'One Shot More'," General Hawley is reported to have said.

There is a tradition, recorded in L. Ashton Thorp, *Manchester of Yesterday* (Manchester, N.H., 1939), p. 262, that Rogers used as a model for one of the figures his old friend Charles Lowell Richardson, paymaster of the Amoskeag Corporation from 1855 to 1899. Another tradition, recorded in Smith, *Rogers Groups: Thought and Wrought by John Rogers* (Boston, 1934), p. 70, states that a neighbor posed for the standing soldier, wearing his old uniform.

The parian versions of this group, standing 19 inches high on an 8-inch base, are believed to be of English or French origin. See the section on parians in Appendix II.

106. THE HOME GUARD / MIDNIGHT ON THE BORDER

Plaster, painted; height 23 inches
Signed JOHN ROGERS/NEW YORK
Patented May 9, 1865
Price: \$15.00; \$10.00 (1877)
Collections: 1, 2, 3, 4, 5, 6, 9

Rogers was working on this group in November 1864 but was interrupted by his own sickness and his brother Henry's wedding in January. The first casts were ready by March 10, 1865. Although a Boston journalist described it as "almost startling in its strength," the group was not a success, Rogers himself describing it as "not very satisfactory." It remained in his catalogue until 1882. There is no record of a bronze master model.

107. THE BUSHWHACKER / THE WIFE'S APPEAL FOR PEACE

Plaster, painted; height 22½ inches
Signed JOHN ROGERS/NEW YORK
Patented October 10, 1865
Price: \$15.00
Collections: 1, 5, 9

Rogers began this group in February 1865 and completed it rather hurriedly just before his wedding in April. Although he had at first considered it one of his best designs, he later admitted that it, along with "The Home Guard," was "not very satisfactory." Although the group was certainly not one of Rogers' best in point of composition, its failure probably is attributable to a poor choice of subject. The "bushwhacker" was a Confederate guerilla in the Border States and Northern patriots possibly found Rogers' attempt to humanize his activities distasteful. "The Bushwhacker" was listed in the 1866 catalogue, but was apparently withdrawn before 1871. There is no record of a bronze master model. Only four copies of the plaster are known to exist.

108. TAKING THE OATH / AND / DRAWING RATIONS

Plaster, painted; height 23 inches; also bronze
Signed JOHN ROGERS/NEW YORK
Patented January 30, 1866
Price: $15.00 (1866); $20.00 (1871–76); $15.00 (1877–95)
Collections:
Plaster: 1, 2, 3, 4, 5, 6, 7, 8, 9
Bronze: Unlocated
Bronze master model: The New-York Historical Society, purchased in 1936 from Katherine R. Rogers

The most admired of all his works, "Taking the Oath" was the first group John Rogers designed after his marriage in 1865 to Harriet Moore Francis. It was inspired by an actual incident in Charleston described to the artist by his wife's uncle David Francis. Seeing in it "a chance to make a magnificent woman — something of the style of Marie Antoinette in the trial scene," he sketched it out excitedly in September 1865 and had it ready in time for the Christmas season. "All who have seen it," he wrote in November, "think it the best I have done, and I think so myself." Rogers sold over three hundred casts that Christmas, even before the bronze master model was cast. "Taking the Oath" retained its popularity long after the war and was still listed in the catalogues of the Rogers Statuette Company in 1894 and 1895.

Apparently Rogers had some bronze casts made of "Taking the Oath," for on February 11, 1866, he reported that the bronzes were progressing slowly but well, but that he did not expect to do any business in bronze thereafter beyond making his master model in bronze. A bronze sold in 1961 by Kennedy Galleries, New York, may be one of these 1866 castings.

"Taking the Oath" has also been reported in

parian and in creamware of Staffordshire type. The origin of these is unknown, but there is no evidence that Rogers had anything to do with their manufacture. The parians are discussed in Appendix II, Section C.

109. UNCLE NED'S SCHOOL

Plaster, painted; height 20 inches
Signed JOHN ROGERS/NEW YORK
Patented July 3, 1866
Price: $15.00 (1866–78); $12.00 (1882); $10.00 (1888)
Collections: 1, 2, 3, 5, 6, 7, 9, 15
Bronze master model: The New-York Historical Society, purchased in 1936 from Katherine R. Rogers

Produced between February and April 1866, "Uncle Ned's School" was immediately hailed as a powerful commentary on the freed Negro's determination to educate himself and improve his lot by his own efforts. F.O.C. Darley, the most popular American illustrator of the day, told Rogers that the group had "more character" than anything else he had done. Henry Ward Beecher, to whom Rogers gave a copy, wrote in acknowledgement: "I am pleased with the complete rendering of the story, with a few means, and without exaggeration. Its simplicity is as agreeable as its errand is noble." The group was listed in Rogers' catalogues until 1888.

110. THE CHARITY PATIENT

Plaster, painted; height 22 inches
Signed JOHN ROGERS/NEW YORK
Patented December 4, 1866
Price: $15.00 (1866–76); $12.00 (1882); $10.00 (1888–92); $8.00 (1895)
Collections: 1, 2, 3, 4, 5, 6, 9
Bronze master model: The New-York Historical Society, purchased in 1936 from Katherine R. Rogers

This sensitive group was produced during the autumn of 1866. It proved to be one of Rogers' most popular works and was listed in all his catalogues. Its special suitability for doctors' offices was pointed out in the *Canada Lancet* (December 1877) and the *Medical Record* (December 1884). The sculptor William Ordway Partridge wrote of "The Charity Patient" in 1896 that it was "as lovely in modern guise as the simple and beautiful works of Donatello, for it is filled with the sweet feeling of that great master. . . . We must commend Mr. Rogers for his happy treatment here of an unhappy costume. The composition is agreeable, the action natural, the expression well rendered, and the whole is a satisfactory, interesting and beautiful work."

111. THE SCHOOL EXAMINATION

Plaster, painted; height 20 inches
Signed JOHN ROGERS/NEW YORK
Patented July 9, 1867
Price: $15.00 (to 1878); $12.00 (1882–92); $8.00 (1895)
Collections: 1, 2, 3, 5, 6, 8, 9
Bronze master model: sold for Rogers in 1897 through his bronze-founder, P. E. Guerin; now in a private collection

Rogers was at work on this as early as February 1867. In the words of an unidentified newspaper of the period, "it represents the visit of a good-natured old school committeeman to a district school. The old gentleman is examining a little girl in arithmetic. She looks on her slate with a prettily perplexed air, which is very charmingly rendered. The schoolmistress, very pretty and very young, looks on, anxious for the credit of her little pupil."

112. THE COUNCIL OF WAR

Plaster, painted; height 24 inches
Signed JOHN ROGERS/NEW YORK
Patented March 31, 1868
Price: $25.00 (to 1878); $20.00 (1882–95)
Collections:
Plaster, Type A: 1, 9, 12
Plaster, Type B: 1, 2, 3, 4, 5, 6, 8, 9, 15
Plaster, Type C: 1, 11, 12, 15
Bronze master model, Type A: The New-York Historical Society, purchased in 1936 from Katherine R. Rogers

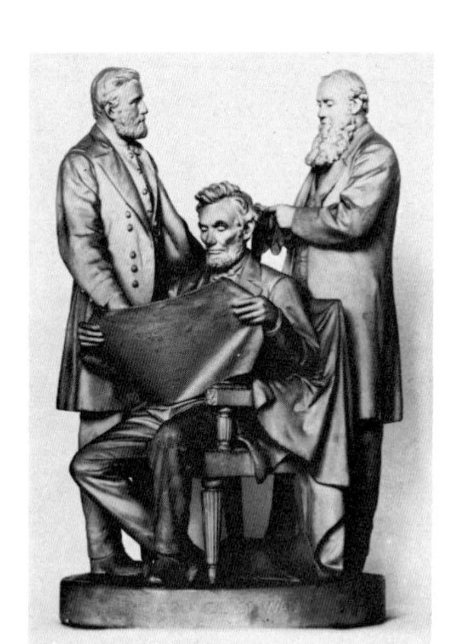

Rogers conceived the idea for this group early in 1867. Its general features were suggested by Secretary of War Edwin M. Stanton, to whom Rogers applied for advice through his wife's cousin, John H. Clifford, of New Bedford, Massachusetts. In a letter to Clifford, May 7, 1867, Stanton thus described one of the most important of Lincoln's councils of war:

> One of the most interesting and appropriate occasions that now occurs to me was the conference at which Lieut. General Grant after returning from his first visit to the Army of the Potomac, laid before the President the plan of operations he proposed to adopt. This was at the War Department, and the group would embrace the three figures of the President, Secretary of War and General Grant. It would require no accessories but a roll or map in the hands of the General.

In his group Rogers followed Stanton's suggestion very closely, varying it only slightly to place the map in the hands of the seated President. The likenesses were done from photographs, which survive in the Rogers papers, and from personal interviews with Stanton and Grant in Washington in June 1867. Rogers may have made a trial bust of Lincoln at this time, for a reporter in 1872 spoke of seeing in Rogers' studio "a life size bust of the good and sad-looking Lincoln" [133].

Patented on March 31, 1868, and put on sale at about the same time, "The Council of War" quickly established itself as a popular memorial of the war. Rogers won high praise for his skill as a portraitist and as a chronicler of the Civil War. The critics noted with special pleasure the sculptor's realistic treatment of Stanton, portrayed in the act of wiping the dust from his spectacles, "a familiar habit with the Secretary when he is thinking hard" (New York *Evening Post,* February 7, 1868).

Even more gratifying to the artist were the comments on his portrait of Lincoln. Secretary Stanton wrote him that "in form and feature" it surpassed "any effort to embody the expression of that great man" that he had seen. Fifty years later, Frank O. Payne, author of *Lincoln in Sculpture,* told the Rogers family that Robert Todd Lincoln had written him "that his family have always regarded John Rogers's group *The Council of War* as the most lifelike portrait of his father in sculpture."

Despite its relatively high price "The Council of War" proved one of Rogers' greatest popular successes. At least sixty copies are extant, divided unequally among three versions.

Type A:

This version shows Stanton wiping his glasses with both hands behind Lincoln's head. This is the original version, since it appears in Rogers' patent application, in the 1868 photograph published by H. Wood, and in the bronze master model. It also appears in Rogers' catalogues for 1872, 1874, 1876, 1878, 1882, and 1888.

Type B:

In this version Stanton is wiping his glasses directly over Lincoln's shoulder. This is the most common of the three types and presumably was stocked the longest. It may date from 1873. In March of that year an up-state New York reporter stated that Rogers was "putting on some finishing touches to a new statuette of Secretary Stanton, from whose son he had just received some later photographs than he had previously possessed." The Stanton photographs found among Rogers papers are mounted on part of an 1872 mail schedule. Type B was illustrated in Rogers' catalogues for 1877,

1890, 1892, and 1894–95, and in the Moulton stereographs published about 1876. No bronze master model has been found.

Type C:

In this version Stanton simply holds his glasses in his left hand and his right arm is dropped casually at his side. There is no evidence by which to date this. It is the rarest of the three types. No bronze master model has been found.

113. COURTSHIP IN SLEEPY HOLLOW / ICHABOD CRANE AND KATRINA VAN TASSEL

Plaster, painted; height 16½ inches
Signed JOHN ROGERS/NEW YORK
Patented August 25, 1868
Price: $15.00 (to 1878); $12.00 (1882); $10.00 (1888)
Collections: 1, 2, 3, 4, 5, 6, 8, 9
Bronze master model: The New-York Historical Society

As early as August 1862 Rogers had thought of making a group based on Washington Irving's "Legend of Sleepy Hollow," but had dismissed the idea because, as he wrote, "Darley seems to have illustrated it so completely that I am afraid I can make nothing very original out of it." By 1868 he had more confidence. "Courtship in Sleepy Hollow," modelled in the spring and patented in August, followed closely Irving's description of the scene without leaning on F.O.C. Darley's popular line drawing, published in 1848. Both the subject and Rogers' skill in presenting it "with accuracy as well as delicacy," ensured the group's success. It was listed until 1888.

This group also exists in parian. The parian at The New-York Historical Society is unsigned, but is inscribed on the back PATENTED AUG. 18, 1868. The origin of the parians is not known; they were probably made in England or France. See the section on parians (Appendix II, Section C).

114. CHALLENGING THE UNION VOTE

Plaster, painted; height 22 inches
Signed JOHN ROGERS/NEW YORK
Patented February 9, 1869
Price: $20.00 (to 1876); $15.00 (1877–82)
Collections: 1, 2, 3, 5, 9

In October 1868 it was reported that John Rogers was working on a group "designed to illustrate the two strongly marked types of southern men — an old Unionist and an ex-Confederate." Perhaps the group was intended to appear about the time of the November presidential election, but it did not go on sale until early in 1869. The subject was not one likely to be of lasting interest, which probably accounts for the disappearance of the group from Rogers' stock after 1882. There is no record of a bronze master model. This group bears an inscription which is found on no other Rogers Group: "The right to photograph this group is not sold with it."

115. SARAH STONE

Portrait bust, plaster or clay; life-size
Destroyed

It is reported in Smith, *Rogers Groups: Thought and Wrought by John Rogers*, p. 116, that in 1868 Rogers made a life-size bust of Sarah Stone, thirteen-year-old daughter of Dr. John Osgood Stone (1813–76). According to Miss Katherine R. Rogers (1955) this was not a successful portrait and was later destroyed. The subject later became Mrs. Morgan Grinnell. In 1931 she gave Miss Rogers a duplicate copy of John Rogers' bust of "John Osgood Stone" [131].

116. THE FUGITIVE'S STORY

Plaster, painted; height 22 inches
Signed JOHN ROGERS/NEW YORK
Patented September 7, 1869
Price: $25.00 (to 1878); $20.00 (1882); $15.00 (1888)
Collections: 1, 2, 3, 4, 5, 6, 9
Bronze master model: The New-York Historical Society, purchased in 1936 from Katherine R. Rogers

Rogers designed this group as a sort of civilian counterpart to "The Council of War" [112], honoring three prominent leaders in the moral crusade against slavery — the poet John Greenleaf Whittier, the editor William Lloyd Garrison, and the preacher Henry Ward Beecher. The fugitive slave mother and child served as an excuse for bringing the three men together and added dramatic interest.

After winning Beecher's enthusiastic approval of the general idea in February 1869, the artist made elaborate preparations before putting it into clay. He interviewed each of his subjects, took detailed measurements, secured several photographs of each, and made life masks of Beecher and Garrison [219, 220]. After modelling the heads, he again visited the three men to check the likenesses. Garrison and Beecher showed more than a passive interest in the project. Beecher, for example, suggested that Rogers show his hand in his vest, because he never buttoned his coat. Rogers chose to ignore the suggestion. Garrison, sensitive about his thinness, had new photographs taken and asked Rogers to destroy an earlier one which he described as an "extraordinary scarecrow likeness . . . which looks as if I had just escaped from Andersonville prison."

Rogers sent the first copies of the completed work to his subjects in October 1869. Garrison pronounced it "a marked success, both in regard to the likenesses and as a work of art," but added a postscript: "All the members of my family concur in the opinion that . . . I am made *too thin in the face*." Whittier reported that the three-year-old child of a cousin cried out "That's Uncle Greenie" when the group was uncovered, but that his friends were disturbed by the absence of whiskers. Beecher's comments have not survived, but the sculptor's daughter reported that, when Mrs. Beecher gave it but faint praise, her husband remarked, "You would have to put a halo around the head to satisfy her."

The public's reaction was enthusiastic. One report told how a famous ex-slave, Sojourner Truth, burst into tears on seeing the group because it reminded her of her own experiences as a fugitive slave. William Cullen Bryant was inspired by this group to write the following to the artist: "You have succeeded in a higher degree than almost any artist of any age in making sculpture a narrative art, and giving to motionless and speechless figures the power to relate their own adventures." The group sold well and remained in stock until the late 'eighties.

The copy pictured in the Smith catalogue (p. 75) and now at the Albany Institute differs in one small detail The bracket on top of the desk is quite plain and concave, not matching the foot bracket, as in all other known copies. This was probably a repair, but the possibility of its being a variant cannot be entirely ruled out.

117. PARTING PROMISE

Plaster, painted; height 22 inches
Signed JOHN ROGERS/NEW YORK
Patented February 8, 1870
Price: $12.00 (to 1878); $10.00 (1882, 1888); $6.00 (1895)
Collections:
Type A: 3, 4, 5, 6, 9
Type B: 1, 2, 3, 4, 5, 9, 10
Bronze master model: none recorded

"Parting Promise" was not one of Rogers' most successful groups, aesthetically or commercially. After being dropped from Rogers' catalogue in the middle of 1888, it reappeared in the 1894 catalogue of the successor company.

There are two easily distinguished versions of this group

Type A: man without mustache.

Type B: man with mustache.

The earlier version, Type A, was pictured in Rogers' patent application, in a Bierstadt stereograph of 1870 and another stereograph of about 1875, as well as in Rogers' 1872, 1874, 1876, 1882, and 1888 catalogues. Type B, although it is the more common of the two, was illustrated only in Rogers' 1877 catalogue and in those of the Rogers Statuary Company, 1894–95. There is no bronze model extant and no record of its sale in 1897, when Rogers sold off some of his master models.

118. THE BATH

Plaster, painted; height 27 inches
Inscribed NEW YORK, but unsigned
Price: $12.00
Collections: 1, 9

This group was listed in the 1894 and 1895 catalogues of the Rogers Statuary Company, successors to Rogers' plaster business, as the "latest statuette from Mr. Rogers' studio." Although the work seems clearly to be from Rogers' hand, his physical condition in 1893 or 1894 almost precludes the possibility that he could have produced it at that time. In fact, the apparent ages of the mother and children in the group strongly suggest that this may have been a work executed by Rogers about 1870, perhaps as a strictly family piece. Its release in 1894 in a plaster version, after Rogers' retirement, was probably a concession to his own need for money or to the successor company's need for a "new" group to freshen its catalogue. The story that it was withdrawn because it was considered "too nude" (Smith, *Rogers Groups,* p. 101) is not supported by contemporary evidence, but might explain why the group was not published when first modelled.

119. JOHN EARL WILLIAMS (1804–1877)

Portrait bust, plaster, painted; life-size
Collections: Society for the Preservation of New England Antiquities, Boston, and Old Dartmouth Historical Society, New Bedford, Massachusetts.

John and Hattie Francis Rogers first met at the home of Mr. and Mrs. John Earl Williams, at Irvington, New York. Mrs. Williams, the former Eunice Burr Thomas, was a cousin of Hattie Francis. Mr. Williams was president of the Metropolitan National Bank of New York. Rogers' bust of Williams was commissioned by the subject early in 1870 and was exhibited at the National Academy in the autumn of the same year. The subject's measurements are noted in the artist's sketchbook.

Two copies of the bust are extant. One was lent by the subject to the Redwood Library,

Newport, Rhode Island, but subsequently was inherited by Williams' nephew, William W. Covell, who presented it to the Society for the Preservation of New England Antiquities. The other copy, discovered in 1913 in the third story of the First National Bank of New Bedford, is now owned by the Old Dartmouth Historical Society. The story of its discovery and identification was told in the New Bedford *Evening Standard*, July 24, 1913.

120. COMING TO THE PARSON

Plaster, painted; height 22 inches
Signed JOHN ROGERS/NEW YORK
Patented August 9, 1870
Price: $15.00
Collections: 1, 2, 3, 4, 5, 6, 7, 8, 9, 15
Bronze master model: The New-York Historical Society, purchased in 1936 from Katherine R. Rogers

The most popular, by far, of Rogers' works, "Coming to the Parson" had an immediate and long-continued success. Total sales in about twenty years, according to Rogers' own statement, amounted to eight thousand copies, approximately one tenth of the artist's entire output. The secret of its success was undoubtedly its appropriateness as a wedding present. The punning title of the newspaper in the minister's hands, *The Union*, was taken from the newspaper Rogers had read as a young mechanic in Manchester, New Hampshire.

121. THE FOUNDLING

Plaster, painted; height 21 inches
Signed JOHN ROGERS/NEW YORK
Patented November 22, 1870
Price: $15.00 (to 1878); $12.00 (1882); $10.00 (1888)
Collections:
Type A: 1, 2, 3, 5, 9
Type B: Private collection
Bronze master model (Type A): Sold for Rogers in 1897 by Guerin; given to The New-York Historical Society in 1961.

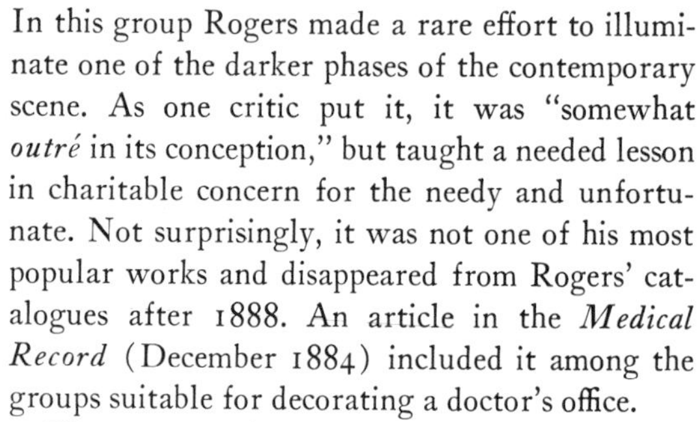

In this group Rogers made a rare effort to illuminate one of the darker phases of the contemporary scene. As one critic put it, it was "somewhat *outré* in its conception," but taught a needed lesson in charitable concern for the needy and unfortunate. Not surprisingly, it was not one of his most popular works and disappeared from Rogers' catalogues after 1888. An article in the *Medical Record* (December 1884) included it among the groups suitable for decorating a doctor's office.

There are two known varieties of this group.

Type A:

Girl's head slightly up, child's head turned toward man. The photograph submitted with Rogers' patent application was of this type.

Type B:

Girl's head slightly down, child's head turned partly toward viewer.

122. RIP VAN WINKLE AT HOME

Plaster, painted; height 18½ inches

Signed JOHN ROGERS/NEW YORK

Patented March 14, 1871

Price: $12.00 (to 1882); $10.00 (1888–95)

Collections: 1, 2, 3, 5, 6, 7, 8, 9, 14

Bronze master model: The New-York Historical Society, purchased in 1936 from Katherine R. Rogers

In December 1870 the New York *Post* reported that John Rogers was modelling a series of three statuettes based on Washington Irving's story "Rip van Winkle." They were shown to his friends the following March and published during the year 1871. The actor Joseph Jefferson, then appearing in his popular dramatization of the Irving story, posed for Rip. Rogers had first seen him in the part in August 1869.

The first statuette of the series showed Rip van Winkle "at home," good-naturedly playing with two village children. In the words of a correspondent of the *Berkshire Courier,* "The easy expression, lazy attitude and ragged costume of the good-natured but vagabond Rip are remarkably perfect, and possess a peculiar interest to those who have witnessed the play, because they were modeled after Joe Jefferson, and his likeness is very striking." William Seymour, a member of Jefferson's company, is said to have posed for the boy (Smith, *Rogers Groups*, p. 77).

123. RIP VAN WINKLE ON THE MOUNTAIN

Plaster, painted; height 21¼ inches
Signed JOHN ROGERS/NEW YORK
Patented July 25, 1871
Price: $12.00 (to 1882); $10.00 (1888–95)
Collections: 1, 2, 3, 5, 6, 9
Bronze master model: The New-York Historical Society, purchased in 1936 from Katherine R. Rogers

The second of the three Rip van Winkle statuettes shows Joseph Jefferson as Rip and William Seymour as the gnome. It was modelled during the spring of 1871. Like the other two in the series it remained in Rogers' stock until the end of his career.

124. RIP VAN WINKLE RETURNED

Plaster, painted; height 21¼ inches
Signed JOHN ROGERS/NEW YORK
Patented July 25, 1871
Price: $12.00 (to 1882); $10.00 (1888–95)
Collections: 1, 2, 3, 5, 6, 7, 8, 9, 14, 15
Bronze master model: The New-York Historical Society, purchased in 1936 from Katherine R. Rogers

This was the last of Rogers' three illustrations of Joseph Jefferson in his most famous role. It was modelled during the spring of 1871. Although Rogers offered the three as a set, they could also be purchased individually. This one is the rarest today.

125. CAMP FIRES OF THE REVOLUTION

Uncompleted design for a large bronze group; presumed destroyed.

After completing the "Rip Van Winkle" series [122–124], Rogers began, during the summer of 1871, an ambitious historical group, half the size of life, intended for reproduction in bronze. Entitled "Camp Fires of the Revolution," it portrayed three famous Revolutionary heroes: Washington, standing with his right hand on the neck of his horse and a spy glass in the other; Lafayette, also standing, with his hand on his sword; and Hamilton, on one knee, with map and compass in hand. The original small clay model was completed in December 1871, but Rogers never completed the full-size model which was glowingly described in the New York *Era* on March 30, 1872. After taking time out to do "We Boys" and "Playing Doctor" [130, 132], he resumed intensive work on "Camp Fires" in September 1872 but seems to have abandoned the project about the end of the year.

For this group the sculptor made every effort to achieve historical accuracy. His research took him to Boston and New Haven in August 1871 and to Philadelphia and Washington in September 1872, to examine portraits, busts, and uniforms not only of Washington, Lafayette, and Hamilton, but of many other Revolutionary figures as well. In a sketchbook at The New-York Historical Society there are twenty-one sketches, with measurements, for this group. He went to just as much trouble to design a suitable horse. As late as October 1872 Rogers even enlisted the aid of Benson Lossing, popular historian of the Revolution, to help solve his historical problems. In the end, however, the project came to nothing, probably because Rogers grew tired of it and felt he could not afford to spend more time on it for an uncertain return. The group was last mentioned, in the Yonkers *Gazette* in December 1872, as possibly to be finished in time for the Centennial. The "Washington" [144] of 1875 may be all that Rogers salvaged from it. See also the so-called mask of Alexander Hamilton [221].

ANATOMICAL STUDIES OF THE HORSE

126. THE SKELETON

127. THE MUSCLES

128. THE ATTACHMENT OF SOME PRINCIPAL MUSCLES

Plaster medallions in high relief; size not known
Price: $5.00 each
No copies located

These studies were modelled by Rogers in 1871 or 1872 from dissections at the Veterinary College of New York, where he made some studies for his abortive "Camp Fires of the Revolution" [125], the first work of his professional years in which he introduced the horse. In 1874 he exhibited these three studies at the National Academy's spring exhibition. They were listed in his catalogues from 1874 through 1882, as designed for the use of students. In 1896 Rogers' cousin, the sculptor William Ordway Partridge, wrote of them in the *New England Magazine:* "Since Mr. Rogers' illness I have been fortunate enough to get possession of a number of casts made from the dissection of the horse by him. I have seen nothing like them in the studios of Europe, and there are few men in this country, among the artists, who know the horse so well as Rogers."

129. JOHN ROGERS (1866–1939), the sculptor's son

Portrait bust, plaster, painted; height 11½ inches
Unsigned
Collection: The New-York Historical Society

John, eldest son of the sculptor, was born in New York in 1866, attended Yale College ('88) and the College of Physicians and Surgeons ('91), and became a well-known New York surgeon, particularly noted as a pioneer in the treatment of goiter. This bust was executed by his father in 1871 when the boy was five. It is inscribed

"Johnnie Rogers/1871." In a letter of November 22, 1874, the sculptor stated that he had "never liked it" and had no copies left. The sole surviving copy was presented to The New-York Historical Society in 1936 by the subject's sister, Katherine R. Rogers.

130. WE BOYS

Plaster, painted; height 17 inches
Signed JOHN ROGERS NEW YORK
Patented May 11, 1872
Price: $12.00 (to 1878); $10.00 (1882–92); $9.00 (1895)
Collections:
Type A: 1, 2, 3, 5, 6, 7, 8, 9, 15
Type B: 1, 5, 6, 9
Bronze master model (Type A): sold for Rogers in 1897 by Guerin; now at The New-York Historical Society.

The original clay sketch-model of this group was completed in March 1872 and the design patented in May. Two New Canaan boys — James E. and Joseph M. Silliman — are said to have posed for it (*New York Herald Tribune*, April 9, 1943, obituary of Joseph M. Silliman). The Sillimans lived on Oenoke Ridge in the house now occupied by the New Canaan Historical Society. John Rogers a few years later acquired the adjoining property and built a house and studio. The house has been demolished and the studio moved to the grounds of the Silliman house.

There are two substantially different versions of this group.

Type A:

The horse's head is down, all four legs in the water; the tail is long.

Type B:

The horse is turning his head to snap at the first boy, his right hind-leg is out of the water, and his tail is bobbed.

Type A is shown in Rogers' patent application, in all his catalogues, 1874–95, on three stereographs of about 1875, and in the bronze master model at The New-York Historical Society. Type B is known only from extant plaster examples, including one given to The New-York Historical Society by Katherine R. Rogers. Both are signed and bear the patent date, but these are differently located on the two types. Type A is more common than Type B.

131. JOHN OSGOOD STONE (1813–76)

Portrait bust, plaster; height 7⅞ inches
Unsigned
Collection: The New-York Historical Society

Dr. John Osgood Stone, a native of Salem, Massachusetts, became a prominent New York physician. Possibly an old family friend, he became the Rogers' "family doctor" after John and Hattie were married in 1865. It was he who first induced them to try New Canaan, Connecticut, as a summer residence in 1868, and it may have been there that the sculptor produced this bust. Although the Smiths in their 1934 catalogue of Rogers' works dated this portrait to 1868, it is more likely that it dates from 1872, since it was exhibited at the National Academy in April of that year.

The original cast, said to have been in bronze, was owned by the subject's daughter, Mrs. Morgan Grinnell of New York City, in 1931. Its present location is not known. A duplicate, in plaster, was presented by Mrs. Grinnell to Miss Katherine R. Rogers in 1931; this later was given to The New-York Historical Society by Miss Rogers. Rogers also did a bust of Mrs. Grinnell as a little girl [115].

132. PLAYING DOCTOR

Plaster, painted; height 14¼ inches
Signed JOHN ROGERS/NEW YORK
Patented October 15, 1872
Price: $15.00; $10.00 (1888)
Collections: 1, 2, 3, 4, 5, 6, 8, 9
Bronze master model: The New-York Historical Society, purchased in 1936 from Katherine R. Rogers

In this group the sculptor for the first time used his own children as models: Johnny, aged six,

Katie four, and Charlie two. Their measurements are noted in Rogers' sketchbook under the date May 1872. "When the public learns that these children are the portraits of the artist's own family," the Yonkers *Gazette* prophesied in December 1872, "it will take a deeper interest in the group." It was a fairly popular one, in fact, particularly as a decoration for doctors' waiting rooms.

One copy at the Essex Institute, Salem, Massachusetts, lacks the "doctor's" spectacles. This may be a real variant or simply a case of accidental loss.

133. ABRAHAM LINCOLN (1809–65)

Portrait bust in clay or plaster, life-size
Unlocated

In a description of Rogers' studio, published in the Yonkers *Gazette* in December 1872, it was stated that "a life-size bust of the good and sad-looking Lincoln looks down from a bracket." This bust, assuming that it was done by Rogers, was undoubtedly an outgrowth of his studies for "The Council of War" [112]. It was also probably this bust which was referred to as a "mask" of Lincoln left in Rogers' studio when he retired (New York *Sun,* May 1895).

134. ROBERT GORSUCH HART (c. 1869–1906)

Portrait statuette, probably plaster; almost life-size
Unlocated

Among the artists in New York with whom John Rogers was most closely associated was the landscape painter James M. Hart (1828–1901). When Hart's son was about four or five years old, Rogers offered to make a statuette of him, almost life-size. So pleased was Hart with the portrait that he painted for Rogers in return a pastoral scene which hung in the Rogers' parlor at New Canaan ever after. The subject, who was born sometime between 1868 and 1871, would have been four or five between 1872 and 1876.

He grew up to be an artist like his father, mother, and two sisters, worked mainly in New York, but died in Mexico.

135. THE FAVORED SCHOLAR

Plaster, painted; height 21 inches
Signed JOHN ROGERS/NEW YORK
Patented April 1, 1873
Price: \$18.00; \$15.00 (1882); \$12.00 (1895)
Collections: 1, 2, 3, 4, 5, 6, 7, 8, 9, 10
Bronze master model: The New-York Historical Society, purchased in 1936 from Katherine R. Rogers

Rogers began this group in December 1872 and had it ready for sale by March 1873. It was well received as "another of those *genre* works that delight all eyes." Its appeal could be even more direct, for at least one schoolteacher of the time, Mr. B. W. Woodward, of West Chester, Pennsylvania, gave this group a place of honor in his home after he married his own "favored scholar."

136. BUBBLES

Plaster, painted; height 40 inches
Signed JOHN ROGERS/NEW YORK
Patented October 15, 1873
Price: \$35.00; reduced to \$25.00 in 1882
Collections: 1, 3, 9
Bronze master model: sold for Rogers in 1897 by Guerin; present location unknown

On March 10, 1873, Mrs. Rogers wrote to her mother-in-law that John was "thinking & experimenting over a quite large, single figure of Charlie (though not *called* so) as a little boy blowing bubbles; for *niches* perhaps. He is often asked for them. I don't know how it will turn out, as he is just starting it & thinking it over." In a later letter Hattie described the full-size figure as "not an entire likeness of C." By June the sculptor was finishing the plaster cast at New Canaan and hoping that it would open to him a whole new field of "*out* door figures" which could "be extended as indefinitely as the groups for *in*doors."

The bronze cast was made in August and the first plaster casts went on sale in October 1873, priced at $35.00. While the figure received the usual excellent notices, it did not prove a very saleable piece. By 1888 it had been withdrawn and it is today one of the rarest of Rogers' published works.

137. FREEDMEN'S MEMORIAL

Design for a statue; presumed destroyed

In May or June 1873 Rogers sent a model for a Freedmen's Memorial to the Rev. Dr. William G. Eliot (1811–87) of St. Louis, a member of the Freedmen's Memorial Commission. Much to his and his family's annoyance, Rogers' model was returned without comment and the commission awarded to Thomas Ball, the prominent Boston sculptor. Rogers' conclusion from this was that "commissions are secured by *wire pulling*." He consoled himself with the thought that not getting the commission would leave him free to pursue more profitable work. His model presumably was destroyed. Ball's famous statue of Lincoln and the Freed Slave was unveiled in Lincoln Park, Washington, D.C., April 14, 1876.

138. GOING FOR THE COWS

Plaster, painted; height 11½ inches
Signed JOHN ROGERS/NEW YORK
Patented December 2, 1873
Price: $10.00
Collections: 1, 2, 3, 4, 5, 6, 7, 9
Bronze master model: The New-York Historical Society, purchased in 1936 from Katherine R. Rogers

In August 1873 Rogers reported that he was working on a new group for Christmas. "The design is very simple," he wrote, "& intended principally to bring in the horse. I shall probably call it Going for the Cows. The horse is nibbling grass near the fence while the boy has jumped off & is interested with his dog at a woodchuck hole, all of which is intended to be so plain that the most careless observer will not fail to see the joke!" Rogers' sketchbook contains a preliminary sketch for the dog, identified as "Dash." One of the

Silliman boys of New Canaan is supposed to have been the model for the boy.

139. HIDE AND SEEK: WHOOP!

"Composition stone," painted; height 46 inches; pedestal 22 inches high, octagonal, available in either composition or in cast iron
Signed JOHN ROGERS/NEW YORK
Patented May 26, 1874
Price: $50.00, plus $15.00 for the pedestal; $30.00 and $10.00 (1882)
Collections: 1, 3, 5, 9
Bronze master model: no record

As soon as "Bubbles" [136] was successfully cast, Rogers began, in October 1873, work on the first of a pair of life-size garden figures. His six-year-old daughter, Katherine Rebecca, posed for the girl. Working on the model in his new studio at home in New York, he had it ready for casting in February 1874. In order to make it strong, light, and impervious to the weather, Rogers experimented with various compositions and finishes and even had to design new machinery for casting so large a figure. The completed model was first shown at the National Academy's spring exhibition in April, was patented in May, and went on sale soon after. In September 1874, after recovering from a severe illness, Rogers remodelled the head and figure and started on the companion piece "Hide and Seek" [141]. During the next two years he made innumerable experiments to find a satisfactory "composition stone" for his lawn figures. His 1876 catalogue announced that the composition had been proved durable by two years' experience. The surface was hardened by a preparation of linseed oil and then painted, making it relatively impervious to water. Pedestals were available in cast iron or composition. The piece was further embellished by a cast iron vase or planter to stand on the tree stump, with a special run-off arrangement to prevent water from discoloring the statue. Although they were listed in Rogers' catalogues until 1890, the "Hide and Seek" figures never sold well and are today quite rare.

140. KATHERINE REBECCA ROGERS (1868–1956)

Portrait bust, plaster, painted; height 8½ inches
Unsigned
Collection: The New-York Historical Society

This bust of the sculptor's six-year-old daughter was executed in September 1874 when Rogers was working on a new model of the girl for "Hide and Seek: Whoop!" [139]. Her mother thought it "just like her" and reported that Katie called it "the group of *me*." Rogers made a number of copies to send to relatives, including his own mother and his aunt, Mrs. Ephraim Peabody, his wife's aunts Mrs. Henry Hoskins of Gardiner, Maine, and Mrs. Charles H. Parker of Boston, and his wife's cousin Susan Francis. His own copy was given to The New-York Historical Society by the subject. It is inscribed "Katie Rogers, Sep. 1874."

141. HIDE AND SEEK

"Composition stone," painted; height 49 inches; pedestal 22 inches high, octagonal, available either in composition stone or in cast iron
Signed JOHN ROGERS/NEW YORK
Patented March 2, 1875
Price: $50.00, plus $15.00 for the pedestal; $30.00 plus $10.00 (1882)
Collections: 1, 3, 5, 9
Bronze master model: no record

Designed as a companion piece to "Hide and Seek: Whoop!" [139], this figure was modelled by Rogers during the summer of 1874. His model was seven-year-old Harry Stimson, whose parents and maternal grandparents (Thomas and Candace Wheeler) were long-time friends of the sculptor and his wife. The Stimsons were summer residents of New Canaan, renting in 1874 a house opposite the New Canaan Library, just south of S. B. Hoyt's greenhouse. Harry grew up to be Henry L. Stimson, Secretary of War under President Taft and President Franklin D. Roosevelt and Secretary of State under President Hoover.

142. THE TAP ON THE WINDOW

Plaster, painted; height 19½ inches
Signed JOHN ROGERS/NEW YORK
Patented December 29, 1874
Price: $15.00; $12.00 (1882); $10.00 (1895)
Collections: 1, 2, 3, 4, 5, 7, 8, 9, 10
Bronze master model: sold in 1897 for Rogers by Guerin; unlocated

This group was released just before Christmas 1874 and attracted the usual enthusiastic praise for its realistic details, its humor, and its "tender sentiment."

143. THE SHAUGHRAUN AND "TATTERS"

Plaster, painted; height 20 inches
Signed JOHN ROGERS/NEW YORK
Patented March 2, 1875
Price: $12.00; $10.00 (1877); $8.00 (1888)
Collections: 1, 2, 3, 5, 6, 7, 9
Bronze master model: The New-York Historical Society, purchased in 1936 from Katherine R. Rogers

This group was designed to capitalize on the popularity of Dion Boucicault, author-director-star of the long-run play "The Shaughraun" (an Irish term meaning vagabond). Boucicault and his dog sat for Rogers in December 1874; the actor's measurements and a sketch of "Tatters" are in the Rogers' sketchbook. In April 1875 a copy of the completed work was presented to Boucicault at Wallack's Theater on behalf of the Irish-American residents of New York "in recognition of the services his literary and artistic work have been to Ireland and the Irish people."

144. WASHINGTON

Plaster, painted; height 30 inches
Signed JOHN ROGERS/NEW YORK
Patented October 19, 1875
Price: $15.00; $10.00 (1882)
Collections: 1, 2, 3, 5, 6, 9
Bronze master model: Metropolitan Museum of Art, New York City, the gift of William Leander Post, 1944

Rogers produced the model for this in the spring of 1875, presumably making use of the many measured drawings of portraits, busts, and uniform details he had made in 1871 and 1872 in preparation for "Camp Fires of the Revolution" [125]. It was designed to meet the rising interest in things Revolutionary as the Centennial year approached. It was also a relatively easy work to turn out while Rogers was devoting most of his energies to promoting and perfecting his large lawn figures. "I do not think you will consider it very interesting," he wrote to his mother on May 16, 1875, "for it tells no story & is simply George standing alone." "Washington" was never a best-seller and disappeared from Rogers' catalogue before 1888. The bronze master model, now at the Metropolitan Museum of Art, was offered for sale to Independence Hall, Philadelphia, in 1931 by Frederick Mitchell Smith of New York. Mr. Smith was advised that the Hall "would be unable to consider the acceptance of the statue even by presentation, as the sculptor, John Rogers, was not born until 1829, and any statue of Washington made after his death would have only the same interest that a copy of an original painting would."

145. CHECKERS UP AT THE FARM

Plaster, painted; height 20 inches
Signed JOHN ROGERS/NEW YORK
Patented December 28, 1875
Price: $15.00
Collections: 1, 2, 3, 5, 6, 7, 8, 9, 15
Bronze master model: The New-York Historical Society, purchased in 1936 from Katherine R. Rogers

Rogers was reported to be working on this group at his New York studio in November 1875. It proved to be second only to "Coming to the Parson" [120] in popularity, with a total sale of 5,000 copies. The sculptor's wife posed for this group, according to her daughter, Katherine R. Rogers.

146. MRS. EDWARD W. LAMBERT

Portrait bust, plaster, painted
Unlocated

In Rogers' sketchbook, undated but probably about 1875, are recorded the head measurements of Mrs. Edward W. Lambert. The subject was the wife of the Rogers' family physician in New Canaan, who lived next to the Rogers house on Oenoke Ridge. The nine Lambert children were playmates of the six in the Rogers household. Mrs. D. W. Richards, a daughter, said of this bust, "We all think it is the best likeness we have of Mother" (quoted in Smith, *Rogers Groups,* p. 119). The bust was owned in 1936 by Mrs. Richards, who lived in South Orange, New Jersey. Its present location is not known.

147. FLOWER BOX

"Composition stone," painted; size unknown
Probably signed JOHN ROGERS/NEW YORK
Patented August 15, 1876
Price: $10.00
No copy located

Rogers produced this oblong window box, decorated in low relief with figures of children at play, during the spring of 1876. It was cast in the same artificial stone material as his lawn figures and vase. Although it was patented and listed in Rogers' 1876 catalogue, no copy is known to have survived.

148. VASE

"Composition stone," painted; height 12½ inches
Signed JOHN ROGERS NEW YORK
Price: $10.00
Collections: 1, 3, 9

On April 5, 1876, Rogers sent his mother a photograph of his new "vase," which was decorated with low reliefs of Santa Claus distributing presents and a game of blind man's buff. Cast in "composition stone," the vase was advertised in his Fall 1876 catalogue, along with an oblong window box [147], both listed as "very suitable for conservatories in Winter, as well as for outdoors in Summer." The vase also could be used with the "Hide and Seek" lawn figures [139, 141] (Essex Institute). Rogers himself used some of these vases, according to his daughter, "holding geranium plants, to stand on the porch rail posts of his New Canaan studio for a few years."

149. JOANNA WILLIAMS

Portrait bust
Unlocated

On April 23, 1876, the sculptor wrote his mother that he had been making a bust of Joanna, daughter of Mr. and Mrs. John Earl Williams of Irvington-on-the-Hudson. Mrs. Williams, born Eunice Burr Thomas, was a cousin of Hattie Rogers. In return for making the bust, Rogers explained, he was to receive an Alderney cow. The measurements for the bust are in Rogers' sketchbook, undated. Rogers also did a bust of Joanna's father; see No. 119.

150. WEIGHING THE BABY

Plaster, painted; height 21 inches
Signed JOHN ROGERS/NEW YORK
Patented November 21, 1876
Price: $15.00
Collections: 1, 2, 3, 4, 5, 6, 7, 9
Bronze master model: The New-York Historical Society, purchased in 1936 from Katherine R. Rogers

On November 3, 1876, the *Boston Courier's* New York correspondent reported that "Mr. John Rogers, author of the inimitable Rogers Groups, those exquisite miniature embodiments of characteristic incidents in American life," had returned from his summer home in Connecticut, "bringing as the result of his vacation a new work which shines even among the most popular of its older companions." This was "Weighing the Baby." According to Miss Katherine R. Rogers (1955), the mother, baby, and mischievous small boy were posed for by her mother and her two brothers, David (born in April 1876) and Charles F. Rogers (aged 6). The group caught on immediately and the first edition was exhausted before Christmas. It was the profits from that season's sales that paid for Rogers' new house on Oenoke Ridge in New Canaan. The *Medical Record* recommended the group (1884) as suitable for doctors' offices.

151. THE MOCK TRIAL / ARGUMENT FOR THE PROSECUTION

Plaster, painted; height 21 inches
Signed JOHN ROGERS/NEW YORK/1877
Patented June 11, 1877
Price: $20.00
Collections: 1, 2, 3, 5, 9
Bronze master model: sold for Rogers in 1897 by Guerin; now in the collection of The New-York Historical Society.

Rogers exhibited two new groups at the National Academy's spring exhibition, April 1877, "Mock Trial" and "School Days" [152]. "The Mock Trial," illustrating a popular parlor amusement of the period, was hailed as a masterpiece in the newspapers but failed to make a hit with the public. It disappeared from Rogers' catalogues between 1882 and 1888. Mr. and Mrs. Chetwood Smith were told by Miss Katherine R. Rogers that the sculptor's sister, Laura Derby Rogers, was his model for the "prosecutor."

152. SCHOOL DAYS

Plaster, painted; height 21½ inches
Signed JOHN ROGERS/NEW YORK/1877
Patented June 26, 1877
Price: $12.00; $10.00 (1888); $8.00 (1895)
Collections: 1, 2, 3, 4, 5, 6, 7, 8, 9
Bronze master model: The New-York Historical Society, purchased in 1936 from Katherine R. Rogers

Two of the Rogers children posed for this group, Katherine (nine) and Charles (seven). Although Rogers showed it at the spring 1877 exhibition of the National Academy and patented it in June, it was not put on sale until the fall of 1877. The press, as usual, hailed it as one of the artist's best works and predicted for it a popularity it did not achieve. A superstitious feeling against monkeys has been said to have affected the sales of this group. Miss Katherine R. Rogers commented in 1955: "The only criticism I ever heard was that some people thought a monkey did not belong in their parlor, but the hand organ and monkey were very popular on the street."

153. THE TRAVELLING MAGICIAN

Plaster, painted; height 23 inches
Signed JOHN ROGERS/NEW YORK/1877
Patented November 27, 1877
Price: $15.00; $12.00 (1895)
Collections: 1, 2, 3, 4, 5, 6, 9, 15
Bronze master model: The New-York Historical Society, purchased in 1936 from Katherine R. Rogers

The earliest reference to this group was a brief, laudatory description published in the *Springfield* (Massachusetts) *Republican,* November 23, 1877. The sculptor's daughter Katherine remembered sitting "sleepily" for the magician's assistant and thought the boy probably was her brother Charles.

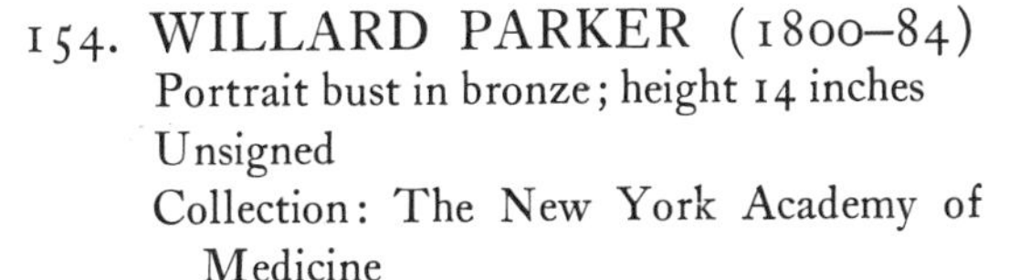

154. WILLARD PARKER (1800–84)

Portrait bust in bronze; height 14 inches
Unsigned
Collection: The New York Academy of Medicine

On November 3, 1877, the *New Canaan Messenger* reported that John Rogers was working on a bust of Dr. Willard Parker. The subject, like the artist, was a New Yorker who had discovered New Canaan in the previous decade and brought his family there regularly every summer. Dr. Parker, one of New York's most notable physicians, was nearing the end of his distinguished career when this bust was executed. The bronze was given to The New York Academy of Medicine in 1930. A duplicate, probably in plaster, was still in Rogers' possession when his New York studio was dismantled in 1895. Its present location is not known.

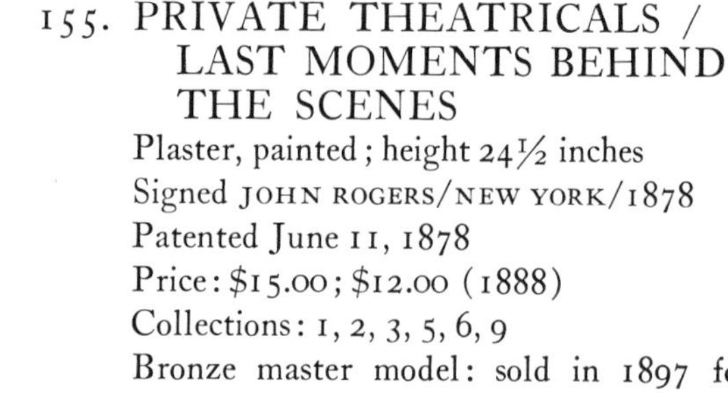

155. PRIVATE THEATRICALS / LAST MOMENTS BEHIND THE SCENES

Plaster, painted; height 24½ inches
Signed JOHN ROGERS/NEW YORK/1878
Patented June 11, 1878
Price: $15.00; $12.00 (1888)
Collections: 1, 2, 3, 5, 6, 9
Bronze master model: sold in 1897 for Rogers by Guerin; unlocated

"Private Theatricals" made its appearance in June 1878. "It is full of expression and life," commented the editor of the *Lyons* (New York) *Republican,* "it is a perfect study of its subject, and in it is shown the same wonderful success in depicting every minute detail that is exhibited in all of Mr. Rogers' works." Miss Katherine R. Rogers thought (1955) that her aunt, Laura Derby Rogers, posed for this group while visiting the Rogers' new house on Oenoke Ridge, New Canaan, in the spring of 1878. It proved only moderately successful and was dropped after 1890.

156. THE PHOTOGRAPH

Plaster, painted; height of "The Photographer," 17 inches; height of "The Sitter," 18½ inches
Signed (each) JOHN ROGERS/NEW YORK/1878
Patented October 15, 1878
Price: $15.00; $12.00 (1882); $10.00 (1888)
Collections: 1, 2, 3, 5, 6, 9, 10
Bronze master models: sold for Rogers in 1897 by Guerin; unlocated

This "group," consisting of a pair of statuettes designed to be posed at opposite ends of a mantel or table, is one of Rogers' most engaging representations of life as it was lived in mid-century America. Mrs. John Rogers posed for the mother and two-year-old David Francis Rogers for the child [see 223]. Their measurements are recorded in the artist's notebook under the date April 1878. Although the *Scientific American* thought "The Photograph" would appeal to "many, very many, mothers," sales proved disappointing and the group was withdrawn before 1892.

157. THE PEDDLER AT THE FAIR

Plaster, painted; height 20 inches
Signed JOHN ROGERS/NEW YORK/1878
Patented December 10, 1878
Price: $15.00; $13.00 (1888)
Collections: 1, 2, 3, 4, 5, 6, 7, 9, 15
Bronze master model: sold for Rogers in 1897 by Guerin; now at The New-York Historical Society

Rogers' "Peddler," issued just before Christmas 1878, was described in *Art and Society* (November 30, 1878) as "one of the cleverest efforts he has made to reproduce in miniature a country scene so familiar as to seem almost commonplace." "Pax," writing in the *Suffolk* (Va.) *Herald,* in December 1884, used this group to illustrate a little Christmas homily on "Men who are stingy with their wives." It was dropped from Rogers' catalogue in 1892.

158. POLO

Plaster, painted; height 21 inches
Signed JOHN ROGERS/NEW YORK/1879
Patented May 6, 1879
Price: $15.00; not listed in December 1888 or after
Collections: 1, 2, 5, 9
Bronze master model: sold for Rogers in 1897 by Guerin; now privately owned

This "very spirited presentation" of what one reviewer called "this new horseback game (equine croquet)" is one of Rogers' technically most ambitious small works and one of his least successful in respect to sales. To avoid breakage of its many exposed parts, the artist had to cast in metal the guidon and some other parts (including the front horse) and paint them to match the plaster. Withdrawn after only nine years, it is today one of the rarest of the published groups. The game of polo, then as now, had a very limited appeal.

159. THE BALCONY

Plaster, painted; height 32 inches
Signed JOHN ROGERS/NEW YORK/1879
Patented November 4, 1879
Price: $25.00; $20.00 (1888)
Collections: 1, 2, 3, 5, 6, 9
Bronze master model: The New-York Historical Society, purchased in 1936 from Katherine R. Rogers.

When Rogers opened his new showroom at 23 Union Square in June 1879, the center of attention was the just-completed clay model of "The Balcony." Both praised and blamed for its elaborate realism, it was also praised for teaching the beauty of charity and for presenting both wealth and poverty in a sympathetic light. Katie and Charlie Rogers posed for the street musicians. For the dog he used "Quiz," a Scotch terrier from Queen Victoria's royal kennels who belonged to a visiting cousin of Mrs. Rogers, Annie Clifford, of New Bedford, Massachusetts. According to a newspaper of the day, "Quiz" had been trained to sit on his hind legs with a piece of meat on his nose "not offering to stir, no matter how long he was kept in that uncomfortable and tantalizing position." This accomplishment made him an ideal model.

160. "IS IT SO NOMINATED IN THE BOND?"

Plaster, painted; height 23 inches
Signed JOHN ROGERS/NEW YORK/1880
Patented June 1, 1880
Price: $20.00
Collections: 1, 2, 3, 4, 5, 6, 7, 8, 9, 14
Bronze master model: The New-York Historical Society, purchased in 1936 from Katherine R. Rogers

Although the clay of this was shown to selected newspapermen in December 1879, it was May 1880 before it appeared on the market. As his first venture in the Shakespeare line since his abortive "Merchant of Venice" [77], "Richard III" [78], and "Hamlet" [97] of 1861–62, Rogers took unusual pains with it, and even exhibited it at the National Academy, as he had his earlier version of the same scene in 1861. It proved to be one of his most popular works. The Rev. Robert Collyer [224], a friend of the artist, posed for Antonio. In a letter of July 3, 1903, Collyer lightheartedly reminded the artist of this: "Your Antonio, well I fall in love with him all over again when I glance at his handsome head, though indeed my wife did say she thought I could afford to lose a pound of flesh and be no worse for it or miss it." There is no contemporary evidence that Edwin Booth posed for Shylock, as stated in Smith, *Rogers Groups,* p. 89.

161. THE REFEREE

Plaster, painted; height 22 inches
Signed JOHN ROGERS/NEW YORK/1880
Patented November 23, 1880
Price: $15.00; reduced to $12.00 (1888)
Collections: 1, 2, 3, 5, 6, 7, 9, 10
Bronze master model: sold for Rogers in 1897 by Guerin; not located

Rogers began modelling this group in April 1880, taking as his models his twin sisters Bessie and Fanny. "The group is one eminently adapted for either parlor or dining room," reported *The Christian at Work,* "as a look at it is calculated to put the most grouty person into a good humor. . . . All our readers who want to make to their friends an acceptable present with which to brighten a happy home, or to bring sunshine into one which is not as happy as it might be, ought to secure this group at once."

162. THE WRESTLERS

Plaster, painted; height 27 inches
Signed JOHN ROGERS/NEW YORK/1881
Patented September 20, 1881
Price $25.00; $20.00 (1888)
Collections: 1, 2, 3, 5, 9
Bronze master model: The New-York Historical Society, purchased in 1936 from Katherine R. Rogers

This group illustrates the wrestling match between Charles and Orlando in Shakespeare's *As*

You Like It, Act I, Scene 2. "Charles is thrown," Rogers' catalogue explained, "for, by a trick well known to professional wrestlers, as they stand facing each other, Orlando suddenly seizes Charles by one arm and whirls him around, which enables him to clasp him from behind and lift him from the ground so as to throw him on his shoulders. Charles tries to break Orlando's hold by twisting open his hands." Although he was, in his daughter's words, "not at all a sports fan," Rogers went to a "prize fight" while he was working on this group, in order to study the correct positions.

163. FETCHING THE DOCTOR

Plaster, painted; height 16 inches
Signed JOHN ROGERS/NEW YORK/1881
Patented December 6, 1881
Price: $10.00
Collections: 1, 2, 3, 4, 5, 6, 7, 9
Bronze master model: The New-York Historical Society, purchased in 1936 from Katherine R. Rogers

This group was inspired by New Canaan's Dr. Richards who, according to Miss Rogers, "did ride and carry medicines in saddlebags and was said to taste them to make sure he gave the right ones." A measured sketch dated June 4, 1881, in the artist's sketchbook, shows that nine-year-old Derby Rogers posed for the boy. The group's suitability for a doctor's office was noted in *The Canada Lancet,* December 5, 1881.

164. JOHN FULTON REYNOLDS (1820–63)

Equestrian statue in bronze; height 12 feet, pedestal 10 feet
Cast by Bureau Brothers
Dedicated September 18, 1884
Location: City Hall, Philadelphia, Pennsylvania, in front of the north entrance

Major-General John Fulton Reynolds, a native Pennsylvanian, was commanding the First and Eleventh Corps of the Army of the Potomac when a sharpshooter's bullet struck him down on the first day of the Battle of Gettysburg. The Reynolds Memorial Association was organized eighteen years later, on July 1, 1881, to secure an equestrian statue of the fallen general for the city of Philadelphia. The principal contributors were Joseph E. Temple ($25,000) and the Commonwealth of Pennsylvania ($5,000 and some old brass cannon). By unanimous vote the Association decided to ask John Rogers to undertake the commission. He accepted with genuine reluctance, because he had no previous experience with monumental sculpture and because he had a constitutional aversion to long-term projects. The $25,000 contract, signed February 14, 1882, called for delivery in two years after acceptance of the working model.

Rogers worked on his several models in a studio built especially for this job in Stamford, Connecticut. "I think the people of Stamford ought to feel indebted to me for furnishing them something of interest to watch & talk about," he wrote; "I have a large glass door in the back of my building and the number of people who take a look in there is quite astonishing." The Philadelphia committee accepted the small plaster model early in September 1882. A year later the finished full-scale model, made out of fifty barrels of plaster, was shown to representatives of the press. After being sawn into about thirty pieces, it was shipped to Bureau Brothers' bronze foundry in Philadelphia. The dedication, originally scheduled for July 1, took place on September 14, 1884.

"The intention of the design," the artist wrote to the president of the Reynolds Memorial Association in October 1884, "was to represent General Reynolds in the front of the battlefield. . . . The horse is startled and shying from the noise and danger in the direction he is looking, while the general is pointing to the same spot and giving directions to his aids at his side."

The critics of the day were somewhat less than enthusiastic about Rogers' first attempt at monumental art. The principal complaint was that the very lifelike and spirited horse made the general look rather insignificant. Although he felt it was "fairly well liked," Rogers himself was aware that the work was far from perfect and lamented that he had not gained his experience "on a less ambitious piece of work." "If any more commissions come along," he told his sister Ellen, "I will try & do better."

165. "HA! I LIKE NOT THAT!"

Plaster, painted; height 22 inches
Signed JOHN ROGERS/NEW YORK/1882
Patented October 31, 1882
Price: $20.00
Collections: 1, 2, 3, 5, 6, 7, 9, 14
Bronze master model: The New-York Historical Society, purchased in 1936 from Katherine R. Rogers

Othello, Act III, Scene 3, provided the dramatic situation for Rogers' third Shakespearean group. Edwin Booth posed for Iago, it was reported in Boston's *Journal of Education,* November 30, 1882; Tommaso Salvini is said to have posed for Othello (Smith, *Rogers Groups,* p. 93).

166. NEIGHBORING PEWS

Plaster, painted; height 18½ inches
Signed JOHN ROGERS/NEW YORK/1883
Patented January 29, 1884
Price: $15.00
Collections: 1, 2, 3, 4, 5, 6, 7, 8, 9
Bronze master model: The New-York Historical Society, purchased in 1936 from Katherine R. Rogers

"I think my group I am at work on here will do very well for Christmas," Rogers wrote from New Canaan on June 10, 1883. "There is some flirtation and some fun in it." The old lady who posed for it, according to the sculptor's daughter, was a Mrs. Allen who summered for many years in a cottage across Oenoke Avenue from the Rogers' house, "the happy second wife of a second husband." The *Miners Journal* (Pottsville, Pa., December 17, 1883) praised Rogers for handling "a church scene . . . with a touch of humor which while doing no violence to propriety in the treatment of the subject adds zest to the artistic beauty of the creation."

167. A MATTER OF OPINION

Plaster, painted; height 21 inches
Signed JOHN ROGERS/NEW YORK/1884
Patented December 9, 1884
Price: $15.00
Collections: 1, 2, 3, 4, 5, 6, 7, 8, 9
Bronze master model: The New-York Historical Society, purchased in 1936 from Katherine R. Rogers

After "General Reynolds" [164] was safely in the caster's hands, Rogers resumed his interrupted "small" work. "I am started on a group which promises some interest though it is not just what I wanted," he wrote to Ellen on February 10, 1884. "It represents a consultation of physicians over an invalid lady — which results in an evident disagreement." He had finished the model by April 23 but did not release it until Christmas. *The Medical Record* illustrated it in an advertisement of Rogers Groups "suitable for physicians' offices."

168. "WHY DON'T YOU SPEAK FOR YOURSELF, JOHN?"

Plaster, painted; height 22 inches
Signed JOHN ROGERS/NEW YORK
Patented February 10, 1885
Price: $20.00
Collections: 1, 2, 3, 4, 5, 6, 8, 9, 10, 13
Bronze master model: The New-York Historical Society, purchased in 1936 from Katherine R. Rogers

One of the most popular of Rogers' works, this illustrates the well known lines from Longfellow's "The Courtship of Miles Standish":

> Archly the maiden smiled, and, with
> eyes overrunning with laughter,
> Said, in a tremulous voice, "Why don't
> you speak for yourself, John?"

Dr. Theodore W. Benedict, of New Canaan, is the source for the statement that his mother, Mrs. Harriet Elizabeth Crissey Benedict, posed for Priscilla. An interesting instance of Rogers' efforts to achieve accuracy of detail is revealed in the following letter to a Mrs. King, of Woodstock, Vermont, dated September 29, 1885:

Dear Mrs. King,

I thought you might be interested in one of my groups that has a spinning wheel in it for, when I was making it last winter I tried to find someone who had ever spun, and your son [Hiram U. King, of the King School, Stamford] made some inquiries of you at my request and I made some alterations from what he afterwards told me. I hope I have it right, though I found some who insisted that the disstaff should be held in the hand. . . .

Rogers even planned to write to Longfellow (May 22, 1884) but the lack of any reply among his papers suggests that this plan was not carried out.

169. "YOU ARE A SPIRIT, I KNOW; WHEN DID YOU DIE?"

Plaster, painted; height 19 inches
Signed JOHN ROGERS/NEW YORK/1885
Patented November 3, 1885
Price: $20.00; $15.00 (1888)
Collections: 1, 2, 3, 5, 6, 9, 15
Bronze master model: The New-York Historical Society, purchased in 1936 from Katherine R. Rogers

The opening of Rogers' "new rooms" at 860 Broadway was marked on April 23, 1885, by a reception at which the artist showed the clay model of his latest work, drawn from Shakespeare's tragedy, *King Lear*. Rogers chose to illustrate the poignant moment in Act IV, Scene 7, when Cordelia is trying to recall Lear's wandering mind to a remembrance of her. This was the least successful of Rogers' Shakespearean groups, probably because of its rather depressing subject. "Because the subject is pleasanter," wrote one reviewer, "I like the previous group, 'Why Don't You Speak for Yourself?' much better." (Howard W. Sexton in *Christmas Greeting,* Bordentown, New Jersey, December 12, 1885). It has been said that Edwin Booth posed for Lear (Smith, *Rogers Groups,* p. 93), but there is no contemporary reference to support this.

170. "MADAM, YOUR MOTHER CRAVES A WORD WITH YOU"

Plaster, painted; height 20 inches
Signed JOHN ROGERS/NEW YORK
Price: $15.00
Patented August 3, 1886
Collections: 1, 2, 3, 5, 6, 7, 9
Bronze master model: The New-York Historical Society, purchased in 1936 from Katherine R. Rogers

"Mr. Rogers has been quite immortalizing himself lately," reported the Lafayette, Indiana, *Evening Call,* June 30, 1886, "by a series of Shakespearian designs, of which this is the latest. The subject is from *Romeo and Juliet* — the fifth scene of the first act. . . . Romeo, in disguise, has lifted his mask, the better to admire her, and as the nurse draws her away with 'Madam, your mother craves a word with you,' he takes the privilege of the sacred character he has assumed and kisses her hand." This was Rogers' last Shakespearean group.

171. PHRENOLOGY AT THE FANCY BALL

Plaster, painted; height 20 inches
Signed JOHN ROGERS/NEW YORK
Patented September 7, 1886
Price: $10.00; $5.00 (1888)
Collections: 1, 3, 5, 9
Bronze master model: no record

This group ("of a somewhat amusing character" as *Geyer's Stationer* described it) represented a tongue-in-cheek comment on the popular "science" of phrenology, the study of the conformation of the skull as indicative of mental faculties. The phrenologist's subject, *Geyer's* also pointed out, appears to be dressed as Poo Bah in *The Mikado,* while his costume is decorated with "three little maids" and other figures from the same opera. "Phrenology" was not a "taking" subject, judging from its early drop in price and present rarity.

172. THE BUGLE CALL

"Large group" in plaster or clay; presumed destroyed

This group was exhibited at the National Academy of Design, Autumn 1886. The review of the exhibition in the *New York Times* of November 21 had this to say about it:

> [John Rogers] has a large group called "Bugle Call," a cavalryman about to mount a prancing horse. He is in full war dress, with a carbine slung behind his back and his steed is in the position most favored by weak painters and sculptors, with both fore feet in the air, that being the easiest way to make an impression of action without onward movement. Mr. Rogers has a bar to support the horse in the model, but states in a placard that the statuette will not need this prop. It may not need it in the sense that without it the horse will fall, but for comfort in looking at the group the pillar will be still desirable. . . . The cavalryman is a conventional type, like the volunteer who stands on a thousand pedestals presenting to rural communities and to inhabitants of towns who ought to know better the same insipid drawing book profile, the same uncharacteristic, cheap features.

Perhaps because of this sharp criticism, Rogers did not put "The Bugle Call" in production. The model presumably was destroyed.

173. THE ELDER'S DAUGHTER

Plaster, painted; height 21½ inches
Signed JOHN ROGERS/NEW YORK
Patented February 8, 1887
Price: $15.00; $12.00 (1888)
Collections: 1, 2, 3, 5, 6, 8, 9
Bronze master model: The New-York Historical Society, purchased in 1936 from Katherine R. Rogers

Despite its patent date, this group went on sale just before Christmas 1886. The story was thus described in Rogers' catalogue: "A Puritan Elder is riding home from Sabbath meeting. He has dropped the reins on the horse's neck and has been absorbed in studying his Bible. His daughter rides behind him on a pillion, while a young man walks by her side and offers her an apple from amongst the hatful he has gathered. This is considered a desecration of the Sabbath by the stern father, who looks at the young man reprovingly."

174. A FROLIC AT THE OLD HOMESTEAD

Plaster, painted; height 22½ inches
Signed JOHN ROGERS/NEW YORK/1887
Patented May 31, 1887
Price: $15.00
Collections: 1, 2, 3, 5, 6, 9
Bronze master model: no record

This group, in what a contemporary called Rogers' "happiest style," proved to be his last truly popular one. Katherine Rogers posed for the young lady. The old lady was Mrs. Morris Ketchum of Hokanum, Westport, Connecticut, widow of a prominent financier and mother of Mrs. Willard Parker, Jr., the Rogers' New Canaan neighbor.

175. ICHABOD CRANE AND THE "HEADLESS HORSEMAN"

Bronze; one-third life-size
Signed JOHN ROGERS/NEW YORK/1887
Price: $1,500.00
Collection: The New-York Historical Society, purchased in 1936 from Katherine R. Rogers

Begun in the late spring of 1887, this group was completed and cast in bronze in time for the National Academy's Autumn exhibition. The design was taken from Washington Irving's tale, "A Legend of Sleepy Hollow." Rogers intended this piece for outdoor or indoor use, possibly in a public park or building lobby, and issued a special circular to advertise it. The price, as listed in the National Academy Catalogue, was $1,500.00, but Ichabod found no purchaser. In 1901 Rogers lent this group, with several others, to the Metropolitan Museum of Art, New York City, where it was displayed for about thirty years.

176. HENRY WARD BEECHER (1813–87)

Plaster, painted; height 24 inches
Signed JOHN ROGERS/NEW YORK
Published 1887; not patented
Price: $12.00; reduced to $10.00 in the Rogers Statuette Company catalogue for 1895
Collections: 1, 3, 9
Bronze master model: no record

The Reverend Henry Ward Beecher died on March 8, 1887. Rogers almost immediately modelled this full-length portrait of the famed preacher who had been among the first to recognize and publicize the sculptor's gift. The statuette was based on a life mask [219] and detailed measurements taken by Rogers in 1869 while preparing "The Fugitive's Story" [116]. Lyman Abbott, in the *Christian Union,* July 7, 1887, wrote of it: "His present statuette, modelled since Mr. Beecher's death, represents the great orator in the act of addressing an out-of-door audience; his overcoat is on, but thrown back, his attitude almost military, and the expression of his face has the felicitous combination of the persuasive and the intensely earnest. . . . There is an inherent fitness," Abbott added, "in calling on one who is pre-eminently the sculptor for the people to represent one who was pre-eminently the orator to the people." Abbott suggested that if Rogers' design was not adopted for the statue to be erected in Brooklyn, he ought to "give it to the larger public as a statuette in plaster." As it turned out, the statue commission went to J. Q. A. Ward and Rogers did publish his own in plaster.

In a letter to Rogers, July 20, 1891, Beecher's widow wrote of this work in the warmest terms: "Just before leaving for Europe, Maj. Pond made me a present of your most excellent statuette of Mr. Beecher & I cannot forebear to tell you what a treasure & comfort it is to me. It speaks to my heart far more than the public one — that turns its back to all old friends — in the City Hall Park. Usually statues disappoint me, but yours does not. A slight change in the lower lip and chin would make it perfect. . . . I hope some day to be able to give each of my children this figure of their father which you have made so true to life."

177. JOHN ELIOT PREACHING TO THE INDIANS

Designs (6) for a monumental statue

Plaster; the first five about 3 feet high, the last about 15 feet

Locations: (A) First Congregational Church, Roxbury; (B) not located; (C) not located; (D) not located; (E) South Natick Historical Society; (F) destroyed

John Eliot (1604–90), minister of the First Church at Roxbury, Massachusetts (now part of Boston), began preaching to the local Indians in 1646 and five years later founded a village of Christian Indians at what is now Natick. His famous Indian Bible was published in 1661–63. In 1887, reportedly at the urging of friends in Roxbury, John Rogers undertook to design a monumental statue of Eliot suitable for erection on the green near Eliot's church. This project occupied much of his time during the next five years and resulted in the six models described below, of which two have survived. Although Rogers' final design was exhibited in New York and Boston and highly praised, efforts to raise money for its perpetuation in bronze were unsuccessful. Financially and emotionally, "John Eliot" proved, for Rogers, a costly failure.

(A)

(A) First Design. A small study in bronzed plaster, Rogers' original design contained four figures in a pyramidal arrangement. Eliot, shown as a vigorous bearded man in a short coat and breeches, stands on an outcrop of Roxbury "pudding stone" (conglomerate). On either side and below him are an Indian woman and man. On the ground between them sits an Indian child with a dead turkey in his lap from which he is removing an arrow. Rogers sent a photograph of this design to his uncle Robert C. Winthrop for comment. Winthrop, while praising the composition, objected to the figure

(B)

of Eliot. "All my historical associations with Eliot would call for a more reverent & venerable figure," he wrote, "& for a costume more in keeping with a missionary preacher." After being exhibited at the gallery of Williams & Everett in Boston, March-April 1888, this model was presented by the sculptor to the Fellowes Athenaeum of Roxbury on May 14, 1888. It is now displayed nearby in the First Church. The model is signed JOHN ROGERS/ NEW YORK/1888.

(B) Second Design. In response to his uncle's comments, Rogers worked up during April and May 1889 a new model with a more saintly Eliot in a long gown. Winthrop thought the changes presented "a great improvement." He felt, however, that the Apostle's head was thrown too far back to be properly seen from the ground and that Eliot looked too long-legged and short-waisted. He suggested the addition of a coat under the gown to break the long straight line of the exposed leg. This model has disappeared, but a photograph survives.

(C)

(C) Third Design. Rogers next altered the angle of Eliot's head and uplifted arm, added a coat under the gown, and shifted the position of his legs slightly. Submitted to Mr. Winthrop's critical eye on May 22, 1889, this version elicited relatively high praise: "I think it decidedly improved. The elaboration of the grape vine had not struck me as excessive, but perhaps it might be slightly diminished. The bunch immediately before Eliot's right foot looks in danger of being crushed. The lowering of the head & the introduction of the *jerkin* are very successful." This model also has disappeared, but is known through a photograph.

(D) Fourth Design. In this model, known only from a photograph, Rogers raised Eliot in relation to the Indian figures, removed the grape vines entirely, and put the child to sleep. Eliot and the rock on which he stands appear to be detached from the rest of the group. This model was probably made during the summer of 1889.

(E) Fifth Design. In this version, also dating probably from the summer or early autumn of 1889, the sculptor eliminated the Indian child and substituted for the open Bible of the other versions a half-closed Bible held open at two places by Eliot's fingers. As in (D) the figure of Eliot is detachable. The model is of bronzed plaster, 36 inches in height, and is signed JOHN ROGERS/NEW YORK. Rogers gave this model to Dr. Ellsworth Eliot of New York City, a descendant of the subject who had been helpful to the artist in his research. Dr. Eliot presented it in 1901 to the Eliot Church in Natick, Massachusetts. Since that time it has been on loan to the South Natick Historical, Natural History, and Library Society.

(F) Sixth Design. The final version of "John Eliot Preaching to the Indians" was exhibited, in the clay, at a reception in the sculptor's New York studio on January 16, 1890. Although at least one critic felt the pose stiff and the modelling lacking in fluency, the consensus was that this colossal "group" was Rogers' most important work. The size was one and a half times the size of life or, roughly, fifteen feet. The surviving photograph shows that Rogers had made further changes in the figure of Eliot, mainly by opening his gown wide and by substituting low shoes for the high boots of the earlier versions. Rogers himself felt that this was the most important work of his career. After casting it in plaster he exhibited it at the National Academy of Design in the autumn of 1891 and at the Boston Museum of Fine Arts in January-March 1892. Despite efforts by the Hon. Robert C. Winthrop, Edward Everett Hale, and others the people of Roxbury and Boston failed to raise a subscription for the statue. When Rogers closed his New York studio in May 1895, the plaster cast of "John Eliot" was broken up and, according to Miss Katherine R. Rogers (1934), the pieces thrown into the East River.

(D)

(F)

178. THE FIRST RIDE

Plaster, painted; height 18 inches
Signed JOHN ROGERS/NEW YORK
Patented September 4, 1888
Price: $12.00
Collections:
Type A: 5
Type B: 1, 2, 3, 9
Bronze master model (Type A): The New-York Historical Society, purchased in 1936 from Katherine R. Rogers

Two versions of this group exist. In Type A the woman is bare-headed, in Type B she is wearing a hat. The hat appears in the description and photograph submitted with Rogers patent application (May 28, 1888); in the 1890, 1892, and 1895 catalogues; and in all known plaster copies but one. The hat is lacking in the bronze master model, in the 1888 catalogue, in the June 7, 1888 issue of *Geyer's Stationer,* New York City, and in one surviving plaster copy. The evidence is inconclusive, but suggests that the hat was an afterthought, added as more in keeping with the "citified" costume of the lady, who is only visiting in the country according to Rogers' catalogue.

179. POLITICS

Plaster, painted; height 18 inches
Signed JOHN ROGERS/NEW YORK
Patented November 13, 1888
Price $15.00
Collections: 1, 2, 3, 4, 5, 6, 7, 9
Bronze master model: The New-York Historical Society, purchased in 1936 from Katherine R. Rogers.

"Rogers, the inimitable, makes a happy contribution to the campaign in clay," reported the New Orleans *Picayune's* New York correspondent in October 1888. The campaign saw President Cleveland unsuccessfully defend his place against Republican challenger Benjamin Harrison. Rogers' contribution was a humorous group which was strictly nonpartisan and appropriate for any future campaign year. This was the last group Rogers patented and the last for which he had a bronze master model.

180. GRANT MONUMENT

Design for a statuary group; not completed

A letter from Robert C. Winthrop to John Rogers, December 18, 1888, strongly suggests that Rogers intended to design a Grant Monument or perhaps simply a Grant memorial group in the manner of "The Council of War" [112]. Winthrop advised the sculptor not to include in his design either President Lincoln or his Secretary of War, Edwin M. Stanton. "I do not believe," he wrote, "that his [Stanton's] figure is likely to promote the popularity of such a work, & Lincoln should not be used as a subordinate figure. Grant, Sherman & Sheridan would make a better trio." Apparently nothing came of this project, except perhaps the models of "Sherman" and "Sheridan" [181, 182] found in Rogers' studio in 1895, after his retirement.

181. WILLIAM TECUMSEH SHERMAN (1820–91)

Model for an equestrian statue, probably plaster

Unlocated

An equestrian figure of General Sherman was listed among the works removed from Rogers' studio when it was sold in 1895. There is no other reference to it, but this model, like that of "Sheridan" [182], may have been part of Rogers' abortive design for a Grant Monument [180] referred to by Robert C. Winthrop in a letter of December 18, 1888. It is also possible that the 1895 reporter mistakenly identified as Sherman one of Rogers' models for his equestrian of "John Fulton Reynolds" [164]. In any case, the model has not been heard of since.

182. PHILIP HENRY SHERIDAN (1831–88)

Model for an equestrian statue, in plaster

Unlocated

When Rogers studio in New York was emptied in May 1895, the works removed from it included an equestrian figure of General Philip Sheridan.

This model, of which a photograph has survived, apparently was given to Rogers' friend, the artist Henry W. Herrick of Manchester, New Hampshire. Rogers' obituary in the Manchester *Union,* July 28, 1904, stated that Herrick had in his home Rogers' "last work," a statue of Phil Sheridan rallying his troops at the battle of Winchester, intended to be cast in bronze. No later reference to this has been found. Miss Katherine Rogers thought the model was made in competition for a commission which Rogers did not get. This is borne out by a letter of Robert C. Winthrop, December 18, 1888, advising Rogers to omit Stanton and Lincoln from his Grant Monument design because "Grant, Sherman and Sheridan would make a better trio" [180].

183. FIGHTING BOB

Plaster, painted; height 34 inches
Signed JOHN ROGERS
Published in October 1889; not patented
Price: $12.00
Collections: 1, 2, 3, 5, 9

The 1888 theater season in New York was marked by a popular revival of Richard Brinsley Sheridan's *The Rivals,* in which Joseph Jefferson starred as Bob Acres. John Rogers approached Jefferson about doing a figure of "Fighting Bob" in December 1888 and executed the model during the first months of 1889. On April 15, Jefferson wrote from Cincinnati: "The statuette of Acres seems to me to be an admirable work, but it has one fault, it looks like a man who would fight instead of a man who would rather not. This renders the figure less humorous than if he was *trying* to look bold. I am glad it is still in the clay and if you can wait I will give you a sitting early in June." Of the final version, Jefferson wrote on August 18, 1889: "I think the likeness has been improved but my family fancy that it looks too old. The strong downward light on my face when you photographed it may have made the lines too deep. But I should call it a success." The photograph referred to (in the papers of John Rogers at The New-York Historical Society) is a close-up of Jefferson in the character but not in costume. Also in the same collection is a full-length commercial photograph of him in costume, in the same attitude as Rogers' figure.

184. CHESS

Plaster, painted; height 21½ inches
Signed JOHN ROGERS/NEW YORK
Published in May 1889; not patented
Price: $15.00
Collections: 1, 3, 5, 6, 9, 10

"Chess," completed in May 1889, was a sophisticated reworking of the youth versus age theme Rogers had used with such success in "Checkers Up at the Farm" [145] and even earlier in "Checker Players" [61]. "The position of the pieces on the board," Rogers' catalogue informed the prospective purchaser, "is taken from a problem given in the frontispiece of Staunton's 'Chess Player's Companion.' The Bishop, King, Pawn and Queen in the second row, and starting from the left hand, are white, and black is to be checkmated in seven moves." The sculptor and two of his sons, Alex and Derby, were avid chess players, according to Katherine R. Rogers.

185, 186. HEAD OF A HORSE

Studies in clay or plaster

At the Autumn Exhibition of the National Academy of Design, 1889, John Rogers exhibited two studies of the head of a horse. These may have been made in preparation for his abortive equestrian of General John Stark [188]. "Vidette," writing for *The Woman's Cycle,* October 30, 1889, mentioned that the sculptor had recently brought a horse into his courtyard studio at 14 West 12th Street and had made "a beautiful model of his head from life. Rogers dotes on equines," this correspondent went on, "and is never so happy in his work as when modelling them." Neither of these studies, presumably in clay or plaster, appears to have survived.

187. JOHN STARK (1728–1822)

Model for a statue, in bronzed plaster; height 26 inches

Signed JOHN ROGERS/NEW YORK

Collection: Essex Institute, Salem, Massachusetts

In 1889 the State of New Hampshire invited designs for a statue honoring General John Stark, New Hampshire's Revolutionary hero, to be placed in State House Park, Concord. John Rogers was one of eleven sculptors who responded. The winning design was submitted by Charles Conrad, but Rogers' model was strongly preferred by certain vocal journalists (see Concord *Patriot,* January 17, 1890, and Portsmouth *Daily Evening Times,* February 3, 1890), who felt that it best represented the vigorous man who led the assault at Bennington in August 1777 crying, "There they are boys! We beat them today or Molly Stark sleeps a widow tonight!" Rogers presented the rejected model to the Hon. Charles R. Morrison of Concord, projector of the scheme for the Stark statue. In 1933 the model was purchased from another private owner in Manchester by the Essex Institute of Salem, Massachusetts. A duplicate, or possibly an earlier or later version of this standing figure was given by Rogers to the Manchester Art Association in May 1895. This presumably was destroyed in the fire that gutted the Kennard Building in January 1902 and obliterated the most complete collection of Rogers' works then in existence.

188. JOHN STARK (1728–1822)

Model for equestrian statue, in plaster

Destroyed

At the same time he was producing his model for a standing full-length statue of General Stark [187], Rogers also modelled an equestrian statuette of the same subject. The New Orleans *Picayune's* correspondent saw it in Rogers' studio in October 1889 and praised the "small sketch model" as "full of spirit, both in man and beast." In January 1890 the City Council of Manchester petitioned Congress to appropriate $50,000 for an equestrian statue after John Rogers' design, to be placed over Stark's grave in Manchester. A bill to this effect was introduced in the United States Senate in 1892, but nothing came of the proposal. The model was on display in the rooms of the Manchester Art Association in May 1895 and is believed to have been destroyed when the building burned in January 1902.

189. UNIDENTIFIED CHILD

Medium and size not known
Unlocated

In a letter to his son Alexander P. Rogers (February 22, 1893) Rogers made a passing reference to an incident which occurred when he was modelling "the little child that went to the Newark Cemetery. I had just finished John Eliot and he was standing over us." This would probably date the incident toward the end of 1889, when Rogers completed his final, heroic-size model of "John Eliot" [177].

190. GROVER CLEVELAND

Portrait bust
Unlocated; possibly not executed

On June 12, 1890, ex-President Grover Cleveland wrote to John Rogers from Marion, Massachusetts, agreeing to sit for the sculptor on his return to New York in September. "Though I have almost flatly resolved to steer clear of gentlemen of your cloth," Cleveland added, "I find myself willing to yield very readily to your suggestion, contained in a letter to Mr. Choate [Joseph H. Choate], which he forwarded to me, adding a powerful word of persuasion of his own." There is no further mention of this in Rogers' papers and it is not known whether Rogers actually did model a portrait of Cleveland.

191. JOSÉ ANTONIO PÁEZ (1790–1873)

Portrait bust; bronze; twice life-size
Unlocated

On June 18, 1890, John Rogers signed a contract with Ramón Páez of New York City, agreeing

to model and cast in bronze a heroic bust of General José Antonio Páez, Venezuelan patriot and president. Rogers was to receive $500.00 on approval of the plaster model and $1,250.00 on delivery of the finished bronze. The bronze bust was exhibited by Rogers at the National Academy's Autumn Exhibition. "Vidette," in the New Orleans *Picayune* for December 2, 1890, described the bust as "a work of great vigor and fine portraiture, which belongs to Venezuela." The bust was designed to stand atop a tall column, but Venezuelan authorities have not been able to determine its present whereabouts.

192. JOSÉ ANTONIO PÁEZ (1790–1873)

Model for an equestrian statue; plaster
Unlocated

Rogers' contract with Sr. Ramón Páez, June 18, 1890, also specified that Rogers agreed to give Páez "a copy in plaster of the equestrian statuette he made of Genl. Páez which Mr. Páez agrees not to reproduce. If it should ever be used as a model for an equestrian statue," the contract concludes, "it is agreed that no one but Mr. Rogers shall make it." Neither Venezuelan authorities nor descendants of General Páez know the fate of this statuette.

193. FAUST AND MARGUERITE: THEIR FIRST MEETING

Plaster, painted; height 22 inches
Signed 14 W 12 ST/JOHN ROGERS/NEW YORK
Published in November 1890; not patented
Price: $12.00 (1890); $10.00 (1892, 1895)
Collections: 1, 2, 3, 4, 5, 9

The first of Rogers' three scenes from Goethe's *Faust,* as popularized in Gounod's opera, this group illustrates these lines from Part I:

Faust. Fair lady, may I thus make free
To offer you my arm and company?
Marguerite. I am no lady, am not fair,
Can without escort home repair.

The lines, quoted in Rogers' catalogue, are from Bayard Taylor's translation (1870). Rogers exhibited this group at the 1890 Autumn Exhibition of the National Academy of Design, priced at $15.00.

194. MARGUERITE AND MARTHA: TRYING ON THE JEWELS

Plaster, painted; height 23 inches
Signed JOHN ROGERS/NEW YORK
Published in 1891; not patented
Price: $10.00
Collections: only two copies are known, both in private collections

Rogers' version of the Jewel Scene in *Faust* was shown at the National Academy's Annual Exhibition, April 1891, along with "Faust and Marguerite Leaving the Garden" [195]. "The expression of the faces in both groups is marvelously lifelike," J. H. Elliott ("Vidette") reported to the New Orleans *Picayune,* April 20, 1891, "and the characteristic painstaking elaboration of costume, details and accessories gives a degree of perfection pervasively gratifying to artistic sense." For some reason, Rogers did not put "Marguerite and Martha: Trying on the Jewels" in his catalogue or in his advertisements. A few copies evidently were sold, however. The National Academy Catalogue listed this group at $10.00.

195. FAUST AND MARGUERITE LEAVING THE GARDEN

Plaster, painted; height 24½ inches
Signed JOHN ROGERS/NEW YORK
Published in 1891; not patented
Price: $15.00
Collections: 1, 2, 3, 5, 6, 9, 14

Rogers' last *Faust* group appeared, with the Jewel Scene [194], in the National Academy's Annual Exhibition in April 1891. It was also listed in Rogers' 1892 catalogue and the 1895 catalogue of the Rogers Statuette Company.

196. PORTRAIT BUST

Rogers exhibited a portrait bust of an unidentified subject at the National Academy of Design, Spring Exhibition, 1891.

197, 198. TWO PORTRAIT BUSTS

Rogers exhibited two portrait busts of unidentified subjects at the National Academy of Design, Autumn Exhibition, 1891.

199. FOOTBALL

Plaster, painted; height 15 inches
Signed JOHN ROGERS/14 WEST 12 ST/NEW YORK
Published in October 1891; not patented
Price: $10.00
Collections: 1, 2, 3, 5, 6, 9

A novel attempt to capture the drama of college football in a small statuette, "Football" was hailed by the Minneapolis *Commercial Bulletin* (December 12, 1891) as "one of the most clever and stirring pieces he has yet produced. There is action clearly set forth, and the prominence now given this game will make it very popular." John W. Boteler & Sons, Washington, D.C., offered a copy of this group as a prize for the amateur club champions of the 1891–92 season. According to the *National Encyclopedia of American Biography* (1948), three of Rogers' sons posed for this group, with William Herbert Corbin (1864–1945), captain of Yale's unbeaten 1888 team and All-American center. All five of the Rogers boys went to Yale, and distinguished themselves in rowing, but none made the football team.

200. STAMFORD MEMORIAL

Design for a monument, probably destroyed

In the fall of 1891 Rogers was approached by a committee charged with securing a monument to memorialize the 250th anniversary of Stamford, Connecticut. Rogers produced a model, about one-eighth the proposed size, which was heartily recommended for adoption by the committee in a report dated January 22, 1892. Rogers' model

featured a central group, eight feet high, depicting the purchase of the site from the Indians in 1642; flanking seven-foot figures represented the Continental soldier of 1776 and the Union soldier of 1861; the whole was to stand on a nine- or ten-foot stone base. The estimated cost was $35,000, of which $13,500 was to be appropriated by the Town and the balance raised by public subscription. Although Rogers' design was accepted and his model displayed during the spring of 1892 in the window of Lyman Hoyt's Sons & Company, Stamford, Rogers sadly admitted in May that the Stamford monument was "about hopeless." For lack of financial support, the project fell through. What happened to the model is not known.

201. LAURA DERBY ROGERS (1879–97)

Portrait bust
Destroyed

When his younger daughter was about twelve years old, in 1891 or 1892, Rogers modelled a small bust of her which, according to her sister (1955), did not turn out very well and was not kept. Laura died at the age of eighteen of typhoid fever. See also No. 225.

202. HENRY E. HOWLAND

Portrait statuette; plaster, bronzed; height 19 inches
Signed JOHN ROGERS/NEW YORK/1892
Collections: Century Association and The New-York Historical Society

Judge Henry E. Howland was the Secretary of the Century Club, of which John Rogers became a member in 1864. This comic portrait with its ill-matched head and body was a present from the artist to the Club on Twelfth Night, 1892. Rogers described it as "a statuette of an officer of the club as seen through Twelfth Night glasses." The Club's formal letter of acceptance, signed by Judge Howland himself on February 10, 1892, is in the artist's papers. The duplicate, also in bronzed plaster, belonged at one time to Miss

Frances Howland; after her death it was given to Alexander Parker Rogers, son of the sculptor, and his widow in turn lent it to The New-York Historical Society.

203. ABRAHAM LINCOLN (1809–65)

Seated statue; plaster and replica in bronze one third larger than life-size

Collection: City of Manchester, New Hampshire

In March 1892 it was reported in the Manchester *Union* that John Rogers had just completed a large seated figure of Abraham Lincoln. The artist exhibited the plaster model at the National Academy in 1892 and at the World's Columbian Exposition in Chicago the following year. It won him a bronze medal at the latter. Two years later, in May 1895, Rogers presented the plaster model to the City of Manchester, personally supervising its installation in the City Library. The statue was moved in April 1902 to less cramped quarters in the main corridor of the city's new high school. In 1910 a bronze replica was made and placed on a granite pedestal in front of the high school, where it remains. The plaster model was then placed in the Hallsville Grammar School.

204. THE WATCH ON THE SANTA MARIA

Plaster, painted; height 15½ inches

Signed JOHN ROGERS/14 W 12 ST/NEW YORK

Published in October 1892; not patented

Price: $10.00; $8.00 (1895)

Collections: 1, 3, 5, 9

The last group "published" by John Rogers honored Christopher Columbus on the four-hundredth anniversary of his discovery of America. Five months later, on February 1, 1893, Rogers announced the sale of his statuette business to William Brush, his foreman, who carried on for several years under the name of Rogers Statuette Company.

205. WILLIAM CULLEN BRYANT (1794–1878)

Portrait bust; plaster, bronzed; life-size

Signed WM. C. BRYANT/BY/JOHN ROGERS/NEW YORK/1892

Collection: The New-York Historical Society, purchased in 1936 from Katherine R. Rogers

Why Rogers should have executed this bust fourteen years after the subject's death is unexplained, although it is possible that it was intended for the centennial of his birth (1894). In any case, it remained in the artist's possession. It was a worthy tribute from the artist to the poet who had written to him in 1869: "You have succeeded in a higher degree than almost any artist of any age in making sculpture a narrative art, and giving to motionless and speechless figures the power to relate their own adventures."

206. WILLIAM CULLEN BRYANT (1794–1878)

Sketch for a seated statue; probably clay

Unlocated

In the New York *Times* of December 17, 1893, Charles de Kay spoke of a "sketch for a seated statue of William Cullen Bryant" by John Rogers as "easy, simple, and very true to life." The younger sculptor William Ordway Partridge singled out the same work for praise in his article on Rogers in the *New England Magazine,* February 1896, p. 715:

> There is in one of the New York studios [wrote Partridge] an original sketch by Rogers of the poet Bryant. It is one of a number of Rogers's sketches or studies which have never come before the public eye. It represents the poet in an easy attitude, sitting in his garden, his head dropped carelessly upon his right hand, as if he had stolen out there from his library to seek the quiet and loveliness of nature apart from the world of noise as well as the world of books. It is a very natural and suggestive study — one of those things in art which look as if they had happened without effort.

Why and when this statuette was made is not apparent, although it is possible that Rogers had Bryant's centennial (1894) in mind when he did this and his large bust [205]. Two Rockwood photographs of Bryant, seated with his head supported by his right hand, are among Rogers' effects at The New-York Historical Society.

207. LANDING OF THE NORSEMEN

Bronze; one-third life-size
Signed JOHN ROGERS/NEW YORK/1893
Collection: The New-York Historical Society, purchased in 1936 from Katherine R. Rogers. The Society also owns the disassembled plaster model.

Rogers' last and one of his most ambitious works, "Landing of the Norsemen" was modelled and cast after palsy had begun to affect the sculptor's hands. In spite of this, Rogers put just as much effort and care into its modelling and its historical details as he had into earlier works. The boat and all the details of the group, his circular announced, were copied "from actual relics found in the burial mounds of the Vikings." The Runic inscription, drawn from the poem *Havamal* (from the ninth century) in the *Edda,* was supplied by Professor William H. Carpenter of Columbia College. The only published criticism of the work was highly favorable. Charles de Kay, in the *New York Times,* May 17, 1893, spoke of it as "uncommonly good in its manly, simple straightforwardness," and appropriate for its intended use in a public park or large building. The bronze cast Rogers lent in 1894 to the Corcoran Gallery in Washington, where it remained until 1901. It was then lent to the Brooklyn Institute of Arts and Sciences for almost thirty years. In April 1902 Rogers offered the original plaster model to the Art Section of the Manchester Institute of Arts and Sciences. It is unlikely, however, that this gift was actually consummated, since The New-York Historical Society has what appear to be the parts of the original plaster model.

208. HENRY WARD BEECHER (1813–87)

Portrait bust, plaster
Private collection

This bust with ornamental base bears the following label: "Copyrighted 1896 by/Rogers Statuette Co./New York." Although there is an obviously close relationship between the bust and both the Beecher statuette [176] and the life mask [217] executed by John Rogers, it is unlikely that Rogers had a direct part in producing the bust as copyrighted. The base, decorated with the American eagle, shield, and olive branch, is notably uncharacteristic. The Rogers Statuette Company was organized by William Brush, foreman of Rogers' factory, to market the sculptor's remaining stock after Rogers retired in February 1893. The company issued catalogues in 1894 and 1895, which included only one previously unpublished work of John Rogers, "The Bath" [118], probably dating from around 1870. "Beecher," like "The Bath," may have been an old work of Rogers dressed up to look "like new," and it is listed here for that reason. The only known copy is privately owned.

Life Masks and Other Casts

Between 1860 and 1891 John Rogers made at least sixteen casts of the faces, hands, arms, or feet of relatives and other subjects. These were done in plaster and used as guides in the modeling of portrait busts or of other works. Since they are not, strictly speaking, "works" of John Rogers, though they are from his hand, they are here listed separately in chronological order.

209. MARTHA DERBY ROGERS (1840–1925)

Cast of hand; August 18, 1860; unlocated

John Rogers' sister Martha was visiting him in New York when this "very nice cast" of her hand was taken. "It is getting dangerous for people to come into my studio now," the sculptor wrote next day, "for I stick them right into plaster after first lubricating them in the way they say Boa Constrictors do."

210. JOHN ROGERS (1829–1904)

Life mask; June 1861; privately owned

On June 8, 1861, Rogers wrote: "I performed quite a feat in casting this week. I had so much confidence in my new plan of casting that I took a cast of my own face all alone by myself & with entire success — showing my whole face including one ear, leaving holes for the eyes."

211. JOHN ROGERS (1800–84)

Life mask; July 1861

This cast of his father's face, taken at Roxbury in July 1861, served to guide the sculptor in his attempt to model a bust of the elder Rogers [84]. It was a very successful cast, according to the artist: "His face is so marked that the resemblance is particularly good." Miss Katherine R. Rogers recalled in 1955 that this cast hung for about sixty years on the wall of Rogers' New Canaan studio.

212. SARAH ELLEN DERBY ROGERS (1805–77)

Life mask; July 1861

This cast of his mother's face, taken at Roxbury during a visit home, was used by Rogers when he was modelling the portrait bust [96] now at The New-York Historical Society.

213. CLARA POMEROY ROGERS (1838–1907)

Life mask; July 1861; unlocated

Rogers' third sister submitted to having a cast made of her face while John was visiting his family in Roxbury in July 1861. The cast turned out spotted, John later reported, and may have been discarded at the time.

214. ELIZABETH BROMFIELD ROGERS (1844–1924)

Life mask and, possibly, a cast of her feet; unlocated

John Rogers' twin sisters, Bessie and Fanny, were among those he "pursued" with his plaster during a visit to Roxbury in July 1861. The cast he made from Bessie's face was one of the most successful, he reported, because he took it in a natural sitting position. He used it in modelling "Air Castles" [80]. He may also have taken a cast or casts of Bessie's feet; in a letter of August 29, 1861, to his mother, he wrote that the girl in "Air Castles" "has got real country girl's feet if they *are* Bessie's."

215. FRANCES STETSON ROGERS (1844–1923)

Life mask; July 1861; unlocated

Fanny Rogers' life mask, taken at the same time as Bessie's (above), was less successful but served to aid her brother's modelling of "Air Castles" [80]. "Jemima," John wrote the girls on August 11, 1861, "shows her gratitude in her improved looks."

216. MRS. GEORGE OSGOOD HOLYOKE

Life mask; October 1862; The New-York Historical Society

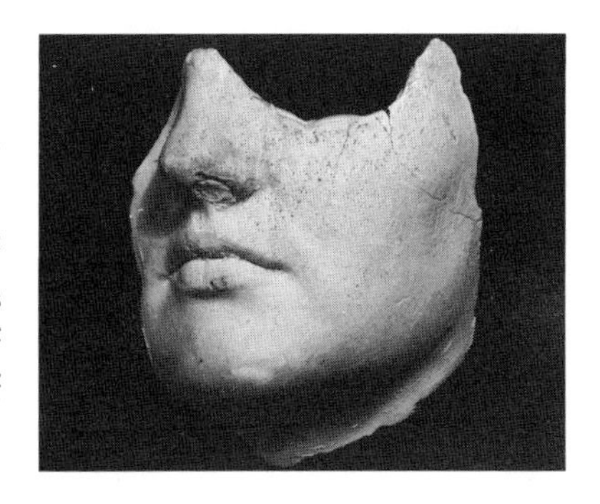

This damaged mask, showing only the lower half of the subject's face, presumably was intended as a guide to the sculptor in modelling his bust of Mrs. Holyoke [95], referred to in a letter of October 5, 1862.

217. EDWIN BOOTH (1833–93)

Life mask; November 1862; unlocated

When he began work on his statuette of Booth as Hamlet [97] in November 1862, Rogers took a cast of the actor's features, fortunately, as it turned out. "Mr. Booth's time is so taken up that he has never given me a fair sitting since the first day," Rogers complained. "If I had not got the cast I should have been entirely unable to proceed."

218. JOHN ROGERS (1866–1939)

Life mask; 1866; unlocated

A life mask of the sculptor's eldest son, born in February 1866, is said to have been made when he was "only a few months old" (Smith, *Rogers Groups,* p. 115).

219. HENRY WARD BEECHER (1813–87)

Life mask, 1869; Plymouth Church, Brooklyn, New York

During the last week of June 1869, after several sittings for "The Fugitive's Story" [116], Rogers suggested to Beecher that further sittings would be unnecessary if he would let a cast be made of his features. Beecher replied (as reported in the New York *Tribune,* May 21, 1887, quoting John Rogers): "If it will be of any service you can take the cast now." When asked if Beecher found the process annoying, Rogers said: "No, Mr. Beecher told me afterward that he nearly went to sleep." Rogers kept the mask in his studio until March 1894 when he presented it to Plymouth Church, Brooklyn, Beecher's church. "A miscarriage of letters" caused a delay of four years in the church's formal acknowledgment of the gift. "Its value as a relic," the Trustees belatedly wrote in April 1898, "so intimately associated with Mr. Beecher's personality . . . and the value of this Mask as a likeness . . . enhances our appreciation of the generous and discriminating impulse that prompted Mr. Rogers to place it in our Archives."

220. WILLIAM LLOYD GARRISON (1805–79)

Life mask; 1869; unlocated

Rogers made a cast of Garrison's face at the latter's home in Roxbury, Massachusetts, on July 7, 1869. Like the Beecher mask (above), it was intended as an aid in completing "The Fugitive's Story" [116]. The cast was listed among others found in

Rogers' studio at 14 West Twelfth Street, New York, when it was dismantled in 1895, after the sculptor's retirement. It may have been one of the items from the studio subsequently sold for Rogers by his bronze-founder, P. E. Guerin.

221. ALEXANDER HAMILTON (1757–1804)

"Mask"; c. 1871; unlocated

When Rogers' New York studio was dismantled in 1895, the New York *Sun* reported a "mask" of Alexander Hamilton among its contents. This was probably a study for "Camp Fires of the Revolution" [125] based on the bust by Ceracchi owned by John C. Hamilton and measured by Rogers in 1871 or 1872. It is possible that Rogers actually made a cast from the original.

222. CHARLES SUMNER (1811–74)

Life mask (?); unlocated

The New York *Sun,* in May 1895, reported a mask of Charles Sumner among the items found in Rogers' New York studio when it was emptied. There is no other reference to such a mask. The mask of "Edwin Vose Sumner" listed in Smith, *Rogers Groups,* p. 114, is probably the same one, misnamed, since there is no other evidence that Rogers did a mask of Edwin Vose Sumner and the Smiths did not list the one of Charles Sumner.

223. DAVID FRANCIS ROGERS (1876–1943)

Cast of arm; c. 1878; privately owned

Miss Katharine R. Rogers identified this in 1955 as a cast made of the arm of her brother David "when he was two or three years old, as a model for a child in one of the groups." It was probably for "The Photograph" [156], published in 1878.

224. ROBERT COLLYER (1823–1912)

Life mask, c. 1879; unlocated

Rogers' life mask of his friend, the Rev. Robert Collyer, was noted in descriptions of his studio in 1887 and again in 1895. The cast was probably made in 1879, when Rogers used Collyer as the model for Antonio in his group "Is It So Nominated in the Bond?" [160]. Collyer's bust measurements were entered in Rogers' sketchbook about the same time. The subject, a Scot who came to the United States in 1850, worked as a blacksmith and Methodist lay-preacher before being called to Chicago in 1859 to serve as Unitarian minister-at-large among the city's poor. The same year he became the first minister of Unity Church, where he stayed until called to the pastorate of New York's Church of the Messiah in 1879. His friendship with Rogers, begun in Chicago in 1859, continued to the end of the artist's life. It was Robert Collyer, at the age of 81, who conducted John Rogers' funeral.

225. LAURA DERBY ROGERS (1879–97)

Life mask, c. 1891–92; The New-York Historical Society

Rogers made this mask of his younger daughter when she was twelve years old, for a bust which was never completed [201]. Laura died of typhoid fever shortly after her eighteenth birthday.

Works Mistakenly Attributed to John Rogers

There are three works attributed to John Rogers in the Smith catalogue of 1934 which the present author believes not to be his work. They are "Bronze Wreath of Leaves and Berries Surrounding Mirror" (Smith, *Rogers Groups,* p. 124), "Fido" (Smith, p. 128), and "Trout Fishing/Landing a Beauty" (Smith, p. 66). The present author concurs with the Smiths in rejecting the seated statuette of William Lloyd Garrison (p. 135). Each of these is considered separately below, along with certain other genre statuary groups which have been or may be wrongly attributed to John Rogers.

MIRROR FRAME

The cast-iron ivy-leaf mirror frame in the collection of The New-York Historical Society was given by John Rogers to his mother as a Christmas present in 1850, during his first year at the Amoskeag Machine Shop in Manchester, New Hampshire. "The mirror frame was cast at the foundry here," he wrote home on December 24, 1850, "& I finished it." If he had also designed the frame himself it seems unlikely that he would have failed to mention that fact. He also did not list the mirror frame among his works when he wrote them down in pencil about 1858 [Nos. 1–45]. The most likely explanation is that the frame was a product of the Amoskeag Foundry operations, to which Rogers, as an employee, was able to add a "custom finish." This interpretation is bolstered by the fact that two duplicates of the Rogers mirror frame have turned up recently. One duplicate, now owned by the New Canaan Historical Society, was pictured in *Antiques,* March 1962, p. 305. The other is in the collection of the Brooks Free Library, Harwich, Massachusetts.

FIDO

Plaster, painted; height 8¼ inches
Inscription: (front) FIDO; (back) JOHN ROGER/204 5TH AVE. NY
Collection: Albany Institute

This little statuette of a puppy was purchased by Benjamin Walworth Arnold in 1932 for $5.00 from a dealer in Albany who had bought it from Miss Henrietta Lyle, formerly of 179 South Pearl Street, Albany. Its authenticity is open to question for several reasons: (1) neither the modelling nor the lettering is like Rogers' other work of 1861–65 (when he was at 204 Fifth Avenue); (2) the figure is not mentioned in any of Rogers' letters; (3) there is an identical figure, unsigned and entitled "Nobody Loves Me," in a private collection in Hannibal, Missouri. Although the evidence is inconclusive, the writer is inclined to believe that "Fido" is not the work of John Rogers, despite the inscription.

TROUT FISHING/LANDING A BEAUTY

In 1934 the Smiths catalogued this as a work of John Rogers (*Rogers Groups,* p. 66, No. 12) on the strength of a stereoscopic view labelled "Rogers Groups/Selected," in the collection of the American Antiquarian Society. The same group is pictured on another stereograph, labelled "Statuary/Rogers Groups/No. 987," distributed by William Y. McAllister, Philadelphia, about 1868 (Essex Institute). The group is definitely not the work of John Rogers, however. Two copies of it in plaster have turned up since the Smith catalogue was published. They bear the signature, on the edge of the base toward the viewer's left, of "Samuel Conkey, New York." A portion of this signature can also be made out on the American Antiquarian Society stereograph.

Samuel Conkey (1830–1904) was a sculptor and landscape painter, born in New York City, who lived for a time in Chicago but returned to New York after losing everything in the Fire of 1871. His only other known statuette is "In the Wilderness," a Civil War subject which he patented in 1866 and exhibited at the National Academy in 1867. A copy is owned by the Society for the Preservation of New England Antiquities. A stereograph, unlabelled, was also published (author's collection). "Trout Fishing" was not patented or exhibited, so it can only be dated approximately, no later than 1868.

WILLIAM LLOYD GARRISON

Plaster; height 25 inches
Collection: Massachusetts Historical Society

This excellent statuette, presented to the Massachusetts Historical Society by a member of the Garrison family, has been wrongly attributed to John Rogers (*Bulletin* of the Society for the Preservation of New England Antiquities, January 1933). It is unsigned and, as the Chetwood Smiths pointed out in 1934 (*Rogers Groups,* p. 135), the treatment of the eyes is uncharacteristic of Rogers, the iris being in relief rather than recessed. Rogers did do a seated full-length statuette of Garrison as part of "The Fugitive's Story" [116] which bears no particular resemblance to this one.

LOTTA AS THE MARCHIONESS

About 1875 this subject was listed on the back of at least three series of stereoscopic views of Rogers Groups. In a surviving copy of the view published by J. W. & J. S. Moulton of Salem, Massachusetts (Essex Institute Collection) the base of this statuette of a carefree but ragged servant girl bears a faint signature which appears to be "J. S.

Hartley." This would indicate that "Lotta" was an early work of Jonathan Scott Hartley (1846– ?). Hartley, a native of Albany, New York, studied there under Erastus Dow Palmer in 1863–64, spent over five years in Europe, and opened a studio in New York City in 1875. He became famous as a portrait sculptor, gaining particular note as the portrayer of actors in character.

Other Misattributions

Besides those which have been wrongly attributed to John Rogers for good, though mistaken, reasons, there are many other plaster groups and single figures extant or pictured on stereographs that have been casually credited to Rogers simply because he is the only well-known sculptor of genre subjects. Even pieces bearing the names of other artists have been ascribed to Rogers. For the sake of the record those "non-Rogers Groups" that have come to the author's notice are listed below.

Caspar Hennecke & Co. of Milwaukee, Wisconsin, produced a line of "Florentine Statuary" in the 1880s and 1890s which certainly outshone Rogers' efforts in quantity if not in quality. Their Catalogue No. 5, 1887 (Landauer Collection, The New-York Historical Society) lists over a thousand pieces in every imaginable form. Hennecke employed mainly European-trained modellers and his genre groups, though well enough executed, are quite different in character from Rogers' work. Some were copyrighted and bear Hennecke's label, but many were not marked and can be distinguished from the products of other statuette factories only if they appear in the Hennecke catalogues. The following are some Hennecke titles of which copies have been reported:

- Faust and Marguerite
- Fast Asleep
- Wolf and Lamb
- By Jingo
- Taking the Cream
- At the Seaside
- First Love
- Family Cares
- You Dirty Boy

J. J. West, Chicago, was an agent for Rogers Groups in 1877–79 but from 1883 to 1885 advertised his own product, marked "West's Statuary." His advertisements in *The Continent* in 1883 pictured "Alpine Hunter" and "The Lost, Found," each at $6.00. "West's Statuary" is stamped on the underside of "Can't You Talk?" in the author's collection.

Perth Amboy Terra Cotta Company advertised in *The Century,* February 1889, a reproduction of Edward Kemey's "Panther and Cubs," at $5.00.

John Deacon produced two baseball statuettes which he patented, with *Carl Muller* in 1868. Muller alone patented two figures of newsboys in 1868 and another pair of baseball figures in 1869.

C. Slater signed a piece called "Mamie's Dead."

Of unknown authorship are the following:

- John Anderson, my Jo
- Tam O'Shanter
- Volunteer's Nurse
- Pets
- Playing Grandma
- Never Mind
- Love's Message
- Home, Sweet Home
- Johnny (soldier)
- Auld Lang Syne
- A Capitol Joke

This list could be extended almost indefinitely, for genre statuary enjoyed great popularity, in Europe as well as in America, throughout the period of Rogers' career. In the United States, however, only John Rogers succeeded in identifying himself with his productions, with the result that he is now credited with the entire output of his competitors. In identifying his work the important thing to remember is that his "published" works in plaster invariably bore his name in block letters. If this is lacking (not just worn off or painted over), the work is not a Rogers Group.

Appendices

Making a Rogers Group

THE PRODUCTION of the Rogers Group typically involved at least ten distinct processes: (1) the choice of the subject and general design; (2) sketching out the design in the rough; (3) making a finished model of the group in clay; (4) taking a pattern cast from the clay model; (5) making the bronze master model; (6) preparing the molds for casting replicas; (7), (8), and (9) the casting, finishing, and coloring of the replicas; and (10) storing or packing the casts. Each of these will be considered separately in the following pages.

1. *Subject and General Design*

As has been shown in a previous chapter, John Rogers was firmly convinced that success in sculpture depended more on the story than on any other factor, even design. His first concern, therefore, always was to find a telling subject. Despite his lament that he had not "the mental capacity to think of them with greater ease," Rogers managed to think of more than seventy usable subjects in thirty-five years, an average of better than two a year. These were drawn chiefly from three sources: the contemporary American scene, American history, and English and American literature.

Rogers made a great point of the fact that he generally thought up his subjects himself. "I used to think," he wrote to his sister Ellen in 1863, "that I should be overrun with suggestions for designs & it quite surprises me to think that I never have had a single suggestion that was of the least assistance to me." Not that he received no suggestions: in his early days in New York he solicited and received a good many from Ellen herself, but her taste tended more toward the ideal and the allegorical than did her sculptor-brother's. Later, according to one of his children, he used to receive many elaborate drawings from strangers for development into groups. These, too, he ignored.

The search for an idea was often a nerve-racking experience, especially as Rogers normally worked on only one at a time, waiting until one group was finished before thinking about the next. In the early part of his career, when he was bent on turning out, as quickly as possible, a wide variety of subjects, this procedure led to some ill-considered choices and to much anxiety. Such was the case in the early fall of 1865 when Rogers, after his long honeymoon trip to Europe, tried to settle down to studio work again. He was particularly anxious for his next group to be "uncommonly good," he wrote, because the last two ("Home Guard" and "Bushwacker") had not been at all satisfactory. The strain of creation put him in a decidedly sickly humor. For several days he felt utterly miserable, suffering from what he called "a sort of dyspepsia on the brain." Then, suddenly:

> Eureka! Hattie, Eureka! [he wrote in jubilation.] I have got a wrinkle which I think is going to make a good group. . . . That is what has been the matter with me for I have felt ever so much brighter & happier since I thought of it. . . . I have been sketching it out but I feel that I am all right on the main idea, and there is a chance to make a splendid group. So now I am happy. . . .

Thus painfully was Rogers delivered of the idea which grew into "Taking the Oath and Drawing Rations," one of the finest of his works.

> I tell you what you must make me do now [the sculptor continued] — that is, to think of a design while I am modelling this one, and not leave it, as I have been in the habit of doing till I have finished the one I have been at work on. You see if I have a sketch by me, I can keep looking at it and altering it for two or three months before I have to go to work on it, and of course, it has all that much better chance of being more perfect in the composition — and I don't get worried & driven so when I need it.

Rogers probably never succeeded in disciplining himself quite so strictly as this, but as the tempo of creation slowed he was able to give more time to thinking about new subjects. Eventually he got into a fairly steady rhythm of two groups a year, one for spring and one for Christmas. Once he had achieved this degree of regularity he was able to save ideas while they matured in his mind. His 1885 group from *King Lear,* for instance, had been in his mind "a long time" before he could get it "to come together right." In earlier days he would have discarded it after a month or so, as he did his scene from *Richard III*. Later he could afford to wait.

Rogers' last words on the subject came near the close of his career, in an 1891 letter to his son Alex, a Yale undergraduate with aspirations to become an illustrator like Charles Dana Gibson. "I have struggled over designs enough," wrote the aging sculptor, "to know how hard it is to strike the right ones and have been almost in despair about it sometimes, but the right thing will come after perhaps throwing away fifty sketches and when you have *found* it it is an *immense satisfaction*."

2. *The Rough Sketch*

Just how did Rogers go about designing his group once the subject was settled on? First, by his own testimony, he fixed in his mind the number and general grouping of the figures, the expression each face was to wear, and the types of faces he intended to use. Next, he made a rough sketch in clay, about one third or one quarter the size of the projected group. This was done, Rogers said, "solely to catch the proper pose of each figure"; faces and expressions were left out. Not all of his preliminary sketching was done in clay. The New-York Historical Society owns a very interesting small sketchbook which Rogers used during the decade of the '70s to set down measured drawings of the human figure, of actual and ideal horses, of historical costumes, and of various other subjects. Most interesting of all, this little book includes measured drawings of a dog and a monkey in the poses taken by the dog in "Going for the Cows" and the monkey in "School Days."

The sketchbook confirms the artist's self-deprecatory remarks at various times on his lack of skill in drawing. "I am so unhandy with my pencil, as I have used it so little, that I cannot more than give a very rough sketch of it," he wrote in 1866, for instance, referring to a sketch of "Uncle Ned's School." The drawings which accompanied his earliest patent applications bear this out.

As late as 1890, there remained in Rogers' studio scores of little modelled sketches of his groups, some of which, he said, had been changed half a dozen times before the work was done to his satisfaction. None of these clay sketches is known to have survived, most, if not all, of them having been destroyed when the sculptor moved out of his Twelfth Street studio in 1895.

3. *The Model*

Once the design was settled to his satisfaction, Rogers began modelling in earnest. This was the part of the creative process that he enjoyed most. "With a lump of clay before me," he wrote at the start of his career, "I should not have a moment's lonely feeling if I did not speak to a human being for a week at a time." Almost twenty-five years later he was just as enthusiastic: "I have constantly resolved, on beginning a new group of late years, that I *would* be patient & take time to study it up well, but when I get started I become interested and excited in my work & feel as if all my energy were bottled up inside me, urging me on to complete it." Rogers was usually at his best when he could work fast. This was one of the characteristics which made it impossible for him to produce good monumental sculpture. After working for several months on "Air Castles," his only marble, he complained: "I don't know how my patience will hold out for I long to get at the clay again."

Rogers almost invariably modelled his figures and groups in clay. St. Gaudens is said to have urged him to try the new waxes which were then coming into favor among sculptors, but there is nothing to indicate that he ever did so, although he did put down in his sketchbook about 1870 a recipe for modelling wax. Even though it had to be periodically dampened and at night covered with a rubber sheet to prevent drying out, Rogers preferred the familiar clay. He also preferred to make his own modelling sticks, of pine with boxwood spoons at both ends and cord around the center for a handgrip.

Except at the very beginning of his career, Rogers regularly had live models to pose for his figures and either live models or lay figures for their drapery. Very often these models were friends or relations of the sculptor (particularly his wife and children), or noted actors (Joseph Jefferson, Edwin Booth, Dion Boucicault), but he also hired models on occasion. Finding models in those days before the advent of the modelling agency was not always easy. When he began "The Fairy's Whisper" in 1860, for instance, Rogers "had a heap of trouble" finding a suitable boy.

> I inquired of grocerymen & policemen & men & boys & women indiscriminately if they knew of any woman who had a child of the size I wanted. They all laughed at the idea as if they didn't know anybody who had not but when I asked them to direct me to some *particular* one they could not think of *one*. Then I applied to the doctors thinking they would have the run of the youthful generation at least but I failed again. So last evening I watched a hole in a tenement house where I saw a fine looking little boy go in. I found his mother at last but she could not talk English, being German. So she rushed up & down street to find an interpreter. I made myself understood at last & she is to come Monday.

Rogers also made use of photographs and plaster life masks to ensure accuracy in portraits of famous persons. Lincoln, Grant, and Stanton in "The Council of War" were done mainly from photographs, Lincoln entirely so. For "The Fugitive's Story," Rogers utilized life masks, measurements, and many photographs in modelling the well-known features of Whittier, Beecher, and Garrison.

Although "the imitation of nature" was one of his chief concerns, he was less interested in revealing the human form divine in his work than in rendering character and expression. In his early years he had had no training in anatomy and had been content to treat his figures almost as caricatures. In Paris and Rome this deficiency was to some extent corrected. Even after settling in New York Rogers pursued his studies a bit further at the New York College of Physicians, where he carefully measured a human skeleton. He also noted the measurements of the "Apollo Belvedere," the "Venus de Medici," and a Mrs. H. W. Moore, but these measurements seem to have been taken mostly to enable him to devise a convenient scale for proportioning his miniature figures. The great skill he acquired in rendering hands and heads certainly betokens a keen gift of observation, but of an interest in the forms beneath the surfaces there is not a hint either in his writings or in his works.

This sort of interest he did show in equine anatomy, however. In the 1870s he made and sold several anatomical studies of the horse and a number of groups designed primarily to show the horse ("Going for the Cows" and "Polo," for instance). He was also interested in Eadweard Muybridge's famous photographs of the horse in motion, though not, apparently, in his human motion studies.

With his human figures Rogers relied to a great extent on a simple formula, the essential point of which was that the face constitutes one-ninth of the total length of the body. To this rule he generally adhered, at least from 1863 on. "Your criticism about the height of my figures is very just," he wrote to a critical relative in 1863. "Some of them have been out of proportion I am well aware, but I do not think it is the case with the man in the Refugee group. . . . I intended him for a six footer & all the proportions were reduced by scale. If you will measure the length of your face & then see how many times it goes into your whole height, I think you will find the Refugee not much out of the way."

The length of time it took Rogers to model his groups varied, of course. At the start of his career he worked very rapidly. On small groups like "The Slave Auction," "Camp Life: The Card Players," and "The Village Schoolmaster" he spent as little as two weeks, but he soon came to feel that he needed to give more time and care to the modelling. His 1862 "Hamlet" took almost six weeks and "Union Refugees" (1862–63) about two months to complete in the clay. The monumental equestrian statue of Gen. Reynolds (1882–83) was eighteen months in the making. Once he got into his stride, from about 1864 on, six weeks to two months was probably usual.

Several descriptions of Rogers' method of working appeared in newspapers or magazines between 1865 and 1890. This one by "Wallace" from the *Lyons* (New York) *Republican* of April 19, 1877, was written at the height of the sculptor's career:

> Mr. Rogers' mode of working is as follows. Upon a stand erected on one side of the room is a long iron rod, upon which is placed the clay in a compact form — the clay being wet in order to make it more pliable and elastic. Taking up one of the tools lying upon the board (which are all made of box-wood and rubber, and of his own manufacture) he commences to mould and shape the image — often the work of many weeks of laborious and concentrated action, requiring not only genius, but the utmost patience and skillful manipulation for the attainment of the desired end. It seems almost incredible that by the simple use of wet clay and a modeling-stick, such exact and perfect expressions can be given to an image: but nevertheless, it is so, and as the writer stands by the side of the master-sculptor, watching how perfectly and deftly he brings out and touches up all the different shapes and shades, now forming an arm or a finger, or moulding a countenance, the expression of which he deftly evokes from what was formerly a stolid lump of clay, he realizes in some measure the hard study, the countless experiments, and the patient strivings, through which Mr. Rogers has attained his present exalted position in the world of art — until now he stands almost alone and unrivalled in the peculiar sphere he has chosen.

4. *The Pattern Casting*

"When the clay model is complete" reported the *Scientific American* in 1865, "a single plaster cast is taken for a pattern, and is finished with the most scrupulous care by the artist." In the early days, up to about 1864, this was the master model from which the molds were made for casting reproductions. After Rogers began to use bronze masters, this plaster pattern was used only in producing the bronze. As a pattern piece, however, it was always produced under the sculptor's eye, often by his own hands, and also finished by him.

5. *The Bronze Master Model*

Starting with the "Union Refugees" (1863), almost all of Rogers' plaster groups were cast from molds made on a bronze master model rather than on the plaster pattern model just described.

"The process of casting in elastic moulds required them to be renewed about once every day," Rogers explained. "This was done by melting the [glue] mold and pouring it over the model where it was left till chilled before it could be opened and handled. This was found to be a very wearing process on the originals, so that Mr. Rogers had to remodel them very often, so he found it necessary to make the originals in bronze, very carefully worked up by hand."

All of John Rogers' bronze work was done at the foundry of Pierre E. Guerin (1833–1911), a native of Brittany, who learned his trade in New York and opened his own foundry in New York City in 1857. Each bronze model cost Rogers from $450 to $1,500 and took up to four months in the casting and finishing. Depending on its size and complexity, each was cast in from three to eight pieces which were then fastened together so that they could be taken apart at the Rogers plaster shop for making the molds.

6. *Molds*

Once the master model, in plaster or bronze, was completed the mass production of copies was carried out in Rogers' own factory at 142 Center Street. Here, up two flights of stairs, in a little back room, half a dozen workmen prepared the molds. "Scattered around the room," wrote one visitor in 1874, "are dismembered Rip van Winkles, headless Scouts, and a generous distribution of fragmentary figures in all stages of finish. In one corner is what seem to be pottery relics from Golgos or the Nile, but which we are informed are plaster cases for the moulds. Each of these cases is divided into two nearly equal parts, within which the bronze cast is admitted, and the interstices filled with liquid glue, which in the course of twelve hours congeals to the consistency of a rubber shoe. The case being now taken off, the glue mould is left, entirely covering the bronze. It is then cut open with a knife sufficient to allow it to be pulled off the bronze . . . and is restored to the case, the parts of which are bound together tightly by cord and dowel pins, and all is ready for the final cast."

The use of glue for the molds was a comparatively recent French invention. As the *Scientific American* pointed out, it was a great improvement over older methods employing wax or plaster. Its elasticity enabled the mold to be drawn off the pattern even where it was undercut and it permitted the mold to be made in two pieces, "thus avoiding a great many seams in the statue, saving labor in finishing, and producing a more perfect and beautiful work."

7. *Casting*

With the exception of his large outdoor groups ("Hide and Seek" and "Hide and Seek: Whoops!"), all Rogers' published groups were cast in plaster. Rogers carried out many experiments with this material, in search of just the right medium. The result was described in 1879 as "a composition of two or three sorts of plaster or ground gypsum, with a mixture of silicious powder to improve its quality." The exact formula is not known.

In 1865 the *Scientific American* thus described the casting process:

> The workman inverts the mold and pours into it a quart or two of a liquid mixture of plaster of Paris and water, shaking it about and pouring all that does not adhere to the inner surface of the mold. He then drops in a number of bent wires, to strengthen the statue at the bends of the limbs and other places particularly liable to be broken, after which he fills the mold with plaster moistened to a soft paste. In about twenty minutes the plaster sets so as to allow the case to be opened, and the glue mold to be pulled off.

W. A. Croffut, writing for the *New York Tribune* in 1879, gave a somewhat different account of the process as seen by him on a recent visit to the Center Street factory:

> This process is peculiar. Instead of being poured in all at once and left to set as iron is into a casting, it takes forty or fifty pourings to make a statuette. The gypsum [plaster] gruel is poured in, washed around hastily in the mould and poured out: after standing a moment, the liquid is poured in again; washed around and poured out, and this monotonous process is repeated over and over and over, for half or three-quarters of an hour, till, by slight accretions the statue is built up on the inside of the mould thick enough to cut off the glue. The statuettes are all hollow, but they are solid enough to be handled with safety.

The differences between these two accounts of the same process probably reflect actual changes in Rogers' casting methods, demanded by the greater size and weight of his later pieces.

8. *Finishing*

Since the statuettes were cast in from three to eight separate pieces, these pieces had to be put together and the joints and seams removed. This was the work of the finishers. They attached the separate pieces by means of wires and finished off the joints with "plaster paste." These operations, along with the removal of seams and other imperfections absorbed a large portion of the labor involved in casting the groups. In 1865 Rogers employed three men to cast as against eight to finish.

9. *Coloring*

After a week in the drying room, the groups spent another week in the coloring-room where they underwent a process which gave them "their uniform clay-colored appearance" and which hardened their surface as well, "so that they will bear washing as well as Parian itself."

The coloring of his groups was a problem to which Rogers had given considerable thought during the early stages of his career. At first he attempted no more than a sort of glaze, achieved by dipping the casts in spermaceti or steerine, but as early as February 1860 he reported that he had been experimenting in the use of slate-colored plaster. Both these processes had to be abandoned, however, as they proved unreliable. The dipped casts sometimes "turned a most horrible mud color" and the colored plaster frequently came out of the molds spotted.

> I have experimented on coloring the plaster ever since I began [he reported in January 1862] & have come to the conclusion that it can't be done. The trouble is that there has to be some alum used in casting in gelatine moulds which has a chemical action on the color & makes them spotted.

Eventually Rogers decided to paint his plaster groups. The first one to be finished in this way seems to have been "The Fairy's Whisper" (November 1860). At first he had left these white, but coated them with a soap solution to make it possible to use them outdoors. Dissatisfied with the effect, he then painted some with a rather rough, nonglossy paint that would resist weathering. The proper way to do this, he said, was to give the group a coat of boiled linseed oil, then "two or three coats of pretty thick paint, put on very carefully & *stippled* so as to have no streaks of paint & give it a nice texture." He later suggested mixing the last coat with turpentine rather than oil, to avoid a shiny look.

The color Rogers eventually fixed on (as early as February 1864) for his groups was what he described as "clay color," made with burnt umber and zinc white. He made no secret of this formula. The following is quoted from a sales catalogue issued by the sculptor in 1892:

> The color can be matched by using Zinc White and Burnt Sienna Umber. They can both be found at any house painter's in the form of a paste which has been ground in oil. Put a little of this Zinc White Paste in a can and add a very little raw linseed oil. Then stir some turpentine in till it is thin enough to use, and color it with Burnt Umber. Two coats are necessary to make it dry without a gloss, but if it still does so, it shows there is too much oil in the mixture, or that it is not fresh and has become "fatty" from exposure. If there should be any difficulty in obtaining the color,

by inclosing fifty cents to MR. ROGERS' address, he will send by express sufficient material to re-color several Groups, with brush and directions on the package, which will enable any painter to use it.

Another formula, found in Rogers' papers, reads as follows: "Tablespoon of zinc white, mixed with burnt umber ground in oil (very little). Thin with turpentine till it is like milk. It grows darker with age so mix lighter than required."

Drab though this color now seems, it was not so regarded eighty or ninety years ago. "Mr. Rogers's Statuary we regard as among the most exquisite works of art that we have ever seen," wrote the editor of *Scientific American* in 1865, "and their pleasing effect we attribute in no small degree to their color."

It was a further recommendation, as Rogers pointed out to his customers, that the groups could be cleaned with soap and water "if care is taken to have it of moderate strength and not to rub too hard."

10. *Storing and Packing*

Finally the casts were stored away on the fourth floor of the Center Street factory to await orders, or they were carefully packed in sawdust in boxes made expressly for the purpose — "so carefully, indeed," it was reported in 1874, "that, incredible as it may seem, not more than one in five hundred is ever broken in transit, such ones being always replaced by the sculptor."

APPENDIX II

Notes for Collectors

BECAUSE they were cast and sold in quantity, John Rogers' "groups" are still eminently collectible. No individual or museum can, perhaps, hope to assemble a truly complete collection of works "published" by John Rogers. Such a collection would include approximately one hundred separate pieces, including eighty-seven titles and at least thirteen variants. Besides these, the avid collector might be lucky enough to find one or more of the missing bronze master models sold for Rogers before his death. Parian copies of Rogers Groups offer another area for specialization; at least seven subjects are known in this material and there may well have been others. Still another way of collecting Rogers Groups, and one which requires much less space and money, is to collect early album photographs, stereopticon views, lantern slides, catalogues, and advertisements of the works of John Rogers.

The following lists have been prepared as practical aids to the collection of any or all of the types of Rogers material listed above. None of them is exhaustive; collectors must complete the picture which is only sketched here.

A. *Checklist of Rogers' "Published" Works*

Listed here in order of rarity, beginning with the most common, are all those works issued by Rogers for public sale of which copies are known to have been sold and which can therefore be considered collectible. The numbers of surviving copies of each work are only approximate, based on the results of a survey made by the author during the writing of this book. Many more copies of Rogers' groups undoubtedly exist, in museums and private collections, but recent additions to the survey indicate that for all practical purposes relative rarity is about as indicated in this checklist. No distinction is made in this list between variants; all copies of a given subject, regardless of variants, are included in the total for that subject. For information on variants, the reader is referred to the catalogue entries themselves. This checklist also includes no parians or bronzes, except spelter copies of "Union Refugees."

Number of known copies	*Subject and Catalogue Number*
Over 50	"Coming to the Parson [120]
	"Council of War [112]
	"Checkers Up at the Farm [145]
41–50	" 'Why Don't You Speak for Yourself, John?' " [168]
	"The Favored Scholar" [135]
	"Taking the Oath" [108]
	" 'Is it so Nominated in the Bond?' " [160]
31–40	"Rip Van Winkle at Home" [122]
	"Going for the Cows" [138]
	"Weighing the Baby" [150]
	"We Boys" [130]
	"Neighboring Pews" [166]
21–30	" 'Ha! I Like Not That!' " [165]
	"Tap on the Window" [142]
	"Rip Van Winkle on the Mountain" [123]
	"Playing Doctor" [132]
	"One More Shot" [105]
	"The Picket Guard" [83]
	"The Charity Patient" [110]
	"The Parting Promise" [117]
	"The Fugitive's Story" [116]
	"The Shaughraun and 'Tatters' " [143]
	"The Town Pump" [89]
	"The School Examination" [111]
	"Courtship in Sleepy Hollow" [113]
	"School Days" [152]
	"Frolic at the Old Homestead" [174]
	"Union Refugees" [98]
	" 'Madam, Your Mother Craves a Word With You' " [170]
	"Politics" [179]
16–20	"The Foundling" [121]
	"Fetching the Doctor" [163]
	"A Matter of Opinion" [167]

16–20	"Returned Volunteer" [102]
	"The Traveling Magician" [153]
	"The Peddler at the Fair" [157]
	"The Photograph" [156]
	"The Referee" [161]
	" 'You Are a Spirit, I Know' " [169]
	"The Wounded Scout" [103]
	"Rip Van Winkle Returned" [124]
	"The Elder's Daughter" [173]
11–15	"Phrenology at the Fancy Ball" [171]
	"The First Ride" [178]
	"George Washington" [144]
	"The Mock Trial" [151]
	"Private Theatricals" [155]
	"The Balcony" [159]
	"Camp Fire: Making Friends With the Cook" [88]
	"Country Postoffice" [99]
	"Uncle Ned's School" [109]
	"Faust and Marguerite Leaving the Garden" [195]
	"The Home Guard" [106]
	"Faust and Marguerite: First Meeting" [193]
	"The Wrestlers" [162]
	"Chess" [184]
	"Fighting Bob" [183]
	"Football" [199]
6–10	"Mail Day" [101]
	"The Village Schoolmaster" [63]
	"Challenging the Union Vote" [114]
	"The Watch on the Santa Maria" [204]
	"Checker Players" [61]
	"The Fairy's Whisper" [71]
	"Hide and Seek: Whoop!" [139]
	"Hide and Seek" [141]
5	"The Slave Auction" [58]
	"Polo" [158]
	"Henry Ward Beecher" [176]
4	"The Bushwhacker" [107]
3	"Sharp Shooters" [90]

3	"Bubbles" [136]
	"The Bath" [118]
2	"Vase" [148]
	"Marguerite and Martha: Trying on the Jewels" [194]
1	"Camp Life: The Card Players" [87]
	"Henry Ward Beecher" [208]
No copies located	"The Farmer's Home" [59]
	"The Fireman" [62]
	"Night" [65]
	"Morning" [66]
	"St. Catherine" [79]
	"Hamlet" [97]
	"Anatomical Studies of the Horse: The Skeleton" [126]
	" " " " " : The Muscles" [127]
	" " " " " : Attachment of Some Muscles" [128]
	"Flower Box" [147]

B. *Bronzes*

John Rogers produced only two works for sale in bronze, "Ichabod Crane and the Headless Horseman" [175] and "Landing of the Norsemen" [207], both one-third the size of life. Only one copy of each was made and these are now in the collection of The New-York Historical Society.

Of the works he produced for sale in plaster or composition, Rogers had bronze master models made for at least forty-eight. The earliest was "Union Refugees" [98], 1863; the latest "Politics" [179], 1888. Of the forty-eight Rogers sold twelve in 1897 through his bronze founder, P. E. Guerin; the remaining bronzes were disposed of by the family long after the sculptor's death. Thirty-eight bronze master models are now in the collection of The New-York Historical Society, two are owned by the Metropolitan Museum of Art, New York, and three are in private collections: "Union Refugees" [98], "The School Examination" [111], and "Polo" [158].

Still to be located are five of the bronze models Rogers sold in 1897:

"Bubbles" [136]
"Private Theatricals" [155]
"The Referee" [161]
"Tap on the Window" [142]
"The Photograph" [156]

In a few cases Rogers is known to have duplicated groups in bronze for sale to special customers. Such was the case with the bronze of "One More Shot" [105] specially made for presentation to Governor Buckingham of Connecticut in 1866. A duplicate bronze, history unknown, of "Taking the Oath" [108] was sold by Kennedy Galleries, New York, in 1961. Others may exist.

No bronze master models are recorded for the following post-1863 groups:

"Mail Day" [101]
"The Home Guard" [106]
"The Bushwhacker" [107]
"Challenging the Union Vote" [114]
"Parting Promise" [117]
"The Bath" [118]
"Anatomical Studies of the Horse" [126–28]
"Hide and Seek" [139, 141]
"Flower Box" and "Vase" [147, 148]
"Phrenology at the Fancy Ball" [171]
"Frolic at the Old Homestead" [174]
"Beecher" [176, 208]
"Fighting Bob" [183]
"Chess" [184]
"Faust" groups [193–195]
"Football" [199]
"The Watch on the Santa Maria" [204]

It should be noted that the absence of any documentary record of bronze master models for these works is not conclusive evidence against their having existed, since two bronzes for which there is no such record have survived: "Union Refugees" [98] and "Washington" [144].

C. *Rogers Groups in Parian*

At least seven of John Rogers' early published works were reproduced in the material known as "parian." This variety of biscuit porcelain developed in England by W. T. Copeland in 1842 was soon made in almost all the Staffordshire potteries as well as at Bennington and Green Point in the United States. Parian was ideally suited for the reproduction of statuary because its fine consistency insured accuracy of detail, while its translucent whiteness and dry, granular texture suggested real marble. A distinctive feature was that parian figures shrank about one-sixth in the firing.

The Rogers Groups of which parian versions have been reported are:

"Checker Players" [61]
"Camp Life: The Card Players" [87]
"Union Refugees" [98]
"The Wounded Scout" [103]
"One More Shot" [105]
"Taking the Oath and Drawing Rations" [108]
"Courtship in Sleepy Hollow" [113]

Of these, "One More Shot" is the most common, with at least a dozen copies reported. "Wounded Scout" and "Courtship in Sleepy Hollow" are next with three copies of each. The others are known by one example each. Except for their size they are identical to the plaster groups. "Taking the Oath" is 19 inches high instead of 23; "One More Shot" 20 inches instead of 23½; "Courtship" 14 inches instead of 16½. The bases vary; some are like those of the plasters, others are more elaborate.

It is my opinion that none of the parian Rogers Groups was actually produced or sold by John Rogers. My reasons for this opinion are that nowhere in his surviving correspondence does Rogers refer to the making or marketing of parians of his groups; and none of the newspaper clippings in his four scrapbooks mention Rogers Groups in parian. Those quoted by the Smiths (*Rogers Groups,* pages 52–53) as mentioning "Parian Marble" actually say "marble" and quite accurately since they refer to "Air Castles" [80], Rogers' only work in real marble. Moreover, neither in his catalogues nor in his advertising did Rogers mention parian copies of his works.

Since Rogers' designs were protected by patent in the United States, it seems unlikely that the parian copies of his works were produced there. The most reasonable explanation, it seems to me, is that they were copied, probably without his consent, by one or more of the English or even French potteries. The opportunity certainly existed, for in 1865 Rogers took some plaster groups abroad and arranged for their sale in London and Paris. "I made an arrangement in London with one of the print dealers," he wrote, "and I suppose they will worry off a few." In Paris he made some sort of arrangement with several of the bronze dealers. If he made any arrangements for parian reproductions, there is no contemporary record of it. In the absence of such a record, the parians cannot be accepted as produced or authorized by Rogers. They are contemporary, however, and aesthetically very satisfying. It would be an interesting study to attempt to identify their source.

Of even more obscure origin and date are two Rogers Groups in creamware: "The Wounded Scout" [103] with a purplish-red glaze and "Taking the Oath" in a cream-colored glaze. Both are privately owned.

D. *Photographs For Albums and For Framing*

Between 1863 and 1868 photographs of Rogers Groups, some of high quality, were published by James F. Aitken, Morris Stadtfeld, J. H. Williams, Hamilton Wood, Jr., Gurney & Son, G. W. Thorne, E. & H. T. Anthony (all of New York), A. A. Childs & Co. (Boston), and Wallis & Abbott (Chicago). In all, twenty-four groups were represented in these early photographs. They were available in up to four sizes: carte-de-visite (2½″ by 4″), which would fit in any photograph album; cabinet (7″ by 9″), medium (11″ by 14″), and imperial (18″ by 22″).

Chart A. ALBUM PHOTOGRAPHS

	Publishers or Distributors								
Subjects	Aitken	Stadtfeld	Williams	Wood	Childs	Thorne	Anthony	Gurney	Wallis & Abbott
"Slave Auction"	X	X	X	X	X				
"Checker Players"	X			X	X				
"Village Schoolmaster"	X			X	X				
"Fairy's Whisper"				X	X				
"Picket Guard"	X	X		X	X				
"Camp Life"	X			X	X			X	
"Camp Fire"	X		X	X	X				
"Town Pump"	X	X		X	X				
"Sharp Shooters"	X	X		X	X		X		
"Union Refugees"	X	X	X	X	X		X		
"Country Postoffice"	X	X		X	X				
"Mail Day"	X	X		X	X				
"Returned Volunteer"	X	X		X	X				
"Wounded Scout"	X	X		X	X	X			
"One More Shot"		X	X	X	X			X	X
"Home Guard"		X	X	X	X				
"Bushwhacker"		X		X	X				
"Taking the Oath"		X		X	X	X			
"Uncle Ned's School"				X	X	X		X	
"Charity Patient"				X	X				
"School Examination"				X	X				
"Council of War"				*X	X				
"Courtship in Sleepy Hollow"				X	X				
"Challenging the Union Vote"							X		

* H. Wood, Jr., published two views of "Council of War," full-face and profile.

As a guide for collectors, the annexed chart lists the twenty-four subjects and the eight known publishers. Under each publisher's name are indicated by *x* the subjects of which he is known to have issued at least "carte-de-visite" photographs. As unrecorded examples come to light, they can be entered on this chart in the same manner.

A few of the later groups were photographed for Rogers by Barcalow ("Weighing the Baby") and Rockwood (the "Hide and Seek" pair, "The First Ride," and "Fighting Bob"), but these were probably for personal use rather than for sale.

In 1877 Rogers advertised at $2.00 bound sets of photographs, reproduced by the Albertype process (photolithography), of most of the groups. As new groups appeared photographs would be sent to the purchasers of the book, for attachment to the "stubs" left in it for the purpose. No copy of this has been located.

E. *Stereopticon Views*

The popularity of the Rogers Group coincided with that of the parlor stereopticon. Between 1867 and 1876 many sets of stereographs of statuary by John Rogers were issued. It would be impossible to describe all of them, since many bear no publisher's name or only that of the local shopkeeper who handed them out as advertising premiums. Some clearly distinguishable sets received fairly wide distribution, however, and are still collectible.

H. Wood, Jr., New York, published in 1867 a set of twenty-two subjects, including two views of "Council of War." He increased the set to twenty-four in 1868 by adding "Courtship in Sleepy Hollow" and "The Fairy's Whisper."

H. Ropes & Co., New York, published in 1867 the same twenty-two subjects as H. Wood, Jr.

A. A. Childs & Co., Boston, published twenty-three subjects in 1868, including only one view of "Council of War." The same list appears on stereographs published by at least three other Boston firms: Dodge, Collier & Perkins; D. B. Brooks & Bro.; and J. L. Bates. Some of these also appear with the names of shopkeepers in several New England towns.

"900 Series" This set published about 1868 contained at least twenty-two subjects numbered from 971 to 992. Some are labelled "Statuary / Rogers Groups," while others are labelled "Statuary / Haughwout & Co." Haughwout's was a big New York store. The most interesting item in this set is 987, "Trout Fishing," which, though labelled a Rogers Group on the card, was actually the work of another sculptor named Samuel Conkey (see page 278).

"$25.00 Series" This set dating from the early 'seventies included at least eight subjects, from "Picket Guard" to "Rip Van Winkle at Home." On the back of each is pasted a printed label describing the group, stating that it is photographed by permission of the artist, and listing the price of "any of the original Groups" as $25.00. One of these was published by De Young's Palace Dollar Store, Philadelphia; the others seen bear no publisher's or distributor's name.

E. & H. T. Anthony, a famous New York photographic house, published a numbered series of Rogers stereographs. Those seen are numbered between 226 and 249 and the subjects range from "Picket Guard" to "We Boys" (1872).

J. W. & J. S. Moulton, of Salem, Massachusetts, published a numbered series (800–833) which ended in 1876 with "Weighing the Baby." Their list included one subject wrongly credited to John Rogers: "Lotta as the Marchioness," a character out of Dickens by Jonathan Scott Hartley.

James Cremer, Philadelphia, about 1875, issued a set of especially good stereographs of Rogers Groups, using the same numbers as the Moultons, but omitting numbers 809, 813, and 826. The very same photographs, poorly printed and numbered 1–30, were issued, without a publisher's name. A set of these has been found on each of which is stamped the name of Alex P. Kerr, Lewisburg, West Virginia, presumably the distributor.

Charles Bierstadt, of New York and Niagara Falls, was publishing Rogers stereographs between 1870 and 1876. Eighteen subjects with his imprint have been recorded, ranging from "Slave Auction" to "Weighing the Baby."

Other sets could, no doubt, be isolated and the relationships established between some of the publishers and distributors, but this is beyond the scope of this book.

In summary, the collector of Rogers stereopticon views can hope to find views of forty-one different groups (not counting variants), from "The Slave Auction" of 1859 to "School Days" of 1877. For the first twenty-four (through "Courtship in Sleepy Hollow") there are more than fifteen different stereographs known of most of these subjects. From then on the choice is limited to about six different sets. The annexed chart lists the subjects and principal known sets. It can be added to as views now unrecorded turn up. This information has been derived largely from examination of the stereograph collections of The New-York Historical Society, American Antiquarian Society, Society for the Preservation of New England Antiquities, Essex Institute, and the author's collection. Mr. Albert L. Partridge, of Watertown, Massachusetts, also provided much helpful information on this subject.

Chart B. STEREOPTICON VIEWS

Subjects	Publishers or Distributors																
	Wood	Ropes	Childs	Dodge, Collier & Perkins	Brooks	Bates	"900" Series	$25 Series	Anthony	Moulton	Cremer	Kerr	Bierstadt	Kilburn	Kuhn	Other publishers	Unidentified
"Slave Auction"	X	X	X	X	X	X							X				2
"Checker Players"	X	X	X	X	X	X				X	X	X					1
"Village Schoolmaster"	X	X	X	X	X	X	X										1
"Fairy's Whisper"	X		X	X	X	X				X							1
"Picket Guard"	X	X	X	X	X	X		X	X	X	X						
"Camp Life"	X	X	X	X	X	X	X										1
"Camp Fire"	X	X	X	X	X	X											2
"Town Pump"	X	X	X	X	X	X			X	X	X	X			X		1
"Sharp Shooters"	X	X	X	X	X	X	X		X		X	X	X			2	4
"Union Refugees"	X	X	X	X	X	X	X			X	X	X	X		X	1	2
"Country Postoffice"	X	X	X	X	X	X	X		X	X	X	X	X		X	3	
"Mail Day"	X	X	X	X	X	X	X		X	X	X	X				2	1
"Returned Volunteer"	X	X	X	X	X	X	X	X	X	X	X	X				2	
"Wounded Scout"	X	X	X	X	X	X	X	X		X			X			2	2
"One More Shot"	X	X	X	X	X	X	X	X		X							1
"Home Guard"	X	X	X	X	X	X	X		X	X	X	X	X			2	
"Bushwhacker"	X	X	X	X	X	X					X	X	X				2
"Taking the Oath"	X	X	X	X	X	X	X			X	X	X					2
"Uncle Ned's School"	X	X	X	X	X	X			X	X	X	X	X			1	3
"Charity Patient"	X	X	X	X	X	X	X		X	X	X	X				1	3
"School Examination"	X	X	X	X	X	X		X	X	X	X	X	X			2	3
"Council of War"*	X*	X*	X	X	X	X	X*	X	X	X	X	X	X			3	6
"Courtship in Sleepy Hollow"	X		X	X	X	X			X	X	X	X	X		X	1	3

Publishers or Distributors

Subjects	Wood	Ropes	Childs	Dodge, Collier & Perkins	Brooks	Bates	"900" Series	$25 Series	Anthony	Moulton	Cremer	Kerr	Bierstadt	Kilburn	Kuhn	Other publishers	Unidentified
"Challenging the Union Vote"									X	X	X	X	X				
"Fugitive's Story"										X	X	X					2
"Parting Promise"										X	X	X	X				
"Coming to the Parson"										X	X	X	X				
"The Foundling"								X	X	X	X	X					
"Rip Van Winkle at Home"								X		X	X	X					1
"Rip Van Winkle on the Mountain"										X	X	X					3
"Rip Van Winkle Returned"									X	X	X	X					
"We Boys"									X	X	X	X					
"Playing Doctor"										X	X	X					1
"Favored Scholar"										X	X	X	X				
"Going for the Cows"										X	X	X	X				
"Tap on the Window"										X	X	X		X			
"Shaughraun and 'Tatters' "										X	X	X					
"Washington"										X	X						
"Checkers Up at the Farm"										X			X				
"Weighing the Baby"										X			X				
"School Days"																	2

* Those marked X* exist in two versions, full-face and profile.

F. *Lantern Slides*

Thomas Hall, of Boston, published lantern slides of fifty different Rogers Groups, as listed in his 1890 catalogue:

*"Fairy's Whisper"
"Fugitive's Story"
*"Council of War"
"Challenging the Union Vote"
*"Taking the Oath"
"Favored Scholar"
"Foundling"
"Coming to the Parson"
*"Courtship in Sleepy Hollow"
"One More Shot"
*"Wounded Scout"
*"Union Refugees"
*"Country Postoffice"
*"Home Guard"
*"School Examination"
*"Charity Patient"
*"Uncle Ned's School"
*"Returned Volunteer"
"Playing Doctor"
"Parting Promise"
"Rip Van Winkle at Home"
"Rip Van Winkle on the Mountain"
"Rip Van Winkle Returned"
"We Boys"
*"Mail Day
*"Town Pump"
*"Picket Guard"
"Going for the Cows
*"Bushwhacker"
*"Village Schoolmaster"
*"Checker Players"
"Sharp Shooters"
"Checkers up at the Farm"
"Weighing the Baby"
"Shaughraun and 'Tatters' "
"Tap on the Window"
"Washington"
"Mock Trial"
" 'Is It So Nominated in the Bond?' "
"Balcony"
"Peddlar at the Fair"
"Private Theatricals"
"Polo"
"Traveling Magician"
"School Days"
"Othello ['Ha! I Like Not That!']"
"Referee"
"Fetching the Doctor"
"Wrestlers"
"Photographer"

The subjects in the above list preceded by an asterisk (*) were also available from Hall as stereopticon views. Hall also offered five "Gem Slides" of Rogers Groups, each containing three views, as follows:

No. 32. "Rip Van Winkle at Home." "Rip Van Winkle on the Mountain." "Rip Van Winkle Returned."
No. 35. "Parting Promise." "Courtship in Sleepy Hollow." "Coming to the Parson."
No. 36. "Mail Day." "Town Pump." "Village Schoolmaster."
No. 37. "Bushwhacker." "Sharp Shooters." "Wounded Scout."
No. 38. "We Boys." "Uncle Ned's School." "Country Postoffice."

It is interesting to note that Hall's lists, published in 1890, contain no Rogers Groups of vintage later than 1882.

Other lantern slide sets of Rogers Groups may well exist, but no other has come to my attention.

G. *Catalogues*

The earliest known catalogue of "Rogers' Groups of Sculpture" dates from 1866. It is not certain whether Rogers issued this himself or whether it was published by one of his agents. The only known copy was sent to Rogers in 1886, as a souvenir, by Archibald Wilson of Poughkeepsie, New York, who subscribed himself "Agent" on the cover. This catalogue illustrated and listed sixteen groups.

The Chicago *Republican* announced on April 12, 1868, that it was about to issue an illustrated catalogue of Rogers' works. No copy of this has been located.

The earliest reference to a catalogue available directly from John Rogers appeared in an April 1869 issue of the *Lyons* (New York) *Republican*. This catalogue has yet to turn up.

Of the catalogues Rogers is believed to have issued each year from 1869 the following are known to have survived: 1870, 1872, 1876, 1877, 1882, 1883, 1888, 1890, and 1892. An 1874 catalogue issued by Williams & Everett, Boston, also exists. The catalogues for 1894 and 1895 at The New-York Historical Society were issued by the Rogers Statuary Company, successors to Rogers' plaster business.

H. *Advertisements*

Illustrated advertisements of Rogers' works began to appear in popular magazines in 1870. Among the magazines in which they are known to have appeared are *Godey's Lady's Book, Every Saturday, Scribner's Monthly, Saint Nicholas, Century Magazine, The Continent, Youth's Companion, American Art Journal, Appleton's Journal, Harper's Monthly, National Journal of Education,* and *Christian at Work.*

Index

Note: Figures in italics indicate pages of entries within the Catalogue of the Works of John Rogers. Figures in brackets refer to identification numbers used in the Catalogue.